mirko ilić
fist to face

by **dejan kršić**

PRINT

PUBLISHED BY
PRINT PUBLISHING

PRINT

Published by Print Publishing
an imprint of F+W Media, Inc.
38 East 29th Street, New York, NY 10016
(212) 447-2100
First edition

For more excellent design information and resources, visit www.printmag.com

ISBN: 978-1-4403-2397-3

16   15   14   13   12   5   4   3   2   1

Distributed in Canada
by Fraser Direct
100 Armstrong Avenue
Georgetown, Ontario
Canada L7G554
Tel: (905) 877-4411

Distributed in the UK and Europe
by F+W Media International, LTD
Brunel House Forde Close
Newton Abbot
TQ124PU, UK

Tel: (+44) 1626 323200
Fax: (+44) 1626323319

Distributed in Australia
By Capricorn LInk
P.O. Box 704 Windsor
NSW 2756
Australia
Tel: (+02) 4577-3555

Designed by Dejan Kršić
Edited by Aaron Kenedi and Buzz Poole
Copyedited by Georgia Cool
Translated into English by Jasmina Ilić
Additional translation by Jele Dominis
and Graham McMaster

Typography used:
Brioni and Typonine Sans
(NIKOLA DJUREK • TYPONINE)

for Andrej & Ivo
Lea & Zoe

Horizontally and Vertically,

Polet no. 67-68-69,

May 22, 1978

Vesna Kesić: Is narcissism blossoming,

Start no. 255, Zagreb, November 1, 1978

Worried labor force,

Danas, no. 167, April 30, 1985,

Studio SLS, PHOTO: Luka Mjeda

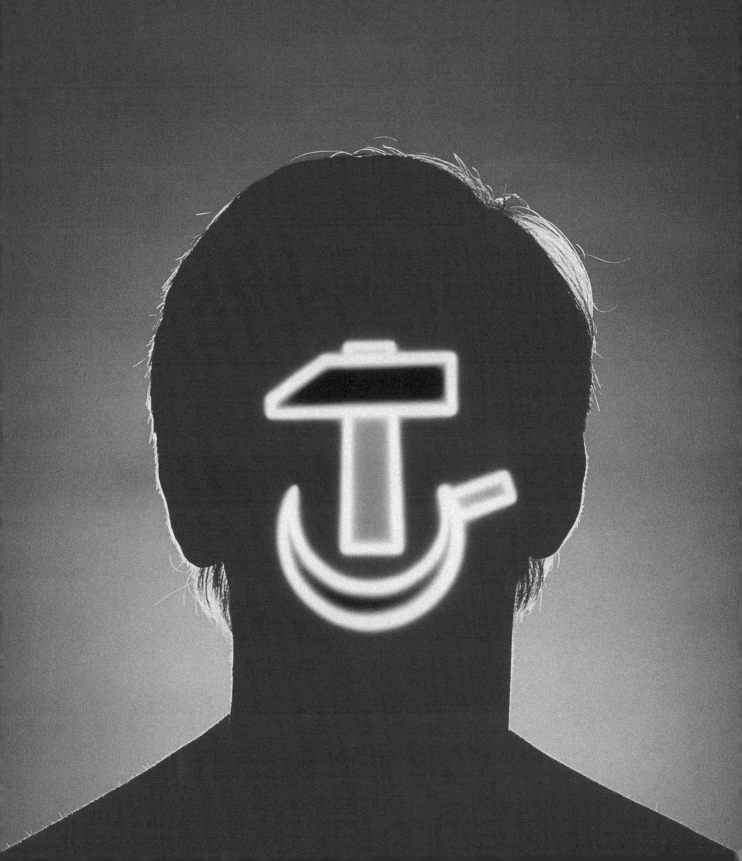

$2.50

TIME

Canada,
Time International,
June 18, 1990,
AD: Rudolph Hoglund

All You Do Is Just Sit Down,
The New York Times, op-ed,
November 26, 1992,
AD & D: Mirko Ilić,
ILLUSTRATION: Milan Trenc

THE NEW YORK TIMES **OP-ED** THURSDAY, NOVEMBER 26, 1992 A27

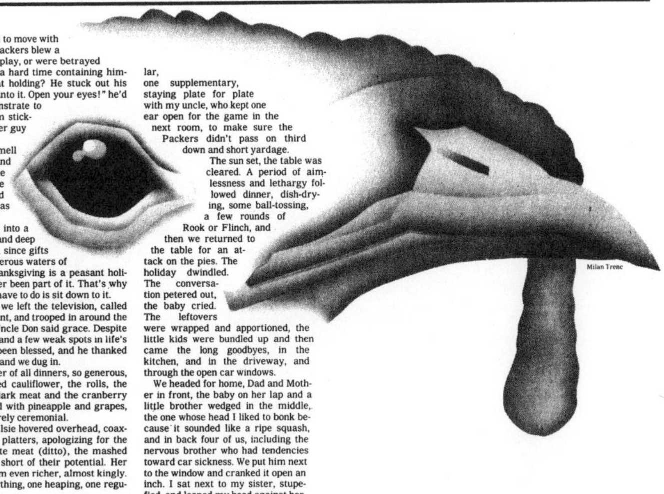

All You Do Is Just Sit Down

By Garrison Keillor

Our family Thanksgiving was as lovely and ordinary as any in America, a day at Uncle Don's and Aunt Elsie's in south Minneapolis, the windows steamed up, our coats piled on a bed, the baby asleep next to them, a Packers-Bears game on television, the little kids tearing around in the basement, the women coaxing the dinner toward the goal line.

Lavish aromas washed into the living room, and next to me on the couch Uncle Don lived and died with the Green Bay Packers. He was a big man, a guard in the days of the single wing, and as he watched the screen he tended to move with the play. And when the Packers blew a big chance with a bonehead play, or were betrayed by inept officiating, he had a hard time containing himself. "Holding! You call that holding? He stuck out his hand and the other guy ran into it. Open your eyes!" he'd holler. And then he'd demonstrate to me how holding differs from sticking out your hand as the other guy runs into it.

We sat and breathed the smell of apple and pumpkin pies, and sage dressing cooking in the great bird's carcass, and the yams baking in butter and brown sugar, a dinner as sweet and plain as life itself.

Christmas takes a person into a realm of poignant memory and deep need and maudlin guilt and, since gifts are involved, into the treacherous waters of taste and judgment, but Thanksgiving is a peasant holiday, and good taste has never been part of it. That's why it is such a comfort. All you have to do is sit down to it.

When dinner was served, we left the television, called the kids up from the basement, and trooped in around the table. There were 12 of us. Uncle Don said grace. Despite some questionable strategy and a few weak spots in life's lineup, nonetheless we had been blessed, and he thanked God for this in a quiet voice, and we dug in.

It was, of course, the dinner of all dinners, so generous, so predictable. The creamed cauliflower, the rolls, the giblet gravy, the light and dark meat and the cranberry mold, a gelatin ring studded with pineapple and grapes, which nobody ate; it was purely ceremonial.

We fed steadily as Aunt Elsie hovered overhead, coaxing us and replenishing the platters, apologizing for the dressing (too dry), the white meat (ditto), the mashed potatoes that somehow fell short of their potential. Her modesty made the meal seem even richer, almost kingly. I ate three helpings of everything, one heaping, one regular, one supplementary, staying plate for plate with my uncle, who kept one ear open for the game in the next room, to make sure the Packers didn't pass on third down and short yardage.

The sun set, the table was cleared. A period of aimlessness and lethargy followed dinner, dish-drying, some ball-tossing, a few rounds of Rook or Flinch, and then we returned to the table for an attack on the pies. The holiday dwindled. The conversation petered out, the baby cried. The leftovers were wrapped and apportioned, the little kids were bundled up and then came the long goodbyes, in the kitchen, and in the driveway, and through the open car windows.

We headed for home, Dad and Mother in front, the baby on her lap and a little brother wedged in the middle, the one whose head I liked to bonk because it sounded like a ripe squash, and in back four of us, including the nervous brother who had tendencies toward car sickness. We put him next to the window and cranked it open an inch. I sat next to my sister, stupefied, and leaned my head against her, testing whether she would allow this. She did. And I fell asleep.

After my aunt died last fall, I bought her dining room table from my uncle, who went South, and now it will hold my dinner, which is like hers and almost as good. Thanksgiving isn't hard to make, which is the beauty of it. You fix a big table full of dinner and plop down and think, Life is good, thank You for this, it could be a lot worse, and I'm grateful it's not.

God bless us. More we do not need. □

Garrison Keillor, host of "American Radio Company," is an occasional contributor to this page.

One Strange Bird

By Margaret Visser

TORONTO

The huge, golden creature we reverently slice and serve for Thanksgiving dinner has a nature and a history as odd as any national symbol could wish. The modern turkey is a deeply enculturated bird; like all festival foods with staying power, it is old and strange, yet typically ours.

"Rugose and carunculated," Audubon called its head and back: all wrinkly and covered with flabby wattles, warts, tubercles and bumps. The weirdest of a turkey's 50 or so caruncles is attached to its face. In the male this cone of flesh, drooping over its bill, can stretch in a trice from one to eight inches.

The whole featherless neck and head changes color as the turkey's moods alter, from white to turquoise to blue, to pink, purple, orange and flaming red. When courting, the flat skin of the male is red and the warty caruncles are a brilliant blue. The bird gobbles. He struts and puffs (a performance called a *pfum*), and his tail feathers display in the manner of a peacock.

The position of the female's head and neck is essential in turkey mating: cocks will display their plumage before a disembodied hen's head crudely carved in wood, provided the object is held at precisely the seductive angle.

Native Americans used the bird's feathers for headdresses, arrows and fans or twisted them on cords and wove them into cloaks and blankets. The black bristle "beard" that hangs from the male's chest was used as a hyssop, for flicking water, in religious ceremonies.

Columbus encountered the bird first on an island off Honduras, where the Indians served some to him roasted. At other Indian feasts, the Spaniards were offered enormous tamales containing a whole turkey each.

The appearance of the living birds astounded, fascinated and confused Europeans, who ended up calling the creature *Meleagris gallopavo*: "guineafowl-chickenpeacock."

The popular name varies from Indian tribe to tribe and from country to country. The English thought the huge new chicken originated in Turkey; the French and Italians called it "from India" (*dinde* and *gallo d'India*), and the Turks themselves call it *hindi*. The Japanese, awed perhaps by all those changing wattles, called it *shichimencho*: "seven-faced."

Turkeys are extraordinarily primitive fowl in certain respects. They seem never to think of looking down when seeking an escape route, and their eyeballs fit so tightly into their sockets that they have to turn their heads to see moving objects.

A deafened female turkey, hearing no sounds from her young, will take them for foreign pests and peck them to death. A turkey with mud on its head may be murdered by its brethren for looking odd. Turkeys often become enraged by unusual rocks, old bones or anything red. At any unexpected noise all males and some females gobble madly.

Geneticists have grossly enlarged the turkey's breast. They have also made the bird delicate, susceptible to cold and wet, almost incapable of copulating (fertilization has to be achieved with human help), and sometimes unsteady on its feet because of its bulging *embonpoint*.

Turkey meat is not only light, the most preferred, but also dark, which lends variety. Darkness in bird meat comes from the myoglobin, which stores oxygen for muscles. Game birds' breasts are dark because they fly. Legs are dark in the domestic turkey because even factory-reared birds have to stand, and so make use of the muscles in their legs.

In 18th-century Europe and North America, turkeys were commonly walked 100 miles or more to market. From the large breeding farms in Norfolk, thousands of birds crowded down the narrow roads to London during the weeks preceding Christmas.

The great black Norfolk gobblers (which the English called "bubbly-jocks") wore shoes for the journey. Their feet were dipped in thick pitch or tied up in sacking and covered with little boots to protect them on the long noisy march south. By the time turkeys arrived upon city dinner tables, dark meat must surely have predominated. □

Margaret Visser is author of "The Rituals of Dinner: The Origins, Evolution, Eccentricities, and Meaning of Table Manners" and "Much Depends on Dinner."

The Two Turkeys

By James Thurber

Once upon a time there were two turkeys, an old turkey and a young turkey. The old turkey had been cock of the walk for many years and the young turkey wanted to take his place. "I'll knock that old buzzard cold one of these days," the young turkey told his friends. "Sure you will, Joe, sure you will," his friends said, for Joe was treating them to some corn he had found. Then the friends went and told the old turkey what the young turkey had said. "Why, I'll have his gizzard!" said the old turkey, setting out some corn for his visitors. "Sure you will, Doc, sure you will," said the visitors.

One day the young turkey walked over to where the old turkey was telling tales of his prowess in battle. "I'll bat your teeth into your crop," said the young turkey. "You and who else?" said the old turkey. So they began to circle around each other, sparring for an opening. Just then the farmer who owned the turkeys swept up the young one and carried him off and wrung his neck.

Moral: Youth will be served, frequently stuffed with chestnuts.

Copyright © 1940 James Thurber; © 1968 Helen Thurber. From "Fables for Our Time," published by Harper & Row.

James Thurber, the humorist, died in 1961.

Essay

WILLIAM SAFIRE

Rating World Spookery

WASHINGTON

There is this "dead drop" in a tree in Farragut Square, just outside my office. Responding to a coded request in this space for assessments of intelligence agencies, some of the world's leading counterspies have dropped off their evaluations of each other's espionage operations.

Here, then, is the first annual international spookery peer review. Gathering and evaluating capabilities are given up to four "cloaks"; covert operations capacity is symbolized in "daggers."

French intelligence, long derided for spying on itself, is regarded as a post-cold-war comer. Because the Gallic ethos tolerates the most flagrant invasion of privacy, Francospooks operate without legislative or press scrutiny, making internal spying easy for 1,500 full-time wiretappers. Operations abroad take the lead in industrial espionage, stealing commercial and technological secrets and selling them to France's private sector. (4 cloaks, 1 dagger)

British intelligence is in an uncomfortable state of "avowal." This means that M.I.6 is at last being publicly recognized and held accountable for mistakes. Its use of the Matrix Churchill company to run arms into Iraq — using the excuse that this kept the West informed about Saddam's buildup — is now being exposed as plainly stupid, embarrassing U.S. and Italian counterparts. But as the Gordievskiy recovery showed, nobody beats the Brits on running agents in place. (2 cloaks, 1 dagger)

Dead drop: data wars.

Chinese intelligence, for 30 years able to penetrate the C.I.A. with a mole (who, as trained, committed suicide when caught), is strongest on "humint," the painstaking gathering of data by individuals. "We send up one satellite to bring back a truckload of rocks," writes an American dead-dropper, "while the Chinese send out tens of thousands of students and businessmen, each to bring back a pinch of sand." (3 cloaks, 1 dagger)

Israeli intelligence, its mission given piquancy by national survival needs, remains strong on covert capability in its region and Europe, thin in Africa. Although Mossad proved to be clean in the Pollard rogue operation, an inability to target Iraqi Scud mobile launchers exposed a shortfall in military intelligence. The still-gutsy agency concentrates its limited budget on the Iranian threat. (3 cloaks, 4 daggers)

Saudi intelligence is strong at the top and able to draw data from global banking sources, but weak in the field, overly relying on paid informants and U.S. expertise in AWACS surveillance. (2 cloaks, 1 dagger)

Japanese intelligence hardly exists; they hire consultants for access. India and Pakistan spy mainly on each other, as do the Koreas.

German intelligence is in flux: still a good team player within NATO, but now no longer shot through by East Germany's Stasi (which once had 80,000 agents, almost in the same league with the U.S. and former Soviet Union). Improving its *Fingerspitzengefuhl* but confused about its mission. Help industry sell arms? Steal stolen French commercial secrets? Retrieve sensitive Stasi files from Russians? (2 cloaks, 1 dagger)

Of the niche agencies, Singapore is better than Switzerland on tracking money flows, Belgium snoops best on European Community affairs, and Norway retains its reputation for the most courageous agents. South Africa has hunkered down.

Of agencies formerly subsidiaries of the K.G.B., the Polish is now the most effective, followed by Czech and Hungarian; Bulgarian hit men suffer for lack of wet work. Cuban and Libyan agents are still paid, but are ideologically unmotivated.

Russian external intelligence under Yevgeny Primakov is as active as ever worldwide. It uses a high-minded control of nuclear proliferation as cover but its mission is to leapfrog costly R&D by stealing military and industrial technology. (4 cloaks, 3 daggers)

The C.I.A.? On Iraqgate, Robert Gates writes to protest that both intelligence committee chairmen "have told me that they could not think of anything I might do on BNL that I have not already done." He's invited me over for a brainwash and rinse next month; I'll report further.

Still the defending champ, but like this year's Washington Redskins, the C.I.A. seems to its peers "kinda flat." (3 cloaks, 2 daggers) □

Leslie H. Gelb is on vacation.

A note of thanks

Sometimes, if we look only at the blazing headlines, it seems we have a lot to worry about. Perhaps we do. But at this time of year, with that special American holiday of Thanksgiving to commemorate, it's also a good time to stop and offer a small note of thanks for what's right with us and our world.

So, thanks...for laughing children wherever the sound rings out...for the game of baseball, and for showing us that we can share it with Canadian friends...for free elections, and record numbers turning out to vote...for trees, and leaves that turn color and fall, and crunch underfoot on a clear, starlit night.

Thanks...for a free press, even if it means we sometimes have to read headlines we don't like...for public libraries with good books and for long winter nights to read them...for the teachers who taught us how to read...for a land that is still rich in natural resources and opportunity...for computers that correct our spelling, balance our checkbooks, and help the kids with their algebra homework.

Thanks...for everyone with a sense of humor to help us laugh our way over the rough spots...for volunteers, who help the helpless...for the energy of the younger generation and the wisdom of the older generation—and the chance to tap the best of both when we need to...for love, at any age.

Thanks...for five-foot, seven-inch basketball players who can play with the big guys...for every day that something happens to make us more tolerant of each other...for the wonders of Niagara Falls, the Grand Canyon, the snowcapped Rockies, autumn in New England, the rolling Mississippi, and all the other scenic delights this country has to offer.

Thanks...for a Gershwin tune, a Cole Porter lyric, and Ella Fitzgerald's renditions...for movies with "Bogie" and "Baby," Tracy and Hepburn, Cary Grant and anybody...for the Marx Brothers...for ice-cold drinks on hot summer days and the smell of new-mowed grass...for November, when sunsets throw a deep, rich orange glow across clouded skies, harvest moons shine boldly, and morning frosts change the tint of grassy meadows—and put an end to mowing.

Thanks...for people who care about other people...for warm kitchens and the smell of coffee brewing on chilly mornings...for weekends with nothing to do and somebody special to do it with...for the Special Olympics, which never fail to inspire us with what the human spirit can accomplish...for working men and women, who carry their briefcases or lunch pails to office and factory day in and day out, and make this country hum.

Thanks...for everything.

And Happy Thanksgiving to everybody!

Mobil®

Impersonating an Officer,

The New York Times Book Review,

2000, AD: Steven Heller

Nike's Power Game,

The New York Times, op-ed,

2000, AD: Nicholas Blechman

A Crude Awakening, *Stanford*, November/December 2006, AD: Amy Shroads

Contents

15   **Preface** by Milton Glaser
17   **Introduction** by Steven Heller

21   **Man of Good Fortune** • The beginning
27   *Studentski list* and *Pitanja* • The conquest of comics • 1976–77

29   **Ink-Stained T-Shirt** • ESSAY BY **Slavenka DRAKULIĆ**

31   **A Black and White World** • The *Polet* Years • 1976–1978
39   **Novi kvadrat** • A new wave before the New Wave
49   **Culture, Politics, and Scene** • The finest hour of the socialist state
55   **A Start at *Start* Magazine** • Illustrations • 1978–85

67   **Gastarbeiter** • ESSAY BY **Rujana JEGER**

69   **Everybody Dance. Now!** • Album cover design • 1979–86
85   **Street Images** • Posters • 1978–86
97   **SLS Studio** • Slow, Bad, Expensive
99   *Danas* **Magazine** • Magazine covers • 1982–85
109   **Before Leaving for New York** • 1985–86
113   **Looking for America** • 1986–87
125   **Self Portraits**

127   **Mirko Ilić—The Eye** • ESSAY BY **Laetitia WOLFF**

129   *Time* **Magazine** • 1986–2006
137   **Media and War** • 1991–96
143   **Op-Ed Pages** • *The New York Times* • Before and after 1992

153   **Caustic Iconoclast** • ESSAY BY **Steven HELLER**

165   **Photoshopping and Digital Illustration** • Oko & Mano • 1993–95 and after
176   **Mirko Ilić Corp.** • From 1995 on
181   **In the Realm of Rendering**

201   **Sex and Lies** • ESSAY BY **Steven HELLER**

205   **The Policies and Politics of Design**
225   **Illustration, the Method**
231   **Designer as Author**

238   **Mirko Ilić — The Eye, Part II** • ESSAY BY **Laetitia WOLFF**

241   **The Books** • Publication design • 1988 to today
263   **Design Is a Good Idea** • Visual identities • 1999 to today
299   **Country Roads Take Me Home** • Work in the post-Yugoslav countries • 1998–2011

Klansmen in the Cellar,
The New York Times Book Review,
March 18, 2001
AD: Steven Heller

R R R R R R R R R

THE LETTER R

The letter 'R' can be the most difficult for type designers to create. When drawn correctly it is rich with subtle details and delicate proportions. The problem is that the 'R' has a more distinct character than it seems to at first glance. It is not a 'P' with a tail or a 'B' with modifications; it is unique among letterforms.

There is an Egyptian hieroglyph on the Rosetta Stone which represents the consonant sound of 'R.' The symbol is called *Ro* and was drawn in the shape of a mouth. In hieratic writing the symbol was modified slightly so that it looked more like a headache capsule.

The Phoenician sign for the 'R' sound was called *Resh*, and bore no resemblance to the Egyptian Ro. Resh meant "head" in the Phoenician language and was represented in their alphabet by what is believed to be a very simple rendering of a human profile facing left.

By 900 B.C. the Greeks had adapted the Phoenician letter and called it *Rho*. The Greeks reversed the orientation of the head's profile (a step in the right direction toward creating our 'R'), and converted the curve of the face into an angular form. (This was clearly a step in the wrong direction as far as the 'R''s evolutionary process is concerned.)

The 'R' further evolved in the hands of the Greeks and ended up looking very much like our 'P.' But it was from an earlier western Greek letterform, in which a short oblique appendage had been added under the bowl, that the Romans acquired the letter.

Recognizing a good thing in this slight differentiation between the 'R' and 'P,' the Romans lengthened the short oblique stroke into a graceful and delicately curved tail which enhanced the letter as never before.

Frederic Goudy thought the 'R' to be the most interesting, and most difficult to replace, of the Trajan letters. The bowl is neither the same size nor the same shape as those of the 'P' or 'B.' The lower contour of the bowl is almost horizontal, while the top contour has an upward swelling. The tail of the Trajan 'R' attaches away from the vertical stroke and ends with a subtle curve and a slight dip below the baseline. The tails of 'R's can begin at virtually any place along the lower contour of the bowl and finish in a tapered point as in ITC Barcelona, curved like the front of a ski as in Gaudy Oldstyle, or in a discreet seal like that in Fairfield.

The 'R' can test the designer's mettle, but when rendered with skill, is an exceptionally beautiful communication tool. Allan Haley

Illustration by Mirko Ilić

R R R R R R R R R

HEADLINE: ITC STONE SANS SEMI BOLD   TEXT: MEDIUM, MEDIUM ITALIC   CREDIT: MEDIUM ITALIC

Preface

By **Milton Glaser**

THE WORK CONTAINED HEREIN is frequently called political, which largely means it is dependent on the changing events of our time for its content. Most of us working under the rubric of professional design have limited or no control of the ideological attitude over the work we do. We are in the service of others.

In those random cases when our client shares our worldview, our most powerful ideas can be expressed. This is a rare but deeply desirable occasion.

One can write such introductions to visual books with the secure knowledge that any narrative will make it more difficult to understand what you're going to be looking at. So, consider this introduction merely an attempt to describe the odd character of Mirko Ilić, a middle-aged man I've been living close to for 26 years. He is a bristling, energetic personality whose dark aura of Eastern-Europeanness rarely leaves him. After chatting with Mirko you begin to believe that everything is a conspiracy. There are satisfactions in this view because it makes every event understandable. Every theory suggests its opposite as well. How else could this perpetual outsider have been working like a mad man all these years?

The self simultaneously seeks and avoids definition.

Mirko's skill and editorial persuasion are obvious. What separates him from much of the field is his commitment to the well-being of his audience. Very often, after a lecture, the question of a designer's responsibility to others is raised. My usual answer to the question is "the responsibility is the same as any good citizen's." What is most evident in this book is the concern expressed by Mirko for the state of mind of his audience and his desire to increase their awareness.

Fervent belief is always risky, but if its opposite is indifference or detached professionalism, the risk may be worth taking. ✖

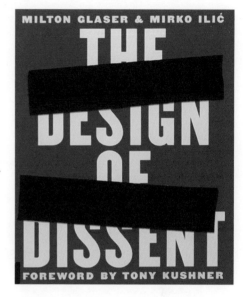

Mirko Ilić & Milton Glaser:
The Design of Dissent,
Rockport, 2005
COVER DESIGN: Mirko Ilić & Milton Glaser

The Letter R,
Upper and Lower Case, 1992,
AD: Milton Glaser,
Walter Bernard
ILLUSTRATION: Mirko Ilić

The New York Times

July 20, 1997 $1.25

Book Review

Copyright © 1997 The New York Times

DARK GENIUS

THE LIVES OF TWO GREAT DIRECTORS

Diane Jacobs on Howard Hawks 10

Stanley Kauffmann on Fritz Lang 11

MIRKO ILIC

Serge Schmemann on Boutros Boutros-Ghali **7**   Francine Prose on Hilary Mantel **9**

Dark Genius, *The New York Times Book Review*, July 20, 1997, AD: Steven Heller

Introduction

By **Steven Heller**

MIRKO ILIĆ OPENED MY EYES. Before him I had never met a Serbo-Croatian; didn't know where Yugoslavia was; had never savored Pljeskavica or Ćevapčići. That part of the world was entirely a blur. Thanks to him, I've since traveled to Belgrade and Ljubljana; learned to pronounce *Pljeskavica* and *Ćevapčići*; studied the geopolitics, art, and culture of the region; and have even been asked to teach design at some of the art schools (who knew there even *was* design, and rather accomplished design at that, there?)—simply because Ilić told his Serb, Croat, and Slovenian colleagues to bring me over and treat me like a king. Whatever Ilić says, they do.

He might as well be called King Mirko. Although he has lived in New York for more than twenty years, he holds beneficent sway over his people in the design and illustration communities. He deserves their respect, too. His generosity of spirit and material is extraordinary. There is nothing he will not do to help young designers garner success. Mentorship? He rarely says no. Advice? He gives it freely, if opinionatedly, without expecting payback. Humor? Among people who have lived through Communist privation and ethnic warfare, his wit is infectious. Inspiration? I've watched as he's packed scores of care packages filled with design books, posters, and other inspirational swag—much of it bought with his own money. Did I say money? He contributes more than he can afford to significant causes.

These acts of goodness are not entirely selfless. He does ask for one thing in return. Honesty. Like Diogenes, who carries the lantern in search of an honest man, Ilić seeks an honest cause and an honest client. He gives the proverbial one hundred and fifty percent to a job and demands as much honesty and respect in return. Ilić has been known to fire those clients that, for whatever reason, do not rise to his standard of integrity. Which means those clients and colleagues who promise license but revoke it when his concepts do not conform to their preconceived vision—or lack thereof.

Ilić does not, however, find it painful to compromise if a better idea rises from the ashes of a rejected one. Yet he refuses to capitulate to rotten notions. And this has cost him dearly. Working in the service field of design, he knows how to communicate a message effectively. He can break through the visual and textual clutter and make cogent, even poignant, graphic messages. The examples in this volume shine with cogency, poignancy, and, most of all, surprise.

What Ilić brings to his work—to his clients—that should be valued is a passion for each thing he concepts. This emotional rigor will allow him to neither repeat past successes nor to succumb to low expectations. Admirable, right? Yet exasperating, too—sometimes.

A story: He was commissioned to design a book I wrote titled *The Swastika: A Symbol Beyond Redemption?* His cover design was smart; he cut the symbol in half and ran the bottom portion on top and the top portion on the bottom of the image area to show that even in this divided form its power to shock was undiminished. For the interior he decided—and here's Mirko at his most conceptual—to replace the word *swastika* with the symbol. This would mean every time the word was mentioned (quite a bit) the

Steven Heller & Mirko Ilić: *Handwritten—Expressive Lettering in the Digital Age*,
Thames & Hudson, 2004
COVER DESIGN: Hoop Design
DESIGN & LAYOUT: Mirko Ilić Corp.

Steven Heller & Mirko Ilić:
The Anatomy of Design,
Rockport, 2007
AD & D: Mirko Ilić; D: Mirko Ilić Corp.

Steven Heller & Mirko Ilić:
Stop Think Go Do,
Rockport Publisher, 2012
DESIGN: Landers Miller Design

Steven Heller & Mirko Ilić:
Genius Moves—100 Icons of Graphic Design,
Thames & Hudson, London, 2001

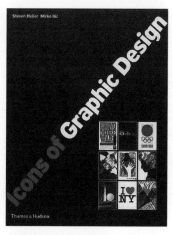

Steven Heller & Mirko Ilić:
Icons of Graphic Design,
Thames & Hudson, London, 2001

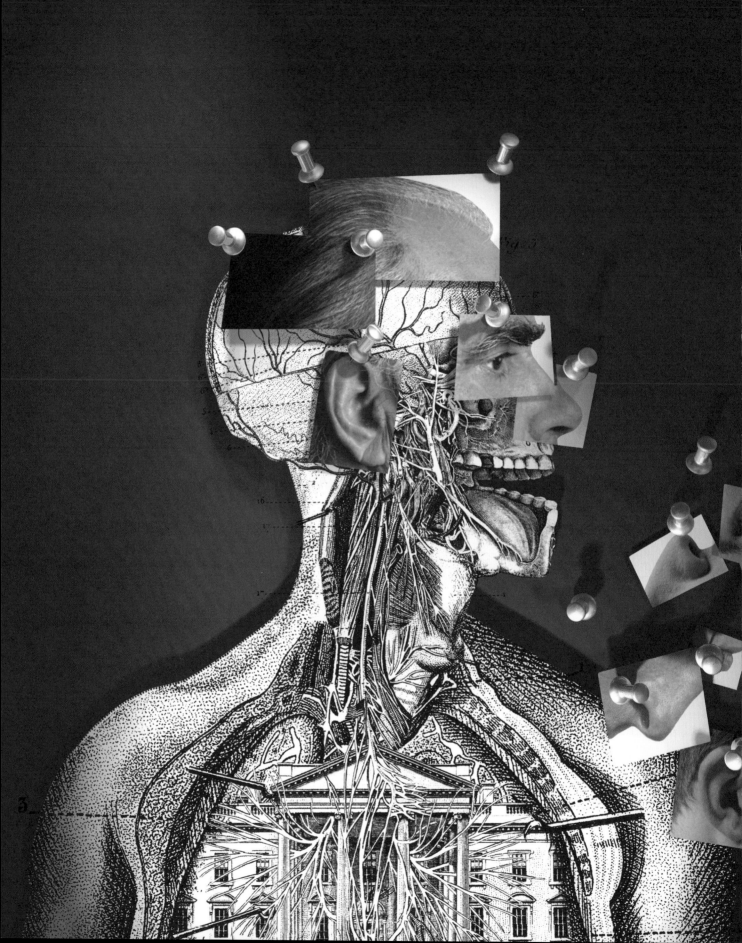

symbol would appear. The publisher was not pleased. I must say, I was wary that this was overkill, but Ilić believed that it was endemic to the thesis of the book. When the concept was rejected, he said we could retain the cover and layout format, but he was quitting the project.

Exasperating? Yes! But he did not leave us in the lurch. It was as respectful as the defiant gesture could be. Integrity? When two immovable forces meet, acrimony can easily result. When the explanation is rooted in adherence to a concept he believed in—a battle fought and lost—it is better to retreat with valor. Ilić has opened my eyes. In his world there is a lot of room for difference, but never the possibility of surrender. ✖

Deep Throat: Mystery Solved,
The New York Times Book Review, 2000,
AD: Steven Heller

Black Hawk Down,
The New York Times Book Review, 1999,
AD: Steven Heller

Picturebook for Dictators, *Studentski list* (Student newspaper) no. 10, Zagreb, February 25, 1976

Man of Good Fortune

The beginning of a career

ACCORDING TO OFFICIAL RECORDS, Mirko Ilić was born on January 1, 1956, in Bijeljina, a small town "on the three border point where Drina flows into the Sava River," where for years nothing exciting happened. The town was known only by those in the agriculture and food industries for its production of plums, until the early nineties when war crimes committed by Arkan's Tigers (a Serbian paramilitary formation) brought it to the front pages of international newspapers.

Like many other famous artists, musicians, writers, and journalists of the Yugoslav baby-boom generation, Ilić was the "child of a military professional." In the former Yugoslavia such an origin dictated certain characteristics, including your social standing as well as your political views, and overall understanding of the world around you.

> **"My mother had a sewing machine and lots of crayons for drawing on fabric. I remember one day picking up one of those crayons when it had fallen down. After many hours of sewing, my mother stood up and saw a drawing of Santa Claus on the floor. Since there was nobody else in the house it meant that I had done it. She was in total shock. 'You did this?!' she asked? She covered the drawing with a piece of carpet to preserve it and show to my father. I remember the importance of that moment because she didn't yell and usually I got yelled at and slapped around. Nobody actually patted me on the back, but I understood that I had done something great, something for my parents to preserve. I still joke about it and I'm still looking to this day for art directors who, when I give them a drawing, will cover it with a piece of carpet. Then, one time when I was maybe five years old, I drew a carriage being pulled by horses. When my grandfather saw it he laughed like crazy. He didn't yell at me for drawing in his book. Instead, he actually showed people. He was so proud of that drawing. Those two moments told me you can show off, and if it works with your parents, maybe it will work with women and bankers. So I went in that direction."**

—MIRKO ILIĆ, "MIRKO ILIĆ & MILTON GLASER: THE KING AND THE JESTER,"

EDITED BY LAETITIA WOLFF, *GRAPHIS* #350, MARCH/APRIL 2004

From Bijeljina, he first moved to Maribor, where he completed his first two years of primary school. He started third grade in Zagreb and then returned to Bijeljina. After fifth grade, the family moved back to Zagreb, where Ilić stayed, finished school, and started his career. Frequent changes of environment marked his way of thinking; he did not belong to anyone, and at the same time he belonged to everyone, so he did not attach values to national, religious, or linguistic differences. He was accustomed to constant adjustment and new situations, which honed his quick wit and sense of humor.

The feeling of not being rooted in a particular nation or local culture and the lack of interest in tradition resulted from these sudden transfers to new environments. He truly lived multiculturalism and belonged more to global media culture (movies, television, pop music, comics ...) than to some ideological notion imposed by the family or state apparatus. "The fact that we were moving around so often made it easier for me to go to America and into the unknown," Ilić said. I did not get to take root, or belong to any group, and xenophobia could not get near me. I cried every time I left friends, but I would soon find new ones. When I was seventeen, I hitchhiked through Europe not knowing any foreign languages, except for a little French. I traveled, and visited some famous comics artists, so it was easier for me later on to contact foreign publishers and send them comics, to start to publish abroad. I was not afraid that someone would tell me to stop trying. I knocked on all doors I had addresses for. I did not have famous or rich parents to help me. All I had was my talent—which was minimal—and my nimbleness."

Ilić began drawing to escape from the loneliness—and probably the related boredom—he felt as a boy: "Since I was an only child and we were constantly moving, sitting in the corner and drawing was my main entertainment. I knew that as soon as I became friends with someone I would soon have to part, so drawing was my best friend. Then I realized that it was easier to do that than some other jobs. If I had learned how to make shoes for these same reasons, I would probably be a shoemaker now."

Ilić doesn't remember exactly how old he was when he first started to draw, but he recalls, "I was small enough to go under a chair, a wooden one with four legs. It had

Father Zdravko, Mirko, grandfather Ilija and
mother Božica Ilić, Maribor 1959

**"My father was in the military, so
I moved through many military
compounds. When they came
home these officers got rid of their
uniforms but not their anger. They
treated their families as conscripts.
Approximately thirty percent of their
children became introverted and in
turn the most successful artists in
Yugoslavia. At the same time forty
percent of them became extroverted
and decided to face the system head
on and become criminals. People who
became artists probably didn't have
a stomach for blood and violence
and they decided to rebel silently: by
drawing, composing, etc. At that time,
if your father was in the military,
you'd move from town to town. Each
time it was a new society, a new
ethnic group; you would be moved
around to a totally different part of
the country. Suddenly it was a totally
different food, a totally different
language, a totally different culture,
and you got dumped in. "**

—MIRKO ILIĆ, "MIRKO ILIĆ & MILTON GLASER: THE KING AND THE
JESTER," EDITED BY LAETITIA WOLFF, *GRAPHIS* #350, MARCH/
APRIL 2004

fantastic white wood on the bottom side, so I doodled on it with a pen."

His mother was first to notice that his doodling was actually quite good and she supported his efforts. Later on, she carefully monitored her son's successes, evidenced by a big book of press clippings from the seventies and eighties that she assembled, which Ilić keeps today in his New York studio.

The beginning of the seventies was quite stormy in terms of Ilić's family life, and though he does not speak a lot about it, it definitely shaped him to a great extent. These were the years of the problematic relationship with his father, who wanted his son to go to a military high school and did not want to hear about an art career. At the same time, the relationship between his father and mother was becoming increasingly tense. In a different scenario, the combination of a dysfunctional family and rebellious teenager would have resulted in yet another promising talent who achieved little. "It's very easy to slip from an artistic to a criminal direction," Ilić once said. "I think I was saved because I had some talent, which my mother recognized and encouraged. When I was fourteen or fifteen, I decided that I'd prefer to be a lover rather than a fighter."

Ilić supported his mother's decision to divorce his father and started to work and earn money. His first paid job was writing numbers on the 6,000 seats of the Dinamo football club stadium. In June 1974, he went to Tunstead International Farm Camp, in Norwich, and worked in the strawberry harvest, after which he traveled around, bought books and comics, and mailed them home.

At that time, local comic-book publishing fell into one of its many crises; publications were being discontinued and local authors were turning to other occupations. The *Omladinskit jednik* (Youth weekly) contained more articles about comics than actual comics: in the centerfold of issue no. 170, from January 1973, critic Darko Glavan wrote about new American comic artists (R. Crumb, Art Spiegelman, Gilbert Shelton). Translations of theorists like Umberto Eco were also being published, and at the end of 1973 the series "Paths and sidetracks of comics" featured various authors discussing the concept of children's comics, classics such as Foster and Raymond, superheroes, and, on two occasions, the new French comics—Reiser, Willem, Wolinski, and Crepax.

Ilić's first published illustration was in *Omladinskit jednik.* "I brought a bunch of drawings to the editors and left them in the newsroom. I did not think it was important to sign them, and after a couple of weeks, one of my illustrations—a mother with a child—was published, but without my signature."

After that, Ilić continuously published his work in youth magazines and then in Vjesnik publications, primarily in the weekly *VUS (Vjesnik u srijedu)* [Vjesnik on Wednesday]. Like many others from the Applied Arts School, he worked part-time at Zagreb-film, the center of Zagreb School of Animation, during the 1975 summer holidays.

"It was a summer job, thanks to Aleksandar Marks. I worked on commercials for Standard konfekcija (a clothing factory), and even a great animation project for the food company Podravka. It was very interesting: live pictures mixed with drawing. I had never animated before, it was too complicated. You had to be there for a hundred years before they would let you make your own movie before you died. However, I realized there that my work habits were not abnormal, and that other people worked during the night as well. I met Radovan Devlić, who worked there more regularly, and several other people who meant a lot to me later on, like Zlatko Bourek who was pretty famous at the time. So this was a valuable experience, and I also earned some money."

The core of the future Novi kvadrat started to gather slowly: Krešimir Zimonić, Igor Kordej, Emir Mesić, and Ilić were a group from the School of Applied Arts. Through his work in the Zagreb Film, Ilić met Devlić and Kunc, and while circulating the *SL*, he met the somewhat older Marušić. This friendship evolved into an intensive theoretical and practical engagement in comics: "I stood at the tram station with Radovan Devlić for hours, and we used to daydream about comics."

It was around that time that Ilić left home: "My mom was relatively young and already divorced, and the custom was to stay with your parents until you finished college, possibly a little longer. But I had prevented her from having a life. I was lucky to be eighteen and to earn enough money to be able to pay for a flat. I soon realized that it was a mistake to rent a one-bedroom apartment. I was the only one of my friends with a flat, so I always had someone coming to the door. Then I realized I couldn't work if someone was always there, so I moved to a two-bedroom apartment. No one was allowed to enter my study, but the rest of the apartment was free to use.

"Until 1979, the School of Applied Arts had five grades. For the final exam we had to make a piece of artwork," Ilić remembered. "We pulled out pieces of paper from a hat and I grabbed 'the history of the costume.' I made a photo of my naked body, and over my private parts I wrote 'The exhibition of historical costumes'. This caused quite a stir, and the women at the school stood in front of the poster and stared. It was kind of a scandal."

Upon finishing at the School for Applied Arts, Ilić wanted to enroll in the Zagreb Academy of Fine Arts, but like many now well-known figures, he was not admitted, which speaks volumes about the character of the institution. "At the suggestion of Duško Petričić I applied to the Belgrade Faculty of Applied Arts," he said. "When I was admitted there, I said 'Thanks but no thanks.'"

Ilić's time in school established his enduring fascination with the poster designer Boris Bućan. It also fostered a friendly rivalry between the two. "I think that I was mostly influenced by—although you can't see it in my work—Boris Bućan. I saw Bućan's work first on the street. Then, one of our teachers said that she would take us to her friend who was a graphic designer. That was the first time we'd seen a graphic design studio, because everybody in the school was a painter. So we went to Bućan and from the moment we entered, I liked it all. He showed us a poster that he made for the theater company Gavella, and the play *Večeras improviziramo* (we improvise tonight). He took the theater logo, extracted the elements, rearranged them, and asked us why the poster looked like it did. I said: 'Well, it's improvising with the logo.' And that's where I took off."

"I liked that approach. I was delighted with the amount of freedom that he had. The school was still teaching us about the experiment Exat 51 group, now and then Polish posters would be mentioned, but curriculum at the School of Applied Arts more or less stopped with Toulouse-Lautrec, like—he was the best designer, and after him everything went downhill with the poster! That's why my education there was much better for illustration than design. They all knew how to make a good illustration. So when I met Bućan,

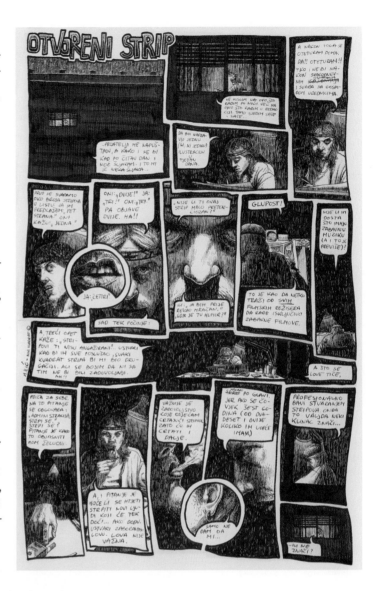

Open Comic,
Polet no. 41, 1977
Comic about drawing of a comic and problems
with editors, publishers and critics.

The picture book of big and small,
Studentski list, no. 11, March 19, 1976

for the first time I saw someone who was truly a designer.

"Another person who influenced me greatly was F. V. Holi. He was the art director at the *Studentski list,* and he was collecting metal printing plates for me because he knew that it was valuable. 'You take it,' he said, 'you will need it.' So I brought my casts, and he designed a catalog for me for an exhibition later on.

"Among illustrators, Duško Petričić was another influence. I don't know if that's evident in my work since it does not resemble his at all. But he's brilliant and it was a great joy for me to see how someone so smart could imbue that intelligence into his work.

"Mihajlo Arsovski and Ivan Picelj came later. Frankly, you can't enjoy Arsovski's design unless you have some cultural reference. Only nowadays are people like Milan Vulpe being discovered. He made a well-known poster for a figure skating championship; it was a bunch of colors, abstract, but when you looked closer, it was a reflection of a skater, upside down.[01] It is quite odd and great. But you can't love something that subtle when you are fifteen! You need more of a punch in the face. We were kids. We didn't listen to chamber orchestras; we liked loud music that would shatter glass. At fifteen, one does not enjoy Bergman, one enjoys Sergio Leone. In a way, everything Bućan did was before the punk movement, but very similar in how he spat in the face of the system. With Arsovski it is a little bit harder to detect what direction he was pushing the boundaries. I would see a Bućan poster on the street and think about it deeply for a week. One single poster of his could literally change your way of thinking. Of course, pop culture had an important impact on me. Movies and Monty Python were greatly influencing everything we were doing at that time, though it seemed to be subliminally. The group would never remember it when talking about it. Of course, the basic things that I devoured in terms of design were album covers. *Hipgnosis* for example. You look at the Pink Floyd cover (the cover of the album *Ummagumma* for instance) and you think, in this picture how did they do this, and this, and that?

"In comics, it was Moebius, but that was later. Before that, it was the American underground that annoyed me because it was imperfect on purpose. They would make something good, and then would screw up the rest, and I was like, 'Nooo …' This desire for perfection always bothered me. However, I was never fascinated by M. C. Escher and those things that people used to worship; it all looked to me like a bad drug trip.

"I never liked Polish posters much either, but Roman Cieslewicz influenced me a lot, although I didn't know much about his work. We met when he was at *Start* magazine. *Start* also made me

01 | It is Bojan Stranić's (1921–1993) poster for the European Championship in figure skating and ice dancing, dated 1974.

aware of Roland Topor, another person who was quite important to me. He made a couple of incredible illustrations, some terribly dark sexual things. He wrote three or four novels, and Roman Polanski's film *Tenant* was based on one of them.

"The writer and musician Davor Slamnig was another influence. I went to elementary school with him. He came from America, and he was really into underground comics, so he used to draw great comics in his notebooks with a pen: a postman rings at the door and peeks through the peephole, through which a kid behind the door shoots an arrow into his eye! These were his comics. I would go over to Davor's home, and he had a bunch of stuff that he brought from America. His dad was a famous poet. I learned a lot from Davor. I didn't like people telling me what to do, but I realized that I could listen to this guy, that it was OK.

"I was lucky to have three or four people in school who were also very interested in comics," Ilić recalled. "They were Krešimir Zimonić, Igor Kordej, and Emir Mesić. Although we already drew comics, we were primarily collectors. We were cleaning other people's attics and taking all the comics that we found there. So at the time I had thousands of comics that I have since given away."

That was a period of large-scale stagnation in domestic comics. "At that time, all of our major comics had been discontinued or were in a process of discontinuing. *Stripoteka* and *Politikin zabavnik* were the only ones being published. So, we could buy two or three a week. We felt the need for comics even if they were the worst ones. This situation forced us to collect old comic books. My collection dated way back, to 1923."

The group was also devouring books, especially foreign illustrated editions about art that, at the time, could be found in the bookstores in the Foreign Literature section. According to Ilić, a single illustration by Brad Holland—"Junkie" for *The New York Times* in 1972, reprinted in an issue of *Graphis*, showed him the full power of illustration and led him to become what he is today.

"We discovered the real thing: a bookstore on Gundulićeva Street. At that time, foreign comics were being sold there. We all felt that comics could—and must—be better, but we were not sure how or why. We didn't have any examples to point to. We were afraid that maybe we were asking for too much. And then we saw those comics in Mladost bookstore: often in color, with high-quality binding. They were absurdly expensive—and instantly they became sacred. Classes were being held at that time in the morning and afternoon, with an hour or two for lunch in between. We used to argue with our parents that we didn't have time to come home for lunch so could we have some money to buy lunch in town? Yes, sure! We would end up with fries from the tourist fast-food restaurant; those foreign editions were between five- and ten-thousand dinars, which in 1972 was a lot of money. So that was how we discovered the American underground and the new French comics. But it was still very difficult to publish anything ourselves. We contributed some ideas to the school paper, but that was pretty much it. We had time to do one frame in a normal format of schoellershammer paper."

In those years, the crowd from the School of Applied Arts used to gather on Marshal Tito Square, in the Kazališna kavana and a nearby cafe, called Zvečevo. In later years, the area became an epicenter of Zagreb's New Wave scene, and Ilić had the majority of his business meetings there. "I think that the biggest jobs in rock music and design were made in *Kavkaz* and *Zvečka*. In a time before cell phones and fax devices, these were our offices." ▶

Joint issue of student magazines in SFRY, May 25, 1976

Studenski list and *Pitanja*

ILIĆ PUBLISHED HIS FIRST COMIC in the February 25, 1976, edition of *Studentski list*. "*Studentski list* featured some good artists, underground comics like R. Crumb. I 'snuck' into SL through some strange connections. I could not get a job as a comics artist; I was just another illustrator. It was done differently back then. They used to wait for an illustration until four in the morning so that it could be taken to the printing office at five A.M.

"Some other people were publishing comics there—but mine they did not want. One day, someone didn't bring the agreed comic and then someone remembered that I drew comics as well, and they told me: 'Bring one page tomorrow.' Of course, I did not like anything I had already done so that night I started to work on a new comic—it was called 'Picture Book for Dictators.' It was pretty good."

This first published comic—despite the fact that at the time he was strongly influenced by American underground comics—shows some features of his work that would become permanenet: strong, clear drawings, media savvy, and frequent portraiture. The next comic, "Picture Book of Big and Small," shows Ilić's interest in meaningful narrative and structural aspects of formal elements such as framing and lettering. "I like to play with sounds," Ilić said. "Each frame contains some kind of sound or noise." A preoccupation with sound and a penchant for testing conventions would soon reach a new level of sophistication through his work published in *Polet*.

Next, Ilić worked on the restored monthly magazine "devoted to society, science, and culture," *Pitanja,* where he met the woman who would become his first wife, the now well-known writer Slavenka Drakulić, who worked there as a secretary of the Head of Publishing-Information Department of CDD (Center for Social Services of the Association of Socialist Youth of Croatia).

Many years later, in a television interview, Ilić said: "At that point, Slavenka had not yet been published. She wrote things for herself, but nothing had been picked up yet. Her sarcastic take on the ideas of all these big shots who worked there was very interesting to me. So we met, started dating; I found out that she had an eight-year-old daughter named Rujana. It did not have much to do with our careers; we were both at the beginning of them. I think we both recognized something in the other. She was reading books that I did not read, in languages that I did not know; she was very smart, educated, and, of course, she was incredibly helpful. I had the instinct, she had the knowledge, and she could explain to me why I did something. I married Slavenka when I was twenty-one years old." ▶

The photo of the original comic table for the Joint issue of student magazines in **SFRY,** May 25, 1977, PHOTO: Danilo Dučak, LETTERING: Nikola Kostandinović

This early comic differs from other comics only in its use of color, all other features are present: a stylish nomadism, playing with the format and the manner of reporting, the theme of the medium of comics itself, until the appearance of the author as "the hero."

OPPOSITE PAGE:

Freedom / Libertad

Student, Belgrade, November 7, 1976

Fokus no. 145, Zagreb 1978

Epic vol 1. #5, 1981

SHAKTI

NOVI KVADRAT

there was a distinctly beautiful
and strong horse

who endlessly
stood in one place.

he waited for a rider.
a rider, not a master,
for each needed one another.

only the rider
could show them the true path,
and only the horse
could carry them there.
there was a disinctly strong horse.

M. ILIĆ

Ink-Stained T-Shirt

By **Slavenka DRAKULIĆ**

I GOT TO KNOW MIRKO IN 1976, when the first issue of *Polet* was being prepared. The editorial office was located on the premises of the magazine *Pitanja* at 10 Opatička Street. In fact, it was just one big room where editors and part-timers and people who had just dropped in to see acquaintances roamed around from morning until night. At any given time there would be at least twenty people in the room. The atmosphere was like that of a café. When *Polet* moved to 3 Savska Street, the social life of the editorial staff shifted to the nearby Kavkaz café. Almost all of today's generation of middle-age journalists got their training at *Polet*. Mirko came every day with a folder under his arm and big bags under his eyes.

Sometimes he would have to draw an illustration on the spot. Being in the middle of the throng of people that didn't seem to bother him.

He was twenty years old, with long blond hair and blue eyes. He wore a T-shirt splotched with Indian ink, jeans, and the obligatory boots. He looked romantic, was very talented, and seemed incredibly self-confident.

Actually, I first took notice of him precisely because of this self-confidence, which at times bordered on arrogance, and only then because of his exceptional talent. Because of this self-confidence, even then he was getting on some people's nerves. Some individuals who are clearly made of different stuff can get on your nerves, people who, you can see, want to do and can do more, who are ambitious, and show through their life and work that the milieu is too little for them. Mirko showed something else as well: that if someone had talent and persistence, he could achieve everything he wanted, regardless of the political system he came from, the milieu he grew up in, or whether you were cold-shouldered by the art establishment. There are people, who are exceptional, who are hard to compare to anyone else, and who are extremely hard to measure, because they will always achieve more and go further.

Sometimes, when I recall the twenty-five years in which I have known him, I think that Mirko's character has been at least as important to his success as his talent. He has this incredible persistence, this will to never stop, to keep on investigating. Some obstinacy, a restlessness, and a need to keep proving himself. And above all, his sheer curiosity. Mirko never stops and he's never satisfied with what he has achieved, whether its a successful new project or the mastering of a new technique. He is always in search of the genuinely new. When he had had enough of the technique of ink drawing, he went over to etching, and meanwhile he was also doing ironical and witty montages for the cover of *Danas*. I couldn't list all the techniques he has used. But I do get the impression that he has never stopped investigating. And in the pursuit of his, he has never given up playing. Only people quite freed of the fear of failure and completely dedicated to work, like him, can be so liberated in the search for new forms of expression. Mirko's curiosity and playfulness are just as great today as they were when he was twenty years old.

It looks as if now there is a new Mirko. But all the same, it is still recognizable as the old, witty Mirko, the Mirko who can't be captured by the cliché.

We don't see each other much today, living on different ends of the world. Nevertheless, I saw him recently in Zagreb, and it seemed that he hadn't changed much, had lost nothing of that youthful fervor. He was even the same physically, except for a few hardly noticeable lines. The only thing is that he no longer wears a T-shirt stained with ink. ✖

> "The most beautiful thing that I have ever drawn in terms of emotions was the comic Shakti. I drew it when I fell in love with Slavenka Drakulić. This was my first major comic and it represented one of the most important shifts in my thinking. For me, the idea that a comic was much more important than the original (which still exists somewhere). The only thing that happens in this comic is a horse. A wonderful, huge, powerful stallion that needs a rider."

—MIRKO ILIĆ, "ENVY PECULIARLY MEASURES YOUR SUCCESS," *DELO SATURDAY SUPPLEMENT*, LJUBLJANA, JUNE 3, 2000

OPPOSITE PAGE:

Shakti,

Vidici no. 3, Belgrade, September 1977;

Polet no. 37, October 21, 1977

Reproduced is the version printed as a poster for the exhibition in the SC Gallery in 1977

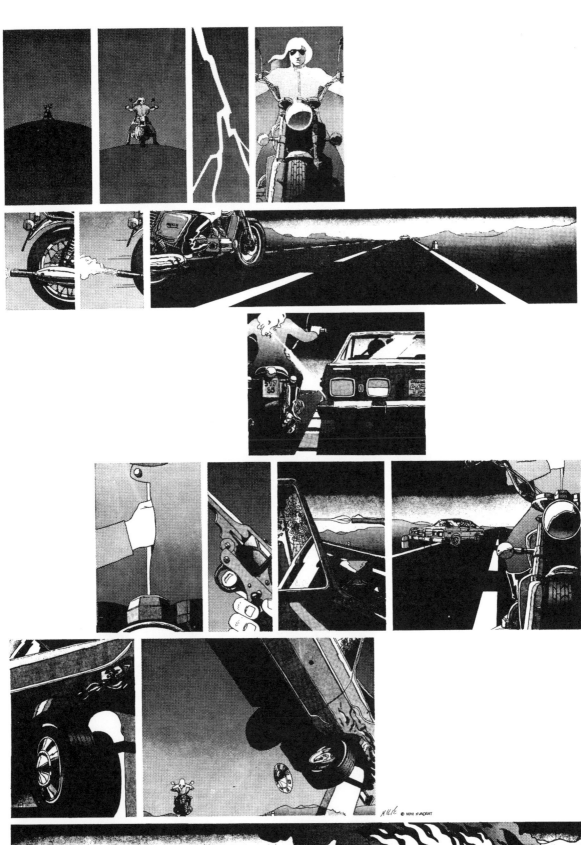

A Black and White World

THE PUBLISHER OF *PITANJA* started *Polet* (the weekly newspaper of the Socialist Youth of Croatia) in the fall of 1976. The design was based on an earlier version of the magazine that had been published in the sixties.

The art direction for the new version was led by the designer Zoran Pavlović, who at that time was employed in the graphic design studio of CDD. Danilo Dučak was the photo editor. *Polet* was printed using letterpress, and the use of photography was rather limited, so the magazine naturally lent itself to illustrations and comics from the very beginning.

Ilić was initially invited by the editorial desk to create illustrations, but the desk also offered him the chance to publish his own comics, and starting with issue number 7, he was formally signed on as the editor of comics and illustrations. He used this opportunity to recruit his colleagues and friends, mostly from the School of Fine Arts, which soon resulted in the formation of the group called Novi kvadrat.

"I heard rumors about *Polet* in *Pitanja*," Ilić recalled. "I spent hours and hours with people who worked on the concept of the newspaper. I was pushing comics through. Of course, the editor, Pero Kvesić, supported the comics, but I don't think he liked the ones I was doing. When the chance to get published appeared, I called Kordej, Zimonić, Skozret, and others. People on the desk liked our comics and we were given more and more space."

The first issues of the magazine rarely had full comics, and the ones that did appear were usually incorporated in the text. Their format varied from one panel to boards of various sizes. In the double issue of the magazine (no. 10–11), three full-page comics and five comics mixed with the text were published.

The new position allowed Ilić to transform his work with the medium. "When we say that someone is the editor of illustrations and comics, it means that he does everything by himself; draws by himself and edits himself! Even then I knew that one person could not change anything and that a group approach was required. So I brought in talented contributors whom I knew and trusted.

"*Studentski list* had an exchange with *Student* from Belgrade, and I went there several times with graphics editor F. V. Holi. Writer Ljubomir Kljakić was a big shot in the youth organization at that time, and he loved and wrote about comics. Knowing that comics in Yugoslavia were theoretically shallow, in order to legitimize the comics in *Polet*, I went and conducted an interview with him about their importance. Then he introduced me to several people in Belgrade, designers Nenad Čonkić, Nikola Kostandinović, Branko Gavrić, and others. So in the summer of 1977, I created an exhibition of my cartoons and Kordej's in the Dom omladine (Youth Center) in Belgrade.

I learned typography from Nikola. He was able to teach me what I could not learn in school. He experimented a lot with design in the magazine *Vidici*, mostly with strange colors and type. I found Milton Glaser's first book at Nikola's. I knew some of his work, but I had not seen everything in the book. What impressed me about Glaser was that he drew, but he drew a little bit this way and a little bit that way. It was different from anything I'd seen before. And, at that time, I had not heard of many other designers since it was not a topic we learned much about in school. We didn't know what happened twenty years ago in our country, let alone further back than that. You had a few of the usual suspects, and that was it."

Our youth is good,
Polet no. 9, December 24, 1976
WRITTEN BY: Zoran Franičević

Untitled (The course of the school reform),
Polet no. 38, October 28, 1977

OPPOSITE PAGE:

Untitled,
Polet no. 53, February 13, 1978

"Mirko Ilić, a very young and energetic artist, became the editor of comics and illustrations at *Polet*, and he began to aggressively impose his ideas about comics and push through the works of like-minded artists. This coincided with the ideas of Pero Kvesić, who (in the first issue of *Polet*) devoted four or five pages to comics, which was unprecedented outside of specialty publications.

So, several domestic comics were to be created each week. Ilić gathered about five or six permanent authors including Radovan Devlić, Nino Kunc, Joško Marušić, Krešimir Skozret, and occasionally Krešimir Zimonić, Igor Kordej, and Ilić, a group that would go on to become Novi kvadrat.

Except within a narrow circle of artists, comics were, until then, mainly considered a pastime for kids and the immature. The authors of the Novi kvadrat contributed crucially to the affirmation of comics for mature readers, and under their sway, comics began to be considered as their generation's expressive means and anyone who respected himself had to be familiar with new releases, new authors, and new trends."

—IGOR MIRKOVIĆ: "HAPPY CHILD," FRAKTURA, ZAGREB 2004

The comics we did were the first things in *Polet* to begin attracting a wider audience—first with the kids, and then a more general audience started showing interest. The solid core consisted of five or six resident authors, but there were others as well.

Ilić describes it this way: "What *Polet* did—which is incredible—is that it paved the way for the kids. The general idea at *Polet* was: here, this is your playground. Everyone who managed to drag themselves in, however damaged, suddenly gained confidence and began to form an actual personal identity. Everyone came with a need to demonstrate what they knew. Although the *Polet* editors claimed otherwise, I always felt that they didn't know what to put in the paper, so they

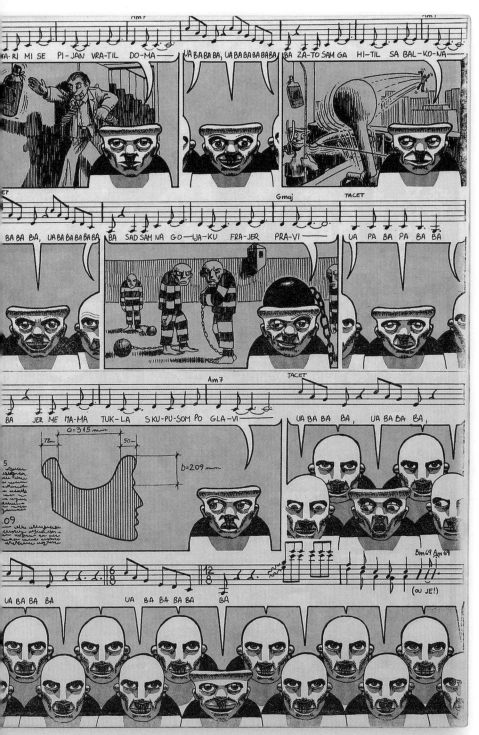

Debil Blues,

MUSIC: Davor Slamnig,

TEXT: Goran Pavelić & Davor Slamnig,

Polet no. 15, February 25, 1977

The original version of the comic is displayed in the Modern Gallery of Zagreb. Only three-quarters of the comic are on permanent display because part of it was lost sometime between when it was donated and when it was framed.

just said, 'let's give it to some kids.' When that started to happen, people began knocking at the door, and it became a place that started to attract a crowd. We were a team at the editorial office, but all clustered in small separate groups, and ours was the illustration team.

"There were a handful of different arts movements that started to gain steam at the time. CKD was theater people and that crew, CDD was the people from the publishing business—primarily members of *Pitanja*. I was in that group, which also included Joško Marušić.

Then the creator of *Polet*, Pero Kvesić, arrived on the scene. He had come from America on a Fulbright fellowship, totally under the influence of under-

From "The History of Human Folly,"
Polet no. 28, May 20, 1977

History of Human Absurdity,
Fokus no. 141, 1978;
Epic Illustrated Vol. 1 No. 1, 1980

"*Polet* **gave us a tiny miracle—Novi kvadrat. At the beginning, we were only filling in the pages that** *Polet* **journalists could not fill in, but when the battle for the pages began, everyone could see that** *Polet* **needed us, because people wanted to read comics. Unfortunately it didn't last long. When the editors realized they could publish photos of hot chicks, comics became irrelevant. However, for a short time, about a year and a half, this was a very important magazine for comics and illustration."**

—MIRKO ILIĆ, "CROATIAN DESIGN IS BETTER THAN AMERICAN,"
NEDELJNA DALMACIJA, SPLIT APRIL 12, 2002

ground comics. A free sex, jeans, an music culture. And it was all very logical to him. We were quite influenced by Europe at that time, but America's influence was starting to creep in a little bit more. Even our Western films were the Italian spaghetti westerns!"

The group started to produce even more comics than they could publish, and Ilić nurtured his managerial gift. He popularized comics and started to push them into other media. Thus the name Novi kvadrat was created, on a panel to promote a new approach to comics and a new generation of comic book authors. Someone asked: "Are you now a new circle of comic book authors?" and Ilić replied: "No, not a new circle, but a square—the new square (Novi kvadrat)." At first, it was just an offhand comment, but when they started to think about formalizing the group, the name stuck. "We needed some sort of name that would protect the quality and be easily remembered."

In September 1977, *Polet* no. 32/33 published the first two comics signed by the Novi kvadrat—Ilić's *Dobitnik* (Winner) and Kordej's untitled comic based on Ilić's idea. In February, 1978 at the Gallery Koprivnica, eight members of the Novi kvadrat first exhibited their work together. And in September 1978, an exhibition was held in Rijeka, with a catalog including the foreword by Slavenka Drakulić and Ilić being published accompanying it.

"We had been appreciated by kids, but the intellectuals did not know about us," Ilić said. "Their equation was: COMICS=NOTHING. And then a few things happened in a short period of time. Renowned critic Veselko Tenžera wrote a short article in *Vjesnik* about the Novi kvadrat explaining how intellectuals were stupid for failing to see what was happening right under their noses, and that in twenty years nobody would remember all of the masters' paintings, but that everyone would remember the Novi kvadrat because it was authentic stuff. At

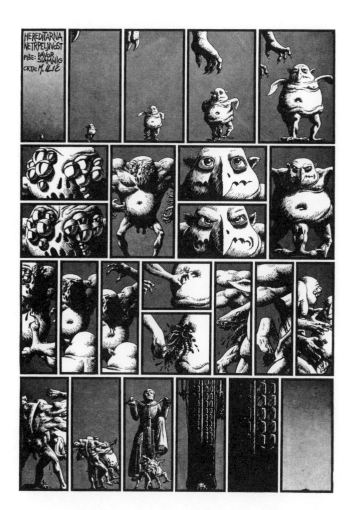

roughly the same time, Belgrade journalist Bogdan Tirnanić appeared in Zagreb. He asked to interview me. When I met him in the hotel lobby I approached him and said: 'I'm Mirko Ilić', he was puzzled, even suspicious, and asked me: 'How old are you?' I told him I was twenty, and he replied, 'Oh, fuck!' We joked later about how that was the moment he realized how old he was. He wrote a two-page article in the magazine *NIN*. Tenžera's and Tirnanić's pieces drew intellectuals' attention to comics. As it is said, if they praise it, then ...'"

"Meanwhile, a science fiction exhibition was organized in the SC Gallery. Someone also was thinking about comics—foreign ones at that—but we got some room there as well and a similar exhibition was held in Belgrade. We started to exhibit more and more. So we went from the alternative student and youth newspapers to being shown in galleries. We had more exhibitions than published comics because that was the only way the intellectual elite could handle our stuff! 'Only if you have it hung on the gallery walls.'"

Ironically, and despite its growing popularity, *Polet* did not do much to promote its contributors. In fact, one could argue that the powers that be were not great supporters of the growing youth-art movement. Only a small ad about a solo exhibition by Mirko Ilić was published in *Polet* no. 44, (December 9,1977). The sixty-fifth issue of *Polet* published the article "It's Not a Circle, it's a Square," which, along with a series of quotes about Novi kvadrat, included a brief conversation with Ilić. "Recently," the author wrote, "*Polet* has begun to realize that it has associates who are the subjects of controversy we think it is high time to present our esteemed colleagues in more detail. As the saying goes: No man is a prophet in his own land."

Two issues later, Ilić published *Okomito i vodoravno* (Vertically and horizontally), his last comic in *Polet*. ▶

Hereditary intolerance,
WRITTEN BY: Davor Slamnig,
Polet br. 22, April 8, 1977

From "The History of Human Folly",
Polet br. 24, April 22, 1977

Born to Be Wild,
Polet no. 35,
October 7, 1977

Novi Kvadrat—New Wave Before the New Wave

I was a punk before you were a punk

IT WAS MORE THAN A QUARTER CENTURY AGO that the Yugoslavian New Wave movement started.

In Zagreb, back in the late seventies, somewhere between the Well of Life,[01] the bustling cafes Veliki and Mali Kavkaz, the increasingly popular youth newspapers *Polet* and *Studentski list*, and the nightclubs, a gathering of young people erupted with a tremendous force of energy, unprecedented and not repeated since. Zagreb became a highly charged place, with the reverberations lasting for years. Many now remember those days with nostalgia. "We were famous and we were young," Ilić said. At the time he was one of the most distinctive and important members of the scene, both as a participant and an instigator. *Polet* was important not only as a news source but also as a medium and a platform for action. While the burgeoning music scene was also attracting attention, it was the comics of Novi kvadrat that introduced the magic of creativity and freedom of thought that connected so powerfully with the youth. Photography and rock came later, during the second wave.

At the same time, just before the eruption of the punk scene, a career in music still seemed like mission impossible for many, while creating comics required only ink, paper, and a great idea. Plus, with Ilić at *Polet,* there was someone of influence who knew the value of good art and was willing not only to publish it but to pay for it as well. Every high school student who read the comics of the Novi kvadrat started drawing comics. All of a sudden people from all around started began forming new collectives, small Novi kvadrat*s*— and not only in Zagreb. "People realized that group work was the only way," Ilić said. "If nothing else, that's a one thing the Novi kvadrat taught." Often, even if nothing came from their drawing, people would continue to work in other creative fields such as journalism, music, theater, or design.

"A popular Slovenian comic at the time became the first album cover for the band Buldožer. We all knew the band's founder, Kostja Gatnik, and he liked what we were doing a lot. But probably the most important person was music critic and concert organizer Igor Vidmar," Ilić said. "In the early debates over the merits of Novi kvadrat, he wrote an article rebutting Darko Glavan's ideas and tried to protect us. We became friends, so I met all the members of Buldožer and another punk band called Pankrti. That's how they ended up playing at my exhibition."

Many people who were there agree that Zagreb's New Wave scene started precisely with Ilić's first solo exhibition at SC in December 1977, where Pankrti played. Another band called Azra—Rock 'n' roll iz šume Striborove (Azra—Rock 'n' roll from Stribor's forest). Azra was a short-lived group but their breakup produced two of the most significant bands on the Zagreb New Wave scene: Azra and Film. At the opening, Azra's leader, Branimir Johnny Štulić, heard a new sound of punk music live for the first time. Hints of this musical epiphany can be heard on his song "The Balkans": "I shave my beard, my moustache, to look like the Pankrti, and if I only had a Fender, we could see a gig ...". The event also had a profound effect on other influential artists of the day. Several decades later Ilić recounted: "It was a shock. They came on stage in white shirts with black ties, and red ribbons tied around their hands they looked like small Slovenian bureaucrats. Suddenly, like in a disaster movie, a wall of noise came toward us. Everybody made

01 | The sculpture of Ivan Mestrovic, in front of the Croatian National Theater, the usual meeting place for young people.

Catalog cover, D: F.V. Holi

"The exhibition in the Student Center Gallery was designed to put comics front and center, and featured concerts and plays. A few bands appeared there for the first time. Azra—Rock'n'roll iz šume Striborove, broke up immediately after their concert there, and two new bands were formed, Azra and Film. Pankrti, out of Slovenia, performed for the first time. One esteemed critic said about their performance that there is no place for punk in Yugoslavia. Interestingly, a year and a half later he was the one who presented Pankrti with an official Socialist Youth award, 7 Sekretara SKOJa."

—MIRKO ILIĆ, "ANTIZID ORIGINATED FROM THE GALLERY WALLS," *VIKEND*, BEOGRAD, JANUARY 27, 2001

From the Saturday night show,
conversation about the *Novi kvadrat*, RTZ 1979

The exhibition photograph from curator and gallery director Želimir Koščević's collection. The author is most likely Vlado Jakelić.

Frames from a 16 mm film recorded by cinematographer Darko Vernić Bundi at the SC Gallery, showing a young, promising, still long-haired, Ilić.

their faces like this":[02] (he grimaces with his mouth wide open). A young, long-haired Ilić can be seen in rare photos from the event, and also in several frames of a student documentary 16 mm film recorded in the SC Gallery at the time of the exhibition.

During these public gatherings and group performances Ilić learned a lesson from the punk movement about the importance of image and appearance, how fashion and behavior could be public performances of their own, and can also contribute to the rebellion. Soon after the opening, Ilić cut his hair short, started listening to The Velvet Underground and the Ramones, and bought the requisite uniform of the period: a black leather jacket and a studded bracelet.

Novi kvadrat's comics introduced explicit themes of sexuality, politics, and everyday life that were new and as yet unseen at that time in Yugoslavia. Their work contained reflections of the interests of the time—from space flights and moon landings to Stanley Kubrick's *2001: A Space Odyssey*. Their comics also helped contribute to the critical examination of the media industry and its habit of commercializing everything.

Overtly questioning the media served as the means to infiltrate, and influence, cultural standards and assumptions. These New Wave artists used galleries and traditional media outlets to raise their questions in a very public context.

It is interesting—and fitting for his career—that Ilić gave his first solo exhibition two years after he published his first comic, and he published his last comic, "Horizontally and vertically," in *Polet* only six months after the exhibition. Right after, Ilić left his position at the magazine.

Under the leadership of new art director, conceptual artist and cinematographer, Goran Trbuljak, *Polet* began placing more emphasis on photography. Although *Polet* had helped the affirmation of the Novi kvadrat, the magazine now began cutting comics from the magazine and moved them to the back page.

In an issue of *Pitanja* dedicated to the Novi kvadrat, Pero Kvesić stated: "The change in the editorial policy brought a new treatment of comics, which was—to put it mildly—awkward. In order to realize this concept, the 'new guys from *Polet*' had to first get rid of Ilić. After that, all authors of Novi kvadrat gradually left *Polet*..." Novi kvadrat's popularity was confirmed by

02 | In the book and documentary movie by Igor Mirković: *Sretno dijete* (Happy Child), Fraktura, Zagreb, 2004, pp. 28

"Comics are like fairy tales for boys. Boys don't relate to the 'happily ever after' stuff. Usually, for boys it's riding horseback into the sunset with the girl they've chosen for the night. And then the next morning brings new opportunities."

—MIRKO ILIĆ, "ENVY PECULIARLY MEASURES YOUR SUCCESS," *DELO, SATURDAY SUPPLEMENT, LJUBLJANA, JUNE 3, 2000*

Fairy Tale,
Polet no. 60, April 3, 1978
Epic Illustrated
Vol. 1 No. 5, 1981

The Victor,
Polet no. 32-33,
September 23,
1977;
Epic Illustrated
Vol. 1 No. 1, 1980

On the Same Side

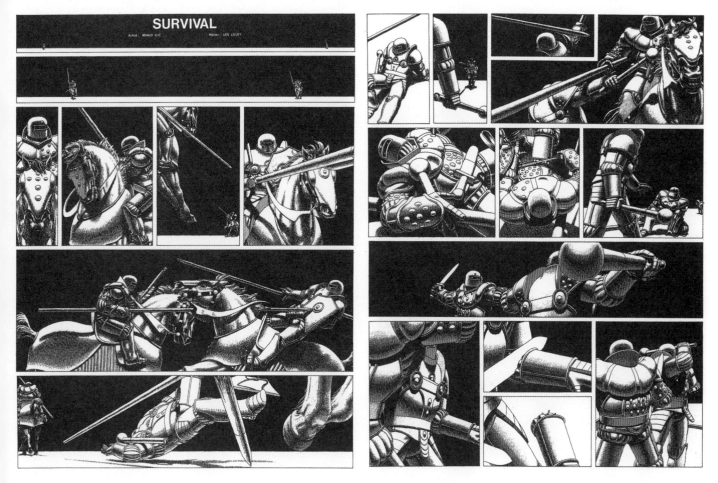

Pages from the comic **Survival**, WRITTEN BY: Les Lilley, *Spunk* no. 1, 1979; *Heavy Metal*, no. 9, 1980

PAGES 43–44:

On the Same Side, originally published in *Strip Vidici 2*, Beograd 1979; republished in *Pitanja* no. 6/7, Zagreb 1979, and *Metal Hurlant* no. 46, Paris 1979

The comic "Na istoj strani" was announced by *Metal Hurlant* to be the most bizarre comic of the decade. Loosely based on the Moebius strip, it presents characters that fight with imaginary enemies on the "other side" of the strip, and get killed from the consequences of their own actions. In the final sentence, the last remaining character says: "All dead. And for such a long time we have fought on the same side. Damn."

the fact that the first printing of their themed issue of *Pitanja* sold out so quickly that the editors went back to press for another 2,000 copies.

At the time of the gradual expulsion of the Novi kvadrat, the new editorial direction included the strong promotion of early, influential punk and New Wave bands, so in a very real sense, Novi kvadrat was indeed a new wave before the New Wave.

After leaving *Polet*, Ilić published comics in specialized local magazines, such as *Strip Vidici* and *Spunk,* and some abroad as well. In 1977 the German magazine *Pardon* published his first cover illustration, and the following year, the famous Italian comic magazine *Alter Alter* published his first comic, "Debil Blues."

He also published work in a number of other magazines, including the Italian *Nuovo Mago* and the French *Charlie*. And in 1979 he published "Na istoj strani" (On the same side) in *Metal Hurlant*.

In 1979, he drew the comic that would be the last he published, "Survival." A story without words, on six boards, it was based on an original screenplay by the famous English scriptwriter Les Lilley (1924-1998). It was published in January 1980 in the American magazine *Heavy Metal*.

He never again completed and published a new comic. Ilić has said on occasion that he hasn't ruled out the possibility of ever doing so, but he doesn't see it as likely. ▶

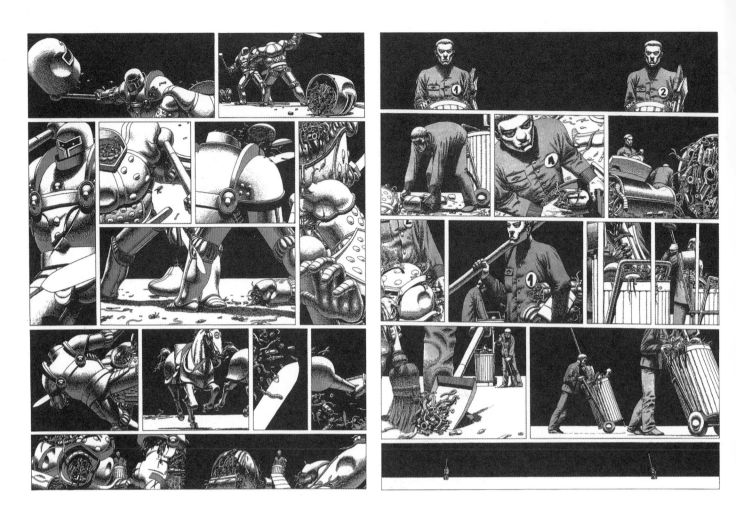

Metal Hurlant

IN LATE 1974, WHILE ILIĆ WAS STILL IN HIGH SCHOOL, artists Jean Giraud (also known as Moebius) and Phillipe Druillet became dissatisfied with how they were being treated by the Parisian magazine *Pilote*. With the young screenplay writer and publisher Jean Pierre Dionnet, they decided to form Les Humanoides Associés, an association of comic book authors. The following year, they started the magazine *Metal Hurlant*. Unburdened by any established rules, their new magazine published comics that used sex, violence, and politics, and examined issues of alienation, boredom, and the emptiness of contemporary life to revolutionize the medium of comics.

The work of this mostly French group was greatly influenced by the American underground scene, psychedelia, and the sexual revolution, but also the political ideas of the counter cultural movement, and the revolutionary turbulences of the sixties antiwar protest. Ilić's interests and work fit cleverly into this new trend in comic book, and from the very beginning were absolutely in line with their ideals, so it is understandable that his work had no trouble breaking through and coming to the pages of European magazines, including *Metal Hurlant*, and later to its American versions, *Heavy Metal*.

Heavy Metal even bought rights to Ilić's last published comic "Survival" for its first animated film, but when *Heavy Metal—The Movie* appeared, in 1981, the animated version of Ilić's comic had been cut.

"They realized that my drawing was too complicated and they gave up," explained Ilić.

"I tried to get my comic 'Survival,' which was published in *Metal Hurlant*, to first be published in the local magazine *Spunk*. This was my childish spite. The comics that I liked the most were always published abroad first and would come to us only later. So I am somewhat adolescently sadistic about this—I first publish my comics here, and then I let them be published abroad. It gives me great joy. Those who want them, want them."

—MIRKO ILIĆ, "COMIC ARTIST, STUBBORN—BOOM! SMASH! BANG!" *POLET NO. 124, ZAGREB, MARCH 5, 1980*

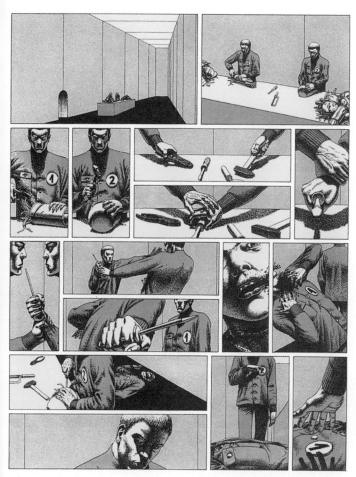

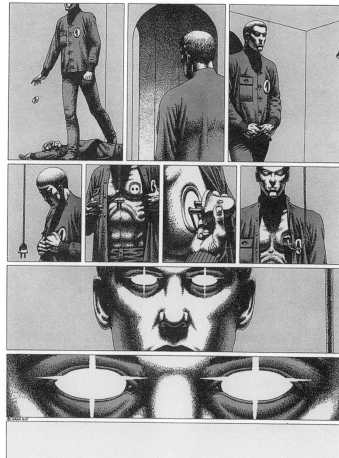

"I eagerly await each new edition of *Spunk* comics magazine, clearly risking each time to see another new horrible comic by Mirko Ilić. Although this time he worked with the well-known foreign screenwriter Les Lilley, I did not notice any major improvements."

—DARKO GLAVAN, "NEW COMIC MAGAZINES—

OLD EDITION," *POLET*, ZAGREB, MARCH 5, 1980

"I have been frequently reproached for many things—usually by people from the industry. They blame me for copying Moebius, almost through tracing paper. At the same time, at the publication he owned, *Metal Hurlant*, he wrote some very positive things about me. After all, many comic books by foreign illustrators resemble each other—take for example a number of people who worked on *Rip Kirby*. No one reproaches them. Foreign artists certainly have influenced us to a great extent. These effects were exaggerated here, because people did not have enough information. On the other hand, except Andrija Maurović, Jules Radilović, and few others, we did not have many of our own original comic book artists. The vast majority copied foreign authors. They were not reproached either, at least not publicly. I think that influences are being overly emphasized. I am positive that I did a couple of things in this medium that surely were new: a music comic ('Debil Blues'), a comic ('On the Same Side') that *Metal Hurlant* declared to be the most bizarre comic book of the decade. If I had not done anything but these two things, it would have been enough."

—MIRKO ILIĆ, "COMIC BOOK ARTIST, STUBBORN—BOOM! SMASH! BANG!"

POLET NO. 124, MAY 3, 1980

"Mirko Ilić's talent and the value of his comics were either overly praised or completely negated. This was probably because Mirko quite persistently and stubbornly follows only one way, his way. His talent may be disputed, but it is undeniable that his energy and ambitions are great."

"RENE BAKALOVIĆ: COMIC BOOK ARTIST,

STUBBORN—BOOM! SMASH! BANG!"

POLET NO. 124, MAY 3, 1980

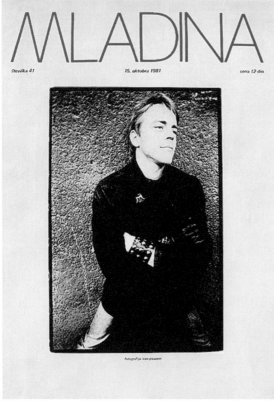

MLADINA

Številka 41   15. oktobra 1981   cena 12 din

fotografija ivan posavec

"Back then, it seemed to me that we were the last screwed up generation. But it turned out that people born between 1953 and 1958 were the only normal ones, the ones who did not know what Stalinism was, what war was. We were demanding from ourselves the same as the Paris students in 1968 were – the impossible. We wanted to be the best not in Zagreb, not in Yugoslavia, but in the world. Our role models were international."

"GREAT SCREWED-UP GENERATIONS," *FOCUS*, ZAGREB, JUNE 2, 2000

Cover of *Mladina*, no. 41,
Ljubljana October, 15, 1981,
COVER PHOTO: Ivan Posavec

48

Culture, Politics, and Scene

The finest hour of the socialist state

TO FULLY UNDERSTAND THE ART AND DESIGN SCENE in the early seventies, it's important to reject some popular myths about Communist repression and cultural prejudices.

"Ilić and the Novi kvadrat appeared around the mid-seventies, a time of reaction to the events of the so-called Croatian Spring of '71, when everyone was afraid to get their hands dirty," Mario Bošnjak, editor of *Start*, said. "Rigid conservative forces had been established, politicians had called out their reserves, there were too many old guys in the war department. All of these factions tried to suppress the cultural uprising. But this political fear was an overreaction in my opinion. In the early '70s no one authorized me to publish erotic stories by blacklisted writers. But I did and I never had any problem from the government, which proved to me that so called blacklists were all in our heads…"

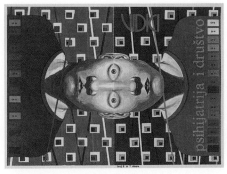

The front and the back page of the themed edition "Psychiatry and Society" of the magazine *Vidici*, no. 8, Belgrade, 1978
AD & D: Nikola Kostandinović

In an interview with Ilić for *Polet,* Ljubomir Kljakić said, "Most student and youth newspapers didn't have to worry about the profitability of their publications since the money had already been allotted to them by the government. That's why so many new publications have appeared in recent years."

Journalist and former editor of *Polet* Denis Kuljiš said, "What is so different today from that time is the amazing amount of money that used to be invested in students and youth culture. Every youth organization in Zagreb had its own newspaper, magazine, or theater; some even started radio stations and sponsored rock festivals. *Polet* created the punk scene and helped invent those bands. It was not private money, all of it was pumped in by the state into that scene. Youth activities were, then, sponsored at the highest level. In fact, the amount of money invested at that time was probably equal to the entire amount allocated to arts and culture by the government today."

"Our resistance to authority became apparent around this time," said Ilić. "It all started with a letter sent to *Polet* by the magazine of the Central Committee of the League of Communists of Croatia asking us to stop printing our anti-government articles. To which we sent a response back, which we published under the title, a reference to a childrens counting-out rhyme 'The Duck Is Sailing Across the Sava River, Carrying a Letter to the Top of the Head, and This Letter Says I Do Not Love you Anymore.'"

Promotional poster for *Polet*, 1979

In an interview Ilić said, "*Polet* was being sponsored by the government, which meant that, ironically, we were a part of the structure. But they made the mistake of inviting us to give a lecture in the political school in Fažana, where on one side was a police vacation resort, and on the other was vacation resort of the CK (Central Committee), and across the channel were the Brioni Islands which housed Tito's summer residence. So here we were one night swimming naked in the ocean, singing anarchist songs. When the police came around midnight to ask us to stop, they could not do anything to us because we were in a protected area. That was when the government hand slapping started. The problem was that the newspaper was way too influential, so, I think, the government wisely decided to reject *Polet*. Slowly at first, the *Polet* staff infiltrated various other newspapers and radio and television stations, and so *Polet* disappeared, but other small *Polet*s popped up everywhere."

As media theorist Marina Gržinić noted in her 2002. article "Punk-strategies, policies and amnesia," "New Wave and punk marked a demarcation between modernity and postmodernity. Postmodernism in contemporar art

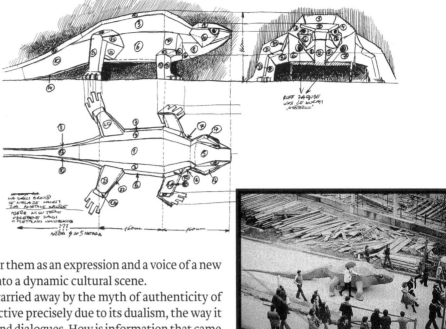

and culture came to Slovenia and other parts of socialist Yugoslavia thanks to the punk and alternative scene in Ljubljana. Radical post-modernism was the result of the punk and underground rock 'and' roll movements."

Regardless of how punk and New Wave were received by the local environment, the bottom line is that they were well received by the youth, which means that on some level there must have been a cultural need for them as an expression and a voice of a new generation, ready to transform into a dynamic cultural scene.

Of course, we should not get carried away by the myth of authenticity of the New Wave scene; it was attractive precisely due to its dualism, the way it used to mix different influences and dialogues. How is information that came from foreign sources —be it the comic magazines and music, *Metal Hurlant*, or the *New Musical Express*—processed in a domestic, local context, how are ideas and strategies shifted from the "low" pop cultural to the "high" elite culture and vice versa?

This New Wave scene, however can—and even should—be seen as the culmination of a process that had its foundation in phenomena and events of the previous decades, such as EXAT 51, the New Tendencies, Gorgona, the Zagreb Music Biennale, Theatre &TD, IFSK, GEFF and experimental films like *Carni val* (Black Wave), the emergence of conceptual art, the SC Gallery, Belgrade SKC, and others.

In the area of popular culture, the period from the 1960s to the '80s was the finest hour of the Socialist state, the moment when the proclaimed aspiration toward Socialist modernization happily coincided with the liberalization of society and aesthetic modernism. It became a cultural scene that was not confined to ethnic, national, or even state boundaries, and local criteria was created, or at least it seemed so to its participants.

This culture created an "imaginary community," not in terms of nation, but in terms of a unique cultural space in which the urban scenes—primarily Belgrade, Zagreb, Ljubljana, Sarajevo and Skopje, Rijeka, Split, Osijek, and Novi Sad communicated with one another, and exchanged ideas and support systems.

A dynamic cultural space gradually formed in Yugoslavia and was circulated by way of a variety of artistic practices that mutually interacted, and were mutually infused with new ideas and enriched. Personalities such as Tomislav Gotovac were linking early Fluxus-inspired events with the *Black wave* (he performed in the notorious movie *Plastic Jesus*), structuralist and experimental film (GEFF), striking and provocative public performances, *Polet*, the New Wave scene and so on. Similar activities were undertaken by the artist Goran Trbuljak, the writer and translator David Albahari, as well as by institutions such as Zagreb's SC Gallery with the Kugla glumište independent theater group and the New Wave band Haustor or Belgrade SKC with the circle around the Srećna galerija (Happy Gallery) led by Slavko Timotijević, *Izgled* magazine, and project-band Kozmetika, photographer Dragan Papić and project *Dečaci* (Boys) that would evolve into the band VIS Idoli.

Interestingly, the first translation of one of the most important books on

For the independent theater group Kugla glumište, Ilić has shaped a figure of a lizard. It appeared for the first time in the theater play "Mekani brodovi" (The Soft Ships), and then in the "Gospodar ledenih strojeva" (The Lord of Ice Machines). The drawing was published in the *Gordogan* no. 1, from the archives of Branko Matan. RIGHT: Photo from the performance of "Mekani brodovi," courtesy of Željko Zorica.

"I remember only that he was one of the first people I met who worked a lot. At that time, it was not cool. Laziness and lack of ambition were cool, so people would actually hide the fact that they worked hard. For instance, I was hiding from my friends that I was really studying; I cursed and blamed the necessity for good grades on the university. Even *Polet* was made easily, by itself, so that Mirko's perseverance—today I would call it focus—was unusual.

At the same time, Mirko was so handsome and the idioculture of *Zvečka* was so macho and puerile, that Mirko's steps of accepting responsibilities—to his work, talent, and marriage—seemed even weirder."

—INES SABALIĆ

contemporary cultural theory, *Subculture: The Meaning of Style* by Dick Hebdige, was published in Yugoslavia shortly after it was released in the UK in 1980.[01] This points not only to awareness of the cultural elite that actively monitored and accepted the world's theoretical achievements and discussions, but also the self-awareness of the New Wave scene of that time, the fact that its own position, its social context and status were reviewed, questioned within and through the work the scene itself. Confirming this is the appearance of the collection of texts, photos, and lyrics *Drugom stranom* (On the Other Side), which back in 1982 and '83 represented an attempt to document and reflect what was still happening.

It is important, especially in the context of nineties events, to stress again that the then evolving cultural scene was developing without respect to national borders, even if those borders meant that the products of the scene—records, magazines, and so on—were rarely distributed internationally, and when they were, their reach was limited. Even if they could not reach the production standards of the West, the authors were imposing global standards of thinking on their own work.

Speaking about this, Ilić said: "I never thought I did comics just for Zagreb—perhaps because I've always been ambitious—I've always worked for the whole world."

The work of Novi kvadrat, or to be precise, the work of Ilić, an author who was published mostly abroad in this period, represented the best-known internationally, something that in this genre could obviously be measured with foreign production.

Remembering those days, in *Polet,* Ilić said, "It was a time of idea exchange, matching intellectual wits... I learned then to be daring and ask for the impossible. We had the feeling that we were shattering institutions, we did not want to succeed here, we wanted to compete with the entire world, because we believed that there were no limits."

A question could be asked today if this "imagined community," because of its relative media success and the creative dynamism of the participants of the scene, a young, intellectual audience, partly made invisible some realities of social life that soon took over the hegemony and consequently ruined the framework within which this culture existed and was possible.

It should be emphasized that it still was a time of strong bipolar division of the world, when the possibility of the decline of the Communist world did not seem probable. Perhaps because Yugoslavia survived Tito's death without threats of foreign invasion or a civil war people believed that changes would go slowly, that nothing will change dramatically.

Except for certain parts of Ljubljana around the ŠKUC Forum, the subculture scene failed to establish any specific infrastructure or organization. Shortly after that, the support for youth culture was no longer sufficient, and their own newspapers such as *Polet* and *SL* were in a constant state of crisis and turmoil. As it was a parasite on the financial and organizational infrastructure of youth and student organizations, with their destruction in the period of the decline of Communism, the scene was on the street, it collapsed and was gone for good.

Speaking about *Studentski list* and *Polet,* the editors often emphasized that there were two fundamental concepts: regional, in which every part of Croatia did have its space that it filled with information about local events (this principle was probably partly wanted by the party structures which were funding youth press),

01 I Dick Hedbige: *Subculture: The Meaning of Style* (Methuen, London 1979), translated as *Potkultura: značenje stila* (Rad, Belgrade 1980). From today's view, it is interesting that the first print run was 3000 copies, but also that the book was translated by the acclaimed writer and translator David Albahari, an influential promoter of postmodernism in literature and person strongly associated with the post-punk/New Wave scene.

"The appearance of the town suddenly changed. Everything was open later, the crowd hung out longer, but for me it all melted into one long day and a very, very long night."

—MIRKO ILIĆ, "IN SRETNO DIJETE (HAPPY CHILD)," *FRAKTURA,* ZAGREB 2004.

Sretno dijete (Happy Child), 2004
Bright light comes out of windows of Zvečka caffe on a poster for documentary movie about New Wave scene in Zagreb.
DIR: Igor Mirković
PHOTO: Luka Mjeda;
DESIGN AND DIGITAL EDITING: Mirko Ilić

and the concept of "urban" model, which focused on what is important to young people regardless of where they live through the universal values of topics. This continuous commitment of the editors to "urban" model of newspapers was instigating cultural production that used referent frames of city scenes, which did not take into account the national context of culture and its ethnic definitions, which will become so important not even a decade later. It is not surprising that in many ways representatives of those scenes appeared as opposition, traitors of the national cause, "witches," "Soros's mercenaries" and members of a cultural emigration. Of course, a part of them was on the "other" side, in roles of editors of *kriegsblatt*, cynical manipulators and war profiteers. Ilić will see typical continuity in this: "They were the same people that were throwing us out from *Polet, Start, Danas...*"

The collapse of the New Wave scene preceded the collapse of Yugoslavia. When Ilić went to America in 1986, the scene was in its late stage, already on the wane, and as the best expression of sublime beauty in the period between the two deaths of Tito's—real in 1980 and the symbolic with the disintegration of his ideological project in the early nineties—works were created by groups gathered in Neue Slowenische Kunst. But this is another story. ▶

V. V. Mayakovsky: Slap in the Face of Public Taste, Theatre 79, 1982
DESIGN: Studio SLS / Mirko Ilić
SILKSCREEN PRINT: Studio S

KUD (Cultural-Artistic Association) Veljko Vlahović, poster,
PHOTO: Slobodan Tadić,
SILKSCREEN PRINT SC, 1980

ПЕФ

ПРО

V. V. MAJAKOVSKI

ŠAMAR DRUŠTVENOM UKUSU

TEKSTOVE ODABRAO I GOVORI: GORAN MATOVIĆ

UMJETNIČKI SURADNICI: TONKO LONZA, ZLATKO BOUREK I ARSEN DEDIĆ

CENTAR ZA KULTURU NOVI ZAGREB · NASELJE FEBRUARSKIH ŽRTAVA 12 – TEATAR '79

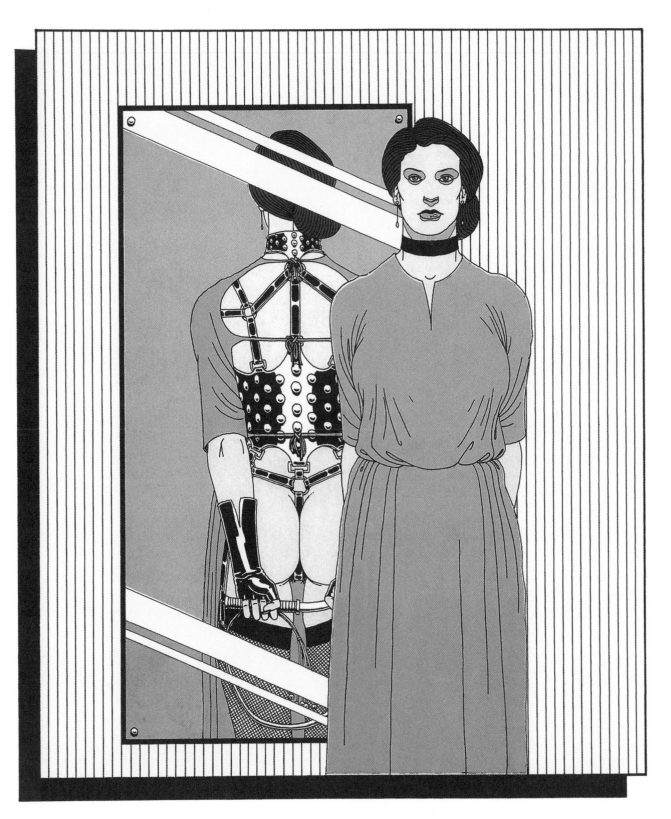

The Ideology of the Hometown Girl

Start no. 269, May 16, 1979. The illustration accompanying an article by Veselko Tenžera on "the phenomenon of nudity that long ago swamped all visual media (*Start* too), and the double standard in 'consuming' such a phenomenon."

AFTER A COUPLE OF YEARS FOCUSING ON comics, Ilić turned away from the comfort of the medium. The reasons are many, but it was due mostly to the bitterness he felt after he was let go from *Polet* and after the break up of the Novi kvadrat. Drawing comics also became a grind for Ilić. Constantly answering to the larger companies and their demands meant "turning the best place on Earth into hell." Besides, as Ilić often says, one of his best qualities is the ability to "know when to leave." In the eighties the comic industry was stalling, perhaps even declining, not only in Croatia and what was then Yugoslavia, but also, in the whole of Europe. New generations were interested in other things, some of the most important comic magazines were dying out. The graphic novel became a more dominant form, favoring a more classical narrative. New techniques in digital animation were combining the comic aesthetic with film more. After making some exceptional breakthroughs in the comic form with *Debil Blues, Shakti, Otvoreni strip* (Open Comic), *Vodoravno i okomito* (Horizontally and Vertically), *Na istoj strani* (On the Same Side), Ilić started looking for new creative challenges in other fields.

By the time he left *Polet,* he was regularly publishing illustrations in Zagreb's *Start* magazine, an illustrated magazine with an unusual past that embodied some of the former Yugoslavia's cultural peculiarities.

It started in 1969 as an automobile magazine. But following the trend of sexual liberalization at the end of the sixties and the beginning of the seventies, it began publishing centerfolds of naked women, which became its recognizable trademark up to its last issue in 1991.

In 1973, after a hundred and five issues, Sead Saračević, was hired as editor-in-chief. Saračević appointed Mario Bošnjak as his editor. Bošnjak had the key position in the daily operations of the magazine, while Saračević brought in many new authors. These were the first steps towards making *Start* a "legitimate" publication, although for years many readers continued to buy it secretly, hiding it when they got home "so the kids didn't see." New so-called high-culture topics were introduced, articles on popular culture were more serious, and the magazine also frequently included travelogues, reports, and political and historical features. Special attention was given to serious and lengthy interviews.

As journalist Vesna Kesić points out: "The popularity of graphic design coincided with that aesthetic development of *Start* and ran parallel to its "depornographization." Zoran Pavlović, a designer from Zagreb, did the first "polishing" in 1973; this was followed by a major one in 1976, which led to a "third *Start*." The latter was done by Roman Cieslewicz, a Polish designer, who was brought from Paris for the two-hundredth issue. [01]

Cieslewicz already had a contact with Zagreb through the designer and artist Ivan Picelj. So in 1973, the SC Gallery (Student Center) together with GZH (Croatian Graphic Institute) published his illustrated book *No!*

"[Art historian and critic] Vera Horvat Pintarić brought Roman Cieslewicz to Zagreb, having first met him in the 1960s when he was going West", said Bošnjak. "That was when he had just redesigned *Elle* Paris. Later he came to *Start* on two occasions, first was for the two-hundredth issue. His slogan for that issue was '200 *Starts* is just a start!'"

At the time, newspaper graphics were getting a lot of attention from *Start*'s publishing house, Vjesnik. This is evident from their

01 | Vesna Kesić: Sead Saračević — *Savoir vivre, Start* no. 500, March 19, 1988

Decisions One Way, Businesses the Other Way

Start no. 306, October 15, 1980

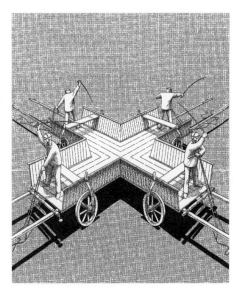

Discussions, Debates, Pamphlets, Apologies

Start no. 397, April 7, 1984

Also published in *Panorama*, May 28, 1984

"The only illustration I did that wasn't published in *Start* was one I drew for an article about Goli otok, a prison camp for political prisoners in the fifties, and the fact that it was finally possible to write about it. However, when I handed in my illustration I 'forgot' that it was possible to write about it, but not to draw."

—MIRKO ILIĆ, "THE WANTONNESS OF A NEW BEGINNING,"
NEDELJNA BORBA, BELGRADE, MARCH 14–15, 1987

**How the Party History
is Being Created**,
Start no. 367,
February 2, 1983

adding new printing presses, and inviting one of the most prominent avant-garde names to redesign the magazine. All of this was partly the result of a general trend to continuously improve the quality of visual communications and newspaper graphics (as reflected in the *Pop Express* magazine designed by Mihajlo Arsovski at the end of the sixties and the design of books and magazines by Zoran Pavlović for CDD/CKD). It was also partly the result of efforts to develop awareness for design (marked by the founding of the Centre for industrial design and its activities, and by the project for visual identity of Zagreb's radio and television station RTZ).[02]

When invited to redesign *Start,* Cieslewicz supposedly said "what do you need me for when you have Arsovski" and after he redesigned it, he even tried to get Arsovski to take it over as the art director but he declined. Years later, in a private conversation, Arsovski commented: "That man sweated blood. I knew that it wasn't for me," and pointed to the fact that the ultimate design did not exactly match his initial plans. "I saw his redesign proposals and what was actually published. It didn't take the editorial team long to water it down!"

The editorial office obviously noticed that too, because Cieslewicz would be invited to redesign *Start* again in 1981.

"Cieslewicz had not really changed us that much, because Zoran Pavlović had already given us a contemporary look", said Mario Bošnjak. "We always had problems with frames, lines, and knock-out type. Cieslewicz pruned the design, simplified it, and removed all knock-out type, which I personally always opposed. He actually taught the whole place to rethink what it was doing editorially and updated everything graphically."

Cieslewicz's redesign of *Start* set standards. Many of his choices seem obvious today. For example, the quality of the photographs became more important than the number of them. A good photograph was worth more than five that were so-so. The design was simplified, all that was redundant was thrown out, giving more place to new visual material as well as illustration—a place Ilić knew how to fill. The editorial office soon realized how much of an effect his involvement had on the quality of *Start* magazine.

After its first redesign in 1978, *Start* appealed to many other illustrators from Novi kvadrat. It is also worth noting that during these years *Start's* circulation was between 180,000 and 200,000 copies.

"Beside Mirko, there was Igor Kordej." Bošnjak said. "We soon run out of space to publish all the works of all these illustrators, so we sent him to illustrate other Vjesnik publications. We had too many good illustrators to publish. We had Radovan Devlić and Krešimir Skorzet—who illustrated smaller columns. Of them all, Mirko had the most powerful ideas; he could get the greatest effect with minimal drawing, unlike Skozret, who had to knock himself out every time. He would give himself so much work that he rarely could finish on time, so part of his illustration would be top quality and the rest would be sloppy, simply because he ran out of time."

Up to this point illustrations in newspapers were usually used to accompany feature columns or topics, rather than news pieces.

Start was, for most of its existence, printed on a rotogravure press, which came out well when printed on quality paper. This printing technology made it possible for the magazine to have both full color and black-and-white pages. High-quality coated paper was imported and usually expensive, so used rarely (es-

02 | From the very beginning, a rotogravure press was used to print *Start* and after 1973, it was replaced with a new rotation acquired for the printing of VUS—Zagreb weekly newspaper, *Wednesday Herald.* Mario Bošnjak: "In those days a scanner was a great wonder. The first scanner was as big as a table and we all went to see it. It was left over from general manager Božo Novak, whose greatest credit is always keeping Vjesnik at the technological top in this part of the world. It was also one of the biggest publishing houses in central Europe. Italy did not have such a big publishing house—it had four or five smaller ones. Now, is that good or not…"

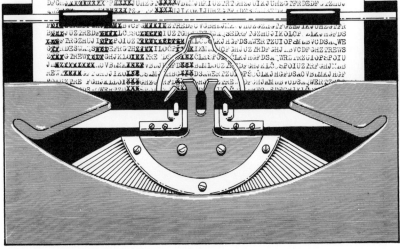

Censorship for Self-Censorship, *Start* no. 340, January 30, 1982

"The fact that in the beginning many authors did not want to sign their illustrations tells a great deal about the status *Start* had. There was a so-called law on pornography: publications deemed as pornographic paid higher taxes. So by using photographs and illustrations, we tried to have an erotic section that would not be seen as pornography. The great painter Josip Vaništa was the first to illustrate an erotic story, but he never wanted to sign any of those illustrations. He drew very sophisticated illustrations, but they were a bit out of context in a newspaper.

I came in for the one-hundredth issue and after another hundred issues, *Start* had become a cultural fact. Sead Saračević was an amazing editor and had full confidence in his associates. A whole generation of people from student newspapers in those days came to work here. The fact that people did not want to sign their work changed with time and they slowly began standing in line to get something published."

—MARIO BOŠNJAK

pecially from the end of the seventies). The low quality of the paper was especially evident on full color pages. This was the reason why black and white illustration had an important position in *Start*. Of course, the lead article had a full page reserved for an illustration, and for years those were usually Mirko's.

Start was really the first modern magazine in the former Yugoslavia. Illustration was not something casually included if there happened to be empty space left on the page, but was seen as an equal part in the presentation of the content. The turning point was the works of Fadil Vejzović, who in 1975 began working as a designer/art editor and a kind of an art director. Vejzović began adapting the style of illustration to fit the theme of the article. He changed techniques and visual languages, introduced the airbrush technique, and did a series of excellent illustrations—at least from an artistic viewpoint

Short Hot Summer—Bonn:
Some Like it Nostalgic,
Start no. 327, August 1, 1981

(the most prominent are the ones from 1976 for a feature series on gulags in Siberia). However, it was the work of young Ilić that brought freshness to *Start.* Simply by using the illustrations as a visual interpretation of the piece, the newspaper illustration became a commentary.

In the five-hundredth issue of *Start,* in a piece dedicated to the history of *Start*'s illustration, editor Marko Grčić wrote:

"Although Fadil Vejzović set out *Start*'s illustration style, he could not, as a painter, bear the inevitable consequence: the need to subsume himself time and time again to the assignment, while at the same time strictly differentiating these activities from those of a painter. Then, however, another new generation of illustrators came, from a milieu closer to journalism—i.e., from comics. They were Mirko Ilić and Igor Kordej. It was already clear from their first illustrations that this was the medium of their artistic destiny. Mirko Ilić is, according to a few important factors, an entirely isolated phenomenon in the history of our illustration—he chose this vocation as a destiny; he is exceptionally creative and is the only one with a truly worldwide reputation. He has something in common with Oto Reisinger, a well-known caricaturist from the older generation. Although the comparison may seem absurd, with both of them their art stands high above what they are able to say about it; they both have an incredible ability to recognize order where everyone else sees chaos or to discern disorder and absurdity where others see order. Often *Start*'s authors and editors became aware of the final impact of an article only when Ilić handed in his illustration for the assigned topic. His drawings are hard, stiff, almost stylized, and ideal for expressing the peculiar Ilić humor, sometimes in the form of cynicism, but mostly giving a clear insight into something that is senseless and at the same time deadly. Ilić has an extremely journalistic way of thinking. When following up on a current story he never picks up an old, already-used-up idea; his artistic reasoning is usually a particular answer to a given—sometimes not well-defined—assignment and since his illustrations always provoke reaction, it seems as though reality itself creates his themes...

As far as *Start* is concerned, perhaps Ilić's most important contribution was to show that editorial illustrations had a life and meaning of their own and should be considered separately from the world of fine art. That was something the Americans recognized far better. However, before becoming a global star of illustration, Ilić rather relentlessly stoked the growing passions of Yugoslavia's youth and helped stir the generation's revolt. At the same time, he was also designing his own personality—a visible one (outfit and haircut) and an invisible one (attitude and world view) to avoid being confused with others. In other words: Ilić had created a new world even before he made his first comic and drew his first (immediately perfect) illustrations within Novi kvadrat. Of course, in true Ilić fashion, he was immediately an outstanding illustrator. It was as if he came out of nowhere."[03]

In May 1982 Ilić began working with the Italian weekly *Panorama,* a step that eventually would take him to New York four years later. ▶

03 | Marko Grčić: Rescue from art, *Start* no. 500, March 19, 1988.

When a Machine Has Feelings,

Start no. 324, June 20, 1981

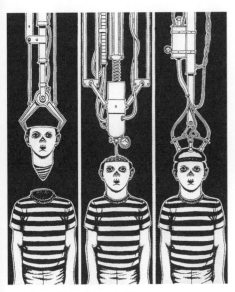

Expensive Children of Summerhill,

Start no. 301, August 6, 1980

Great Sin on the Small Screen,

Start no. 325, July 4, 1981

Pedagogical catechism against sex,

Start no. 376, June 18, 1983

"As we moved from a student press to a professional press, young artists began doing the opposite of what we were doing. I found these results satisfying. Let them think I'm old, that my work is not good, that it's time for new ideas—I like that. Let them fight me with their work. That was the reason I brought illustrator Igor Kordej, a colleague, to *Start*—to be my rival. Up to that point I did two illustrations per issue; after he came I did only one. But Kordej was my guarantee that I would keep on doing a good job and that I would not withdraw into my own shell. This was a rivalry in the best possible sense: sometimes I had a better trick, I drew a better illustration, I got a better idea, and so on. That was the way we helped each other. The easiest thing to do is to sit back in a comfy chair and live peacefully for the rest of your life. But who needs that?"

—MIRKO ILIĆ, "SLOW, BAD AND EXPENSIVE," *ZUM REPORTER* NO. 846, BELGRADE, FEBRUARY 10, 1983

Are Yugoslavs Lazy,
Start no. 420, February 23, 1985

Measure Against Measure,
Start no. 257, November 29, 1978

Consumer Sold to Consumption,
Start no. 258, December 13, 1978

SEV - Unity of Opposed Interests,
Start no. 403, June 30, 1984

Do We Need Foreign Capital,
Start no. 378, July 16, 1983

"Mirko brought with him an important thing—a new perspective on the function of illustration. He was really the first to treat illustration as equal to the text, not as a secondary part of an article. Illustration did not copy the idea, rather it developed and commented on the ideas in the text. Mirko was definitely the first among our illustrators to do something like that. What Arsovski and Bućan did for graphic design in Yugoslavia, Mirko did for illustration—he turned a new page. Nothing was as it used to be. First, there was astonishment, then acceptance, and then came copying. They tried to copy Mirko too, but that was a bit too hard. You could copy what was less important—the technique and the drawing, but you could not copy the way he thought. Thanks to his enormous artistic and conceptual capacity, illustration became something completely different from what it used to be in Croatian journalism. He would receive the text and then he would perhaps call me to tell me what kind of a surprise he had for me. In my time none of his illustrations were ever rejected..."
—MARIO BOŠNJAK

From Rags to Riches,
Start no. 254,
October 18, 1978

**Is Justice Made
of Paper?**,
Start no. 257,
November 29, 1978

**Who Is Not to Be in the
Communist League**,
Start no. 370,
March 26, 1983

Yugoslav Foreign Currency Dilemmas,
Start no. 421, March 9, 1985

OPPOSITE PAGE:

Amateurs by Profession
Start no. 265, March 21, 1979

**With a Car Through the
Wall**, *Start* no. 316,
February 28, 1981

CIA pushing drugs?
Start no. 262,
February 2, 1979

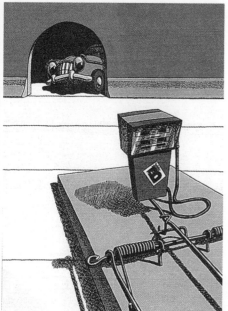

Balls and Flippers for Colorful Takeoffs

Start no. 250, August 23, 1978

Second Youth of the Old Music

Start no. 290, March 5, 1980

Sexual Side of the Brain

Start no. 315, February 14, 1981

The Reality of a Californian Dream, *Start* br. 342, February 27, 1982

Illustration with Slavenka Drakulić's text, *Duga*, Belgrade, 1982

First illustration published in foreign magazine, German satire magazine **Pardon**, 1977

The state does not strike back, *Start* no. 352, July 17, 1982

Knowledge at a Higher Price,

Start no. 293, April 16, 1980

Milisav VESOVIĆ / MO

Cernenko e i militari

Panorama no. 962, September 24, 1984,

AD: Franko Lefevre,

ILLUSTRATION: Mirko Ilić

Terrorism and Mafia

Panorama no. 990, April 7, 1985,

AD: Mirko Ilić & Franko Lefevre,

PHOTO: Luka Mjeda

"Those illustrations from *Start* were seen by the people from *Panorama*, and they liked them a lot, so their manager for international affairs came to Zagreb, contacted me, asked me to send him copies, which I did, but after that there was silence. I thought I was forgotten, when suddenly *Panorama* appeared, with my illustration. Later they called me in for a visit, and so I used to draw illustrations in my hotel room. They purchased a range of my works from *Start*, which was quite a nice way of showing that what I was doing was not one of those things called 'They live only for today, throw them away and it's over.' They still find them interesting even though I made them four years ago. In addition, they say that they are very convenient since they can be used for some other texts."

—MIRKO ILIĆ, "SLOW, BAD, AND EXPENSIVE," *ZUM REPORTER*, NO. 846, BELGRADE OCTOBER 2, 1983

Gastarbeiter

By **Rujana JEGER**

DO YOU WANT TO GO TO VENICE WITH ME, my father asked. Of course, I said (actually screamed). *Mirko, mom, I'm going to Venice,* I said. But on the day of the departure, I had a very high fever and a horrible cough and I couldn't go. I cried and cried. Father went anyway and met up with my new stepmother. (A year later he moved to Canada with her).

"Don't cry," Mirko said. "As soon as you get better, I will take you to Milan, ok? Milan?" OK, OK, I said and obediently drank tea with honey and took two aspirin. A few weeks later, good to his word, we boarded the night train to Milan. Mirko had a Walkman and was listening to Lou Reed's album *Transformer.* He soon fell asleep, and I listened to his Walkman all night long and watched dark shadows pass on the ceiling. We woke up in Milan. In the lobby of a small cheap hotel where Mirko had stayed several times before, we had a problem: I was 15 and, even though he was my stepfather, he was only 27. He seemed too young to be my father, and since we didn't share the same last name, they didn't want to let us share a room and we had no money for two. Mirko was irate. "I am her father!" he yelled, *"Io sono il Padre, capisci?"* Confronted by this surge of anger, the clerk gave in.

We threw our things into the room and went out for a coffee and cake. Then we boarded the bus and went to the publishing house. After an eternity on the bus, we arrived at a huge skyscraper standing on columns, surrounded by a lake full of swans. The editorial departments of a number of fashion magazines that Mirko did work for were there. The foyer teemed with models. Interesting people crowded the elevators, chaos ruled each floor. A tall blonde with short hair offered us a chewing gum. Later on I saw her pictures in *Amica.* While Mirko was working, I was chewing my gum and listening to the Walkman. It was all "A Walk on the Wild Side" for me. After that we had some spaghetti and returned to the hotel. Mirko unscrewed the chandelier, put in a 100-watt bulb, set the table in the middle of the room and said: "OK, now you go to sleep, I have to draw a little bit!" Only then I realized that we were not tourists but *gastarbeiter.*[01] He handed me a new Peter Gabriel tape. I plugged myself in and fell asleep. In the morning I found him asleep with his head on the table. We went to Mondadori where he introduced me to some people from the fashion industry. Someone asked me if I wanted to be a model. I had puffed red hair and tight overalls with a leopard pattern. I thought they were joking and stared at the floor. Peter Gabriel had given me strength to endure their gazes. In the afternoon we strolled through the Piazza Duomo and crawled through small streets full of exclusive boutiques. In one of them I tried to choose between leopard and black high top sneakers, but was unable to decide. Mirko bought both for me. I was happy. Spaghetti ... 100-watt light bulbs... Walkman...

He worked hard every night, all night long. In the afternoons we would go to the movies, and once we even went to a club, with some fashion people. I did not dance, I just looked around. I don't think that Mirko was very in to the scene either. He was half dead from all the work. But he wanted to give me something, to be my father, there, in Milan, when we were *gastarbeiter.* →

01 | Gastarbeiter is German for "guest worker" (or "guest workers"—the plural is the same as the singular). It refers to migrant workers who had moved to Germany mainly in the 1960s and '70s, seeking work as part of a formal guest worker program (Gastarbeiterprogramm). The word is commonly used in the region of former Yugoslavia to mean locals working abroad.

Rujana Jeger, daughter of Slavenka Drakulić and Ilić's step-daughter, posed for the cover of **ARA—Artistic work action Belgrade '81** (Jugoton 1981, LSY-61650), a compilation LP of ten New Wave bands from Belgrade: Radnička kontrola, Bezobrazno zeleno, Profili profili, Defektno efektni, Urbana gerila, Petar i zli vuci, U škripcu, Pasta ZZ, Via Talas, TV moroni.
D: Studio SLS, PHOTO: Radovan Sredić;
MAKE UP: Dinka Završki

Prljavo kazalište: Prljavo kazalište, Suzy 1979, LP 332, PHOTO ON THE BACK COVER: Siniša Knaflec

Prljavo kazalište:

My Father Was in the War

Suzy 1979, SP 1212

"The term 'star' is relative. When I lived in Zagreb, just as I was starting out, I was designing covers for a well-known group in Croatia. Their front man, still in high school at that time, was sitting at my home shaking his head, dubiously watching my design concept. He was being very dramatic, overacting, pondering. Then Slavenka Drakulić, to whom I was married at the time, entered the apartment, and my client, seeing his professor, got up briskly and stuttered that everything was fine. The cover became wonderful, and he greeted his teacher and slipped away. The 'star' was, in fact, playing hooky so that he could come to me for a meeting. So much for the stars."

—MIRKO ILIĆ, "I LIKE TO MAKE A FUSS," *GLORIA* NUMBER 384

Everybody Dance. Now!

RECORD DESIGN IN YUGOSLAVIA underwent a rapid change in the mid seventies. Pop and rock acts gradually started to take center stage and a new criteria was being imposed for the record industry. Bijelo dugme—the band of now internationally famous Goran Bregović—set new standards in the Yugoslav record industry. All of a sudden, what band members looked like, the sound and lighting of concerts, album-cover design became the main focus. Soon enough, with development of early TV video clips, even concerts lost their role as the primary way a band was experienced. Instead, their main purpose was to promote a record. The twelve-inch record was no longer seen as a mere collection of hit singles, but as a well-rounded creative structure of an author and the product of collaboration. Musicians, as well as critics and audiences, were paying more attention to the role of a producer, arranger, recording engineer, and also album-cover designer. In other words, which had become common practice in the West (starting in the mid-sixties with the Beatles' *Revolver* and Velvet Underground and Nico "banana album" with Andy Warhol's cover), had also taken root in Yugoslavia. It was a modernist paradigm shift in which the album is perceived as a whole creative package of artistic expression, with design being just as important part as the songs and production. And with Ilić's generation it became common practice. And let us add that record sleeves that were their main path into the art and design. For instance, influence of Barney Bubbles early seventies covers for British space rock band Hawkwind is obvious in his early SF comics and illustrations.

In late sixties, album covers were first seen as mere packaging but then gradually they were regarded as art. Despite the occasional involvement of some well-known designers, such as Mihajlo Arsovski, Ivan Picelj, Boris Bućan, and Borislav Ljubičić, it was only with Dragan S. Stefanović's high-profile work for Bijelo dugme that the role of designer and his work actually attracted the attention of the audience. Around the same time, in 1974, the young music critic and art history student Darko Glavan organized the very first Yugoslav exhibition of foreign album covers in the Gallery SC in Zagreb. Another important milestone was the emergence of the first album by the Slovenian band Buldožer, *Pljuni istini u oči* (Spit in the eye of truth) (ALTA / PGP RTB 1975). The cover design for the album loosely follows the conceptual album *Thick as a Brick* by Jethro Tull. Designed as a newspaper that included comics, illustrations, short stories, and fake advertisements, its raw, black humor, and complex relationship with the contents of the record brought a new spirit to the Yugoslav music scene. The design was signed by Slavko Furlan, but in accordance with the general newspaper format, it was primarily the collective work of band members and their friends.

When Ilić started to design record covers, the most important record company in Yugoslavia at the time was Jugoton in Zagreb.[01] Most of its record covers were done by the photographer and designer Ivan Ivezić, who was basically a one-man in-house design studio. In hindsight, Ivezić's work deserves further exploration but he was primarily a talented photographer who willingly met the music industry's narrow requirements for design at the time. That being essentially a photograph of the artist on the front cover, with the back cover containing information about the songs, usually with some radical colorful composition of geometrical

01 | Nine record publishing houses operated in Yugoslavia with ten labels and five records' factories – Jugoton and Suzy in Zagreb, RTB and Jugodisk in Belgrade, ZKP RTV Ljubljana, Helidon from Maribor, Diskoton and Sarajevodisk from Sarajevo and Diskos from Aleksandrovac primarily focused on folk music.

Prljavo Kazalište: **Black and White World**,
Suzy 1980, LP 343, PHOTO: Marko Čolić

Prljavo Kazalište: **Hero of the Street**,
Suzy 1981, LP 363, ILLUSTRATION: Igor Kordej

Bijelo dugme:
Till You Turn 100,
Jugoton 1980, LSY-10003
PHOTO: Željko Stojanović
Slides of plastic surgeries
through VPA
(Vjesnik's Press Agency)

"For some reason or another
the Bijelo dugme record cover
had to be finished immediately.
So I had just few hours to find
a model willing to pose semi
nude, so I had to persuade
some girl in front of the
Zvečka caffe. That was the way
we had to work."
—IGOR MIRKOVIĆ, "SRETNO DIJETE,"
FRAKTURA, ZAGREB, 2004, STR. 59

abstractions. Today these "reverse sides" look much more interesting than the often naive and funny photographed covers, which were shot without any stylist or makeup artists, and very often in brutal natural light without any retouching.

It was the so-called New Wave movement that radically changed this practice, by improving production quality and opening the door to more creative approaches and new designers, including Ilić. While he might have been the biggest name to enter the field at the time, others included Igor Kordej, Bachrach and Krištofić, design partnership Aux Manière, and musician/artists with diverse multimedia interests, like Ivan Piko Stančić, Goran Vejvoda, Vladimir Jovanović, Koja, and Srđan Gile Gojković.

The growth of the area's music scene was rapid. In 1976 Jugoton worked with only eight Yugoslav rock bands releasing eight singles and six LP records. In 1981 that grew to twenty-five bands, thirty singles released, and sixteen LP records. While typical record releases at the time sold between ten and twenty thousand copies, the best selling local performers at the end of the decade, (bands such as Bijelo dugme, Novi fosili, Srebrna krila, and singer Zdravko Čolić) were selling between two hundred and four hundred thousand records. The leader of Bijelo dugme, Goran Bregović, once said that they sold more records than there were record players in Yugoslavia.

First privately owned publishing house in Croatia, Suzy, was established in 1973. It was the licensing partner of the American CBS group and opted for long-term investment in a small number of performers. They repped bands like Parni valjak and Prljavo kazalište exclusively, and sales ranged from fifty to one hundred thousand LPs and audio cassettes sold.

Ibrica Jusić + Dog: Room 501, Two Persons,
Jugoton 1983, LSY-63146, PHOTO: Luka Mjeda

The early eighties was an era of affirmation of the most important Yugoslav New Wave performers, first through singles and compilations, and then through solo albums. But these artists did not appear out of nowhere. This "sudden" breakthrough of the New Wave scene was preceded by long years of struggling musicians and a fomenting music scene. It's just that now they were all given a chance to publish their work. Ironically, this focus on local talent was a by-product of the Yugoslav music industry not being able to afford to license foreign artists rather than a conscious appreciation of what was happening in the local music scene. The economic crisis of the time created a flourishing cultural structure, (alas, we never figured out—with the exception of Goran Bregović—how to translate that cultural capital to an international level).

The design of the album covers was extremely important for both the evolution of design in Yugoslavia and the awareness of its importance, and for Ilić's personal development from an illustrator to a professional designer. He collaborated on commercial projects, showed discipline in fulfilling of industry requirements, complied with notoriously tight deadlines, and even when not particularly enthusiastic, he created inspired work.

Drago Mlinarec: Everything is OK,
Jugoton 1979, LSY-66057
PHOTO: Boris Dučić

With the general scarcity up to this point of creative record-cover design on the local pop scene, Ilić's work represented something new. He used all possible methods and approaches, styles and techniques—black-and-white and color photography, toning, airbrush, illustrations, photomontages, collages, etc. —to purposefully eschew a clearly recognizable style. All of this was before computers, so each custom typeface had to be drawn, arranged from Letraset or even from Xeroxed copies of letter forms, and prepress production had to be done by the printing house, which often resulted in less than ideal final products.

"Mirko is always striving to find a new detail that changes the whole idea," said Luka Mjeda. "At the conceptual level, but also during production. What

New Wave: Azra, Film, Parlament, Parni
Valjak, Prljavo kazalište, Suzy 1980, LP 347,
D: Mirko Ilić, PHOTO: Dražen Kalenić,
MODEL: Dejan Kršić

Various Artists: Your Choice — 26 Hits for
the Big Party, Jugoton 1983, LSY-61880

can be easily done today with a computer was not possible at that time, so he explored various printing techniques, which others had not thought of, probably because they didn't know it was an option. He did not have to do this, as many other designers did not, but he wanted to expand the possibilities. The longer he was in that business, the more he learned about all technical details."

Due to the limited resources that publishers were willing to invest, most records had only a single package. Additional inside covers, paper bags for the plate, specially designed label for the record, gatefold covers or supplements like posters, were rare, and reserved only for best-selling performers (Mišo Kovač, Bijelo dugme, Srebrna krila, Oliver Mandić …) and records where the commercial success was unquestionable or irrelevant. Although, designers occasionally managed to push more complex solutions, such as embossing (Bijelo dugme, Prljavo kazalište, Igor Savin), die-cutting of the cover (Parliament), or even such extravaganza as three different versions of covers for *Doživjetu stotu* (Live until 100) by Bijelo dugme.

In general, the production standards at that time were still relatively low, and Ilić was trying to raise them by hiring art photographers, make-up artists, and stylists.

Although he created most of his covers with Luka Mjeda, he also collaborated with well-known art and fashion photographers, including Danilo Dučak, Andrija Zelmanović, Dražen Kalenić, Željko Stojanović, Slobodan Tadić, and Saša Novković. Even so, he was often forced to use supplied images regardless of their quality. For the Skopje band Leb i sol's album Kalabalak, there was no time or money to organize a photo shoot, so Ilić transformed the poor-quality images they did have into a collage and multiplied the heads of the musicians, turning the cover image into wallpaper-like texture.

From 1979 to about 1986, Ilić designed between one-hundred-and-fifty and two-hundred single and LP records for Jugoton. He also worked for Suzy, Helidon, PGP RTB, Diskoton and others. It was almost one record jacket per week.

Many of them were simply still portraits of performers, where Ilić's contribution mostly came down to background choice, setting, framing, and a typographic solution for the record title and the artist name. To bring some life to the designs he often used abstract graphical, colorful elements (lines, nets, grids, squares, triangles, stars). The superficiality of such decorations often faithfully reflected the content of the music – especially when it came to the pop and easy-listening or folk music acts, who still looked at LPs as collections of individual songs with no clear substantive focus.

When he was able to design covers for more inspiring performers, even when he had to work within same limitations, he made some interesting work. One standout is his courageous decision to picture Josipa Lisac from the back—with the (now terribly) politically incorrect use of a dead fox, a reference to the singer's nickname and album title which loosely might be translated as "Foxy Lady". His reassembled portraits of quite inconspicuous and publicly unknown members of the New Wave band Stidljiva ljubičica are a clever reference to the album *More Songs About Buildings and Food* by the Talking Heads. Interestingly, years later, he applied a similar technique to an illustration about plastic surgery.

Surprisingly, his illustrated covers were very rare, as is the case with his many *Danas* magazine covers later on. Clearly this was the result of his conscious desire to move away from his reputation as solely an illustrator. Occasionally he did use drawings, but mainly when designing record covers for children, and often these have withstood the test of time better than the albums where he had to work with photography in low-quality production levels.

Though probably the most famous pop music covers Ilić did were hand-

Various Artists:

Everybody Dance. Now,

Jugoton 1981, LSY-61588

"According to Jugoton's specifications, the cover should primarily protect the record from scratching. It is also used, among other purposes, to advertise the record. According to research, an unknown band will sell 30 percent more records if the cover is good. But if a band is famous and it releases a record with a plain white cover—like the Beatles—it will sell anyway.

As far as our designs, it really depends on the band or the individual, what they think their covers should look like and to what extent the designer is capable of fighting with them to convince band of something else. Small bands don't complain too much because they know that they are still small, so they suffer the terror imposed by designers. But once they become big, they dictate what they want and it will most likely be their dear and beautiful faces."

—MIRKO ILIĆ, RADIO 101, AN INTERVIEW, APPROX. 1984

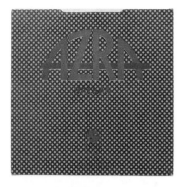

Azra: And What Should I Do / Balkan,
Suzy 1979, SP-1218

Azra: Mon ami / Deep Inside You,
Jugoton 1984, SY-23981, D: SLS

Idoli: Bambina / A Stranger in the Night,
Jugoton 1983, SY-23946, SLS

Zana: Check Pants / My Grandpa,
Jugoton 1981, SY-23753

**Stidljiva ljubičica: I Love You /
My Friend Goes to the Army**,
Jugoton 1981, SY-23798
PHOTO: Dražen Kalenić

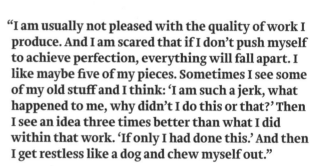

> "I am usually not pleased with the quality of work I produce. And I am scared that if I don't push myself to achieve perfection, everything will fall apart. I like maybe five of my pieces. Sometimes I see some of my old stuff and I think: 'I am such a jerk, what happened to me, why didn't I do this or that?' Then I see an idea three times better than what I did within that work. 'If only I had done this.' And then I get restless like a dog and chew myself out."
> —MIRKO ILIĆ

Prljavo kazalište: Black-and-White World,
Suzy 1980, SP 1240, PHOTO: Marko Čolić

Film: You Radiate Rays through the Air,
Jugoton 1983, SY-23934,
D: Studio SLS, PHOTO: Luka Mjeda–SLM

**Slađana & Neutral Design: Mickey, Mickey /
Das Licht von Kairo**, Jugoton 1983, SY-23947,
D: SLS, PHOTO: Luka Mjeda

**Aerodrom: When My Thoughts
Wonder Off**, Jugoton 1980, SY-23631,
PHOTO: Dražen Kalenić

Xenia: The Threesome / For the Last Time,
Jugoton 1984, SY-24039,
D: Studio TIM, PHOTO: Zvonimir Atletić

**Zabranjeno pušenje: I Don't Want to Be
a Kraut**, Jugoton 1984, SY-23978,
D: Studio SLS, PHOTO: Zvonimir Atletić

drawn—the airbrushed tongue for the debut album of Prljavo kazalište and the Svi marš na ples compilation. The cover of Prljavo kazalište's debut LP was his second album cover and his first use of the (decidedly nonpunk) airbrush technique. Avoiding the literal transfer of punk aesthetics (despite the safety pin) and the use of current visual clichés of that time (blackmail typography, expressive black-and-white photography, screaming surfaces of plain Day-Glo colors), Ilić embraced the method. One song on the album was titled "Some boys," and as an ironic comment on the Rolling Stones' hit record at the time, Some Girls, Ilić reinterpreted their logo. The stuck out tongue was one of common punk poses of the day. This adaptation of the Stones' logo became the icon most strongly associated with the band and they still use it today (although these days, the band is considered more of a dinosaur than defiant group of provocateurs from the workers' suburbs).

If Paket aranžman, the joint debut LP of the three main bands on the Belgrade scene (Idoli, Šarlo akrobata, Električni orgazam), marked a major breakthrough of New Wave, the compilation *Svi marš na ples* represented its commercial inauguration. The cover features simple but clever illustrations ironically portraying the fashion sense of each band. The overall (and very accurate) effect, as well as the image's ability to convey a collection of quite diverse groups and songs, was achieved with minimal means.

Ilić said that he was most satisfied with the work of his when he had total creative freedom. Often these were more low-key editions, such as compilations, children's records, or editions of classical music. "Little things made me happy. I was happy with Svi marš na ples, and there were several children's records that I made, some with Kordej, some by myself, like *Šegrt Hlapić*... There was a classic record as well, a Zagreb wind trio in which the coat of arms of Zagreb was converted into three trumpets..."

In contrast to these relatively small projects, perhaps Ilić's best known for a commercial album was the cover for *Doživjeti stotu* by Bijelo dugme. The design concept was based on the title track, but also as an ironic reference to the "rejuvenated" New Wave sound and the image of the band members. The idea of the cover also relied on the previous covers made by Dragan S. Stefanović that always featured some close-up of female body. Different versions of the cover for *Doživjeti stotu*—breasts, lips, eyes—are a reference to Stefanović's series. As a marketing gimmick, three versions were created. It was a confirmation of the stature of the band among the growing competition and also a bold statement: "Who could afford this, except the Dugme?" Also, it must have been an idea that was in the air, because at the same time several international albums came out with similar tricks.[02]

Today, Ilić's covers are often undergoing a transformation of their own, mostly because they are being tampered with. Quite often his art is reused

Stidljiva ljubičica: **Look Back at Me**,

Jugoton 1981, LSY-63110,

D: Studio SLS, PHOTO: Radovan Sredić

U škripcu: **New Years**,

Jugoton 1984, LSY-61868,

D: SLS, PHOTO: Luka Mjeda,

COSTUMES: Đeni Medvedec

and manipulated without his permission. New generations see those record covers mostly in some bastardized version on a CD reissues. So not only has the format been drastically reduced, but also often the designs are reframed, with sometimes two records reprinted on the same CD. Parts of different covers get merged, and sometimes—as in the rerelease of *Svi marš na ples*—typography is changed for no apparent reason. All of this reveals not only the lack of respect for cultural capital, but also the lack of importance given to the design, as well as the weak copyright protection designers receive.

"I don't get too upset about it," Ilić said. "But I would appreciate it if they would at least sent me a copy of a new CD when it is released." ▶

02 | Zones: *Under Influence* (Arista, 1979) – the only one who really has completely different versions, while others produce only color mutations; Squeeze: *Cool for Cats* (A&M/Polygram 1979); Split Enz: *True Colors* (design Noel Crombie, Mushroom/ A&M 1980); Genesis: *Abacab* (Charisma 1981); Split Enz: *Waiata* (A&M 1981).

The Cadillac: It's Only Rock'n'Roll, Suzy/CBS 1982, 85709, D&ILL: Studio SLS – Igor Kordej & Mirko Ilić

Rock Begins, Vol 2, Suzy/Atlantic 60025, 1980, PHOTO: Željko Stojanović

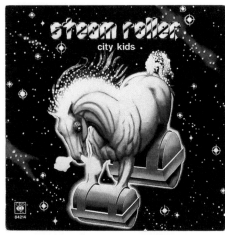

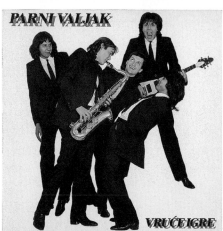

Steam Roller: City Kids,
Suzy/CBS 1979, 84214

Parni valjak: Hot Games,
Suzy/CBS 1980, LP 84814,
PHOTO: Dražen Kalenić

Parni Valjak: Catch the Rhythm,
Jugoton 1984, LSY-63208,
D: Studio SLS,
PHOTO: Josip Strmečki

Parni valjak: The Concert,
Suzy/CBS 1982, 88593,
D: Studio SLS,
PHOTO: Jasmin Krpan,
Davor Pačemski

"It is very difficult for a kid to pay twenty-eight thousand dinars for a double album of Parni Valjak songs that he has already heard. I persuaded the band to print a free ticket on the cover, and when the band was on tour one really could go to the concert with it. It was a good trick for kids to get something for free. I screwed up the design; that ticket should have looked better, like a coupon, or a bond, I did not really work hard on it, but the idea was good."

— MIRKO ILIĆ

Josipa Lisac: Lisica, Jugoton 1982,
LSY-63136, PHOTO: Željko Koprolčec

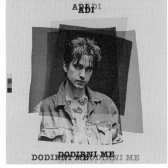

Adi: Touch Me, Jugoton 1982,
LSY-63134, PHOTO: Željko Koprolčec

Early use of bodypainting
at the sleeve of **Andrej
Baša: Between Heaven
and Earth**, Jugoton 1982,
LSY-61689
Studio SLS, PHOTO: Željko
Koprolčec

Daniel: Julie / I Was Naive,
Jugoton 1983, LSY-63156
D: Studio SLS, PHOTO: Luka Mjeda

**Oliver Mandić: I Would Like to Scream Your
Name**, Jugoton 1985, LSY-63241,
D: M. I, PHOTO: Ivan Mojašević

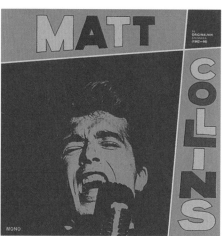

Crveni koralji: Rock'n'Roll zbirka 1963-1966,
Jugoton 1985, LSY-62010,
D: TIM, F: Luka Mjeda

Matt Collins: 16 Original Tracks,
Jugoton 1981, LSY-61613

PJEVAM PJESNIKE

ARSEN DEDIĆ

Arsen Dedić:
I Sing the Poets,
PGP RTB 1980, 2520044,
PORTRAIT: Boris Dogan

A portrait of Arsen Dedić
was, besides being printed
on a separate cardboard
and inserted in the album
covers, also embossed on
the cover of the album
released in 1980 by PGP RTB
in cooperation with RTZ
(Radio-television Zagreb)
and Goranovo poljeće
poetry festival.

Leb i sol: Kalabalak,
Jugoton 1983, LSY-63158,
D: Studio SLS,
PHOTO: V. Serafimov

Zana: Back on the Train,
Jugoton 1983, LSY-63188,
D: Studio SLS,
PHOTO: Luka Mjeda,
MAKE UP: Višnja Trusić

Izazov: The Chalenge,
Jugoton 1982, LSY-63126,
D: Studio SLS,
PHOTO: Željko Koprolčec

Zamba: Low Punch,
Jugoton 1983, LSY-63169,
D: Studio SLS,
PHOTO: Luka Mjeda/SIM

Daniel: Tina and Marina,
Jugoton 1985, LSY-63224,
D: Studio TIM,
PHOTO: Luka Mjeda,
MAKE UP: Snježana Pletikosa

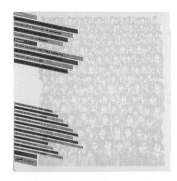
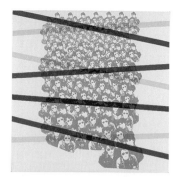
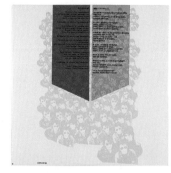
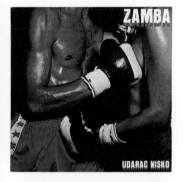

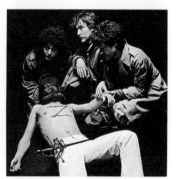

FESTIVAL
ZABAVNE
GLAZBE
SPLIT '82
Split Song Festival

Split '82 Festival,
Jugoton 1982, LSY-69037/8,
D: Studio SLS
PHOTO: Željko Koprolčec

FESTIVAL ZABAVNE GLAZBE
SPLIT SONG FESTIVAL

USTANAK I MORE
SPLIT '83

Split '83 Festival,
Jugoton 1983, LSY-12003/4,
D: Studio SLS,
PHOTO: Luka Mjeda

Revolution and Sea:
Split '83 Festival,
Jugoton 1983, LSY-61826,
D: Studio SLS
PHOTO: Luka Mjeda

CHILDHOOD

IGOR SAVIN

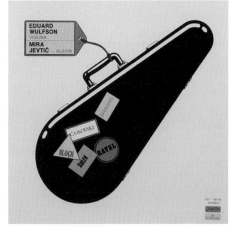

Igor Savin: Childhood,
Jugoton 1984, LSY-61719

On the album cover for minimal-ambient-electronic album *Childhood* by composer Igor Savin, embossed square frames that listeners will feel rather than see, underlines the objectivity; i.e., the objective nature of the album cover and the insistence upon the subtleness of the drawing that looks childlike with discrete letters of pure, prime colors.

Eduard Wulfson, violin / Mira Jevtić, piano,
Jugoton/Fonoars, LSY-66149

Arbo Valdma: Fuga coronat opus,
Jugoton/Fonoars 1980, LSY-66107

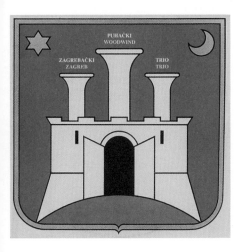

Zagrebački Wind Trio,
Jugoton/Fonoars, LSY-66155

Ivana Brlić-Mažuranić: Strange stories of apprentice Hlapić, Jugoton 1982, LSY-68080,
D & ILLUSTRATION: Mirko Ilić, Studio SLS

Kaj nam pak moreju: The Zagreb Cabaret between Two Wars,
Jugoton/Discothalia 1982, LSY-69041/2,
ILLUSTRATION: Aleksandar-Šaca Marx

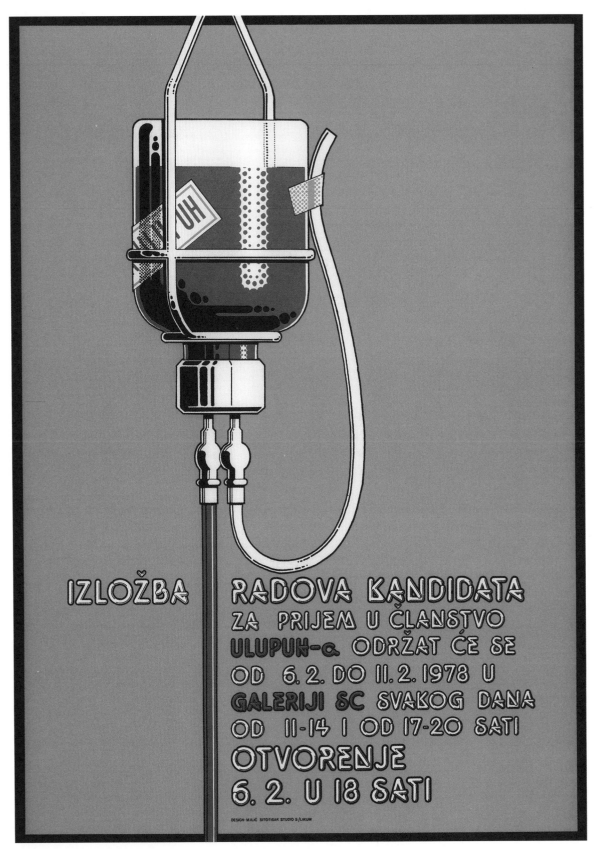

IZLOŽBA RADOVA KANDIDATA ZA PRIJEM U ČLANSTVO ULUPUH-a ODRŽAT ĆE SE OD 6.2. DO 11.2.1978 U GALERIJI SC SVAKOG DANA OD 11-14 I OD 17-20 SATI OTVORENJE 6.2. U 18 SATI

DESIGN: M.ILIĆ SITOTISAK STUDIO S/LIKUM

"If you're from Eastern Europe and you tell someone in the West that you design posters, they think that you must mean Polish posters. Unfortunately they have become a symbol of the whole of Eastern Europe. As if a hundred million people should design a poster that exact same way." —MIRKO ILIĆ

An exhibition of works of candidates for the membership to ULUPUH, poster, 1978 SILKSCREEN-PRINTING Studio S

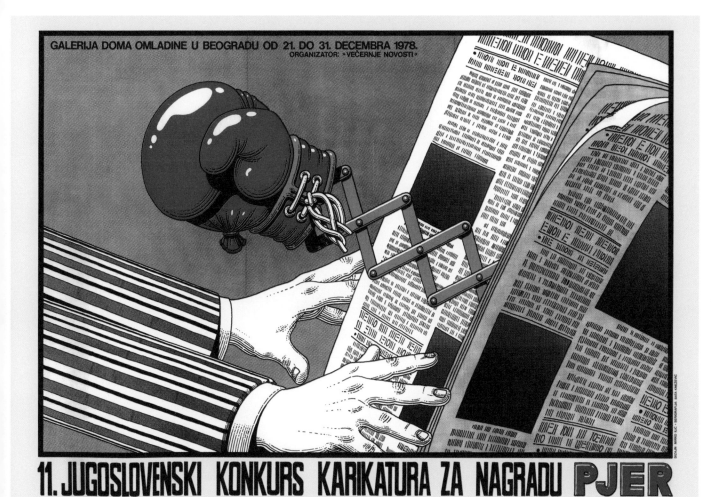

11. Yugoslav caricature contest for the Pjer prize, poster, 1978, AD: Dušan Petričić, SILKSCREEN: Bata Knežević

"Sometime in the mid-seventies, he appeared one day in my office in *Večernje Novosti*. A young punk with short name and an even shorter last name—Mirko Ilić.

I do not know why I remember that he was missing a large rectangular piece from the pajamas he was wearing beneath an unbuttoned leather jacket. Probably because the lack of fabric was a counterbalance to everything else that Mirko possessed: energy, talent, confidence, audacity, spirit...

His appearance, combined with the rich content of his portfolio, has left little doubt that he is a remarkable artist. Even from that first encounter with Mirko and Mirko's drawings, I was without any doubt able to determine the most important characteristic of his layered art persona: He can think!

For me, it's always been the most precious ingredient of any human creation. In the artistic space that Mirko is moving through, among thousands of great illustrators and excellent craftsmen, that delicate feature has a special meaning.

Since at the time I ran the PJER competition for the best newspaper caricature, through the organization of *Večernje Novosti*, I was not even a bit hesitant about to whom to offer the realization of the poster. It was one of the first professional engagements that he was offered and I am particularly proud of that. Many years after our first meeting, an unfortunate coincidence of historical, social, and political circumstances brought me and my family to Toronto. And by some strange universal order, my first professional commission on the new continent, I received from Mirko, who was the art director of the op-ed pages in *The New York Times* at that time. Thus, our longstanding friendship, which lasts to this day, made a full circle in the best way. Mirko has opened many important doors at this stage of my professional life."

—DUŠAN PETRIČIĆ

"It is completely different, designing posters and painting. It usually takes some time for a painter to achieve any level of acclaim, while a poster designer might get more immediate recognition. But when you finally do get noticed in the painting world, it lasts for a long time. I'm not sure how many young designers, even in Zagreb, if asked a question about Boris Bućan, would think of the poster designer, and not of Boris Bućan the painter."

—MIRKO ILIĆ

2. YUCON

2.-4. 11. 1979.

GALERIJA STUDENTSKOG
CENTRA ZAGREB, SAVSKA 25

ORGANIZATOR KLUB PRIJATELJA
BELETRISTIKE I ZNANSTVENE
FANTASTIKE »SFera« - ZAGREB

design: m. ilić   lišak- EC grafički servis studentski centar zagreb

Poster for the second YUCON,
silkscreen SC, 1979

In the mid seventies, the Gallery SC held SF Fairs, the first organized gatherings of science fiction fans which soon turned into real sci-fi conventions that were massive in scale. They changed the name first to YUcon and then in 1983 to SFeraKon which they are still called.

"I was asked to come up with a poster for the science fiction festival, and I remembered the film *Innocence Unprotected*,* where acrobat Dragoljub Aleksić hangs by his teeth from a trapeze below an aircraft flying over Belgrade. That's our science fiction. That's our Superman!" —MIRKO ILIĆ

* *Innocence Unprotected*,
DIR: Dnušan Makavejev,
Avala Film,
Belgrade, 1968

Street Images

Posters · 1978–86

FOR HIS EXHIBITION OF COMICS in the SC Gallery, Mirko printed a poster of *Shakti* in silk screen in the large B1 format.

"An architect and promoter of design, Bernardo Bernardi, actually fell in love with that poster," said designer Boris Ljubičić. "He recognized something in it and asked Ilić to make a poster for the annual exhibition of candidates for the admission of new members to ULUPUH (The Croatian Association of Artists of Applied Arts). It could be said, and might even get Mirko offended a bit, that Bernardi in this way indirectly revealed him to others as a new talent."

The exhibition was held in February 1978 at SC Gallery, and as he was not a member of ULUPUH either then, Ilić has—of course—used that very poster as the submission of work to apply for candidacy, and he was indeed admitted.

Thus, Ilić's professional design career started at the end of 1978. Around the same time, by commission from Dušan Petričić, he designed a poster for the eleventh Yugoslav caricature contest for the *Pierre* prize in Belgrade, and became a permanent designer with Theatre &TD, in Zagreb, known for its high-quality posters and visual identity designed by Mihajlo Arsovski.

"After Arsovski, Boris Bućan worked there, but it did not last long. He made two posters for a play about Don Juan, pink and blue, male and female, and got into an argument over that right away. Then Željko Borčić worked there for a couple of years; he gave up for his own reasons, and I came after him. I have often used silk-screen printing studio at SC; I think someone brought me there and said—here, try him."

Staying within the same horizontal poster format limits and silk-screen printing techniques, he has made an interesting variety of works, and very few of these are similar. Although the majority of posters were drawn by hand, he frequently changed styles and techniques, and he soon began to use photography and collage or montage of available materials along the lines of a sewing pattern. ▶

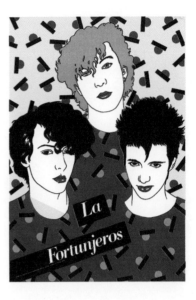

La Fortunjeros, band poster, 1982

Aerodrom (Airport), band poster, silkscreen, 1980.

Telephone, dual-format poster for the ongoing performance of the group in the SC Club, screen printing, around 1979/80

Marx / Freud &
Lenin / Einstein
for Beginners –
the comic strip,
CDD – Zagreb /
SIC – Belgrade
1980, promotion
posters,
silkscreen,
2×120×70 cm

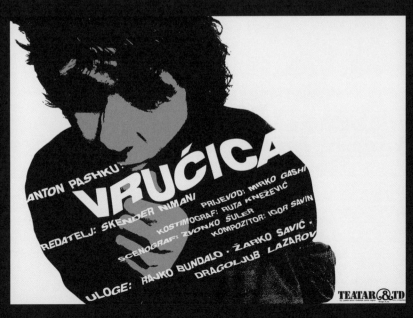

Andras Suto: The Star at the Stake, 1978
Program booklet is co-signed with Vjekoslav Fabić-Holi

Jean-Claude Danaud: Handmade, 1979

Anton Pashku: Fever, 1980

All posters for Theater &TD: Graphic studio SC, format app. 70×100 cm. Program booklets were made in various formats, associated with the content of the performance and poster designs.

"At an exhibition at the Zagreb Art Pavilion in 1992, I wanted to show some of my posters for Theater & TD. But they had thrown away their complete poster archive, including the works of Mihajlo Arsovski, Boris Bućan, and Željko Borčić. When I checked with the companies that had printed the work, I was told they had gone out of business and sold their entire archives as scrap paper. Then I discovered that the Graphic collection of the National library, which should have had copies, didn't have a clue about it, and that the Theatrical institute, which by default should have collected all theater posters didn't know where anything was either."

—MIRKO ILIĆ

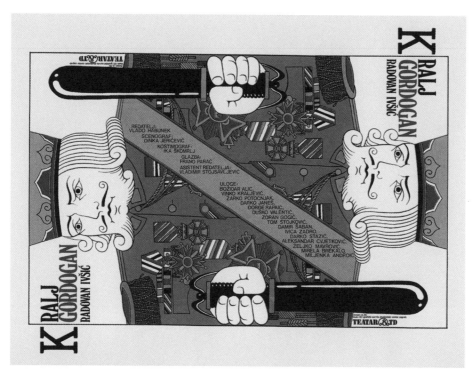

Radovan Ivšić:

King Gordogan, 1980

Tom Stoppard:

Travesty, 1980

Edward Bond:

Summer, 1982

Slawomir Mrozek:

On Foot, 1982

Dario Fo: The Accidental

Death of an Anarchist, 1979

ON THE RIGHT PAGE:

Will Shakespeare &

Tom Stoppard: Hamlet, 1981

Anthony Burgess:

A Clockwork Orange, 1981

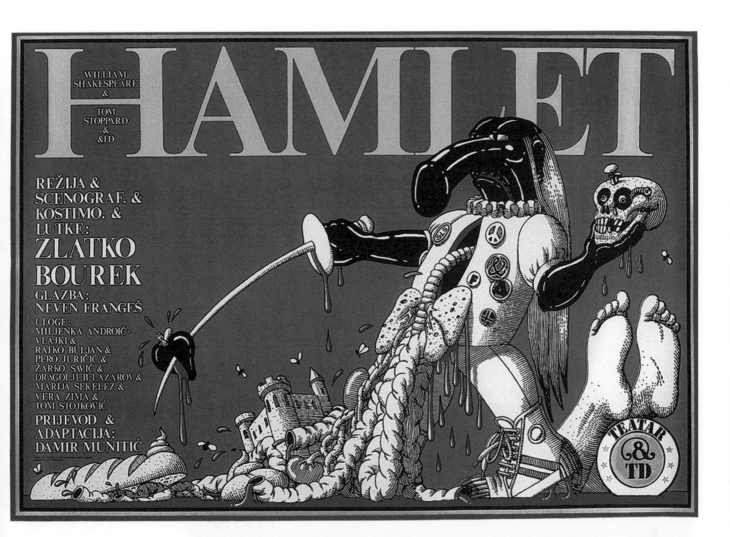

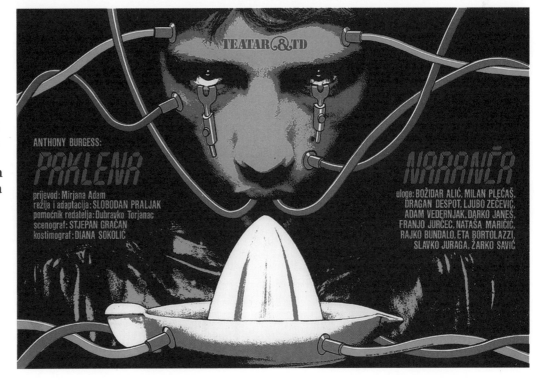

"Long ago Dejan Kršić worked as my first assistant. So back in 1981 he appeared on the poster for the play *A Clockwork Orange*. When we were preparing a retrospective exhibition we realized that it was directed by Slobodan Praljak. The very same Praljak who was a general in the Croatian army in Bosnia and is currently on trial for war crimes at the Hague, charged with, among other things, the destruction of the four-hundred year-old Mostar Bridge, a cultural monument. And thirty years ago he used to direct avant-garde theater. Isn't life strange?" —MIRKO ILIĆ

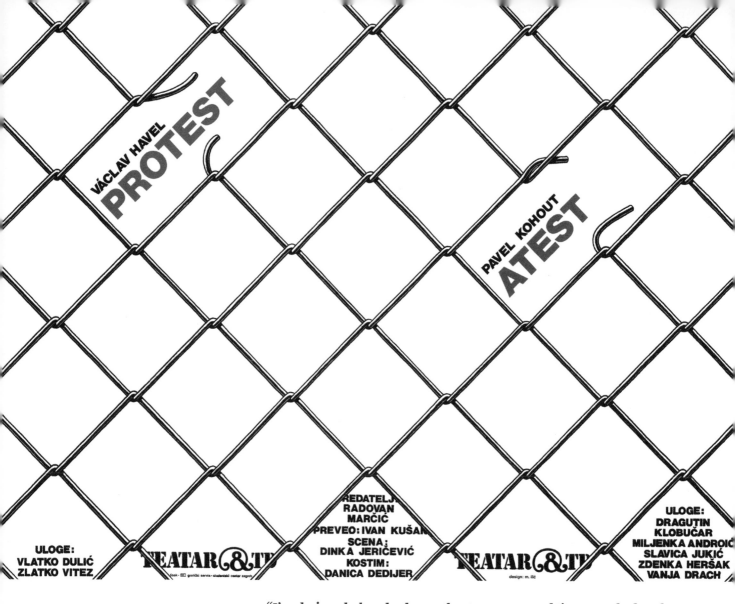

VÁCLAV HAVEL PROTEST

PAVEL KOHOUT ATEST

ULOGE:
VLATKO DULIĆ
ZLATKO VITEZ

REDATELJ:
RADOVAN
MARČIĆ
PREVEO: IVAN KUŠAN
SCENA:
DINKA JERIČEVIĆ
KOSTIM:
DANICA DEDIJER

TEATAR & TD

ULOGE:
DRAGUTIN
KLOBUČAR
MILJENKA ANDROIĆ
SLAVICA JUKIĆ
ZDENKA HERŠAK
VANJA DRACH

Václav Havel: Protest /
Pavel Kohout: Atest, 1981
Poster for double bill performance of two
short plays by Czech dissident writers. At
the time Havel was in prison, and decision to
set up his play was kind of moral support.

"I've designed a hundred or so theater posters and I've never had to show my
sketches to clients. I just took the final designs directly to the printer. At that
time, theaters didn't have to survive by selling tickets, so a bad poster had
no real impact on their survival. Plus, I knew that if someone came to me for
work, they're interested in my thinking as much as in my design."
—MIRKO ILIĆ

Hans Krendlesberger:
Target, 1979

Dubravko Jelačić Bužimski:
Lord of the shadows, 1979

Athol Fugard:
Sizwe Bansi is Dead, 1979,
F: Željko Stojanović

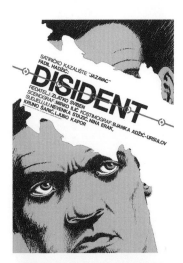

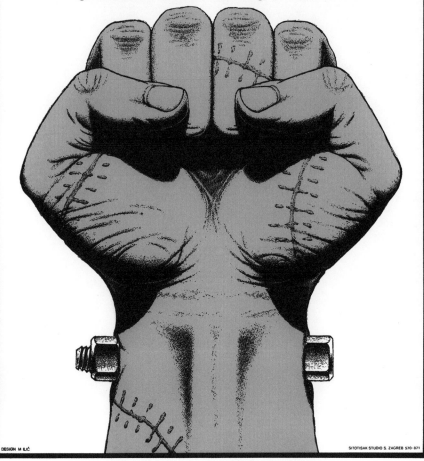

Radoslav Pavlović: Chauvinist Farce, 1983

Fadil Hadžić: Dissident, 1984

Days of Satire 1985, 1985

Fadil Hadžić: Gods are Tired, 1985

All posters for the Theatre of satire Jazavac, 50×70 cm, silkscreen, Studio S

"In the play *Exit*, there is a quote: 'The fact that you did not succeed is not because you're stupid and they are smart. You are not successful because you are not talented and they are. The reason you failed can't be because they are constantly working and you're not doing anything. It is because you are a Serb, or a Croat, or Albanian, or because you are old or young or blond ...' It means that every reason you can think of to make an excuse for why you failed is a good reason. And in principle, you are always hated by those who did not succeed. I do not think I have succeeded yet. I think that I am still to succeed."

—MIRKO ILIĆ, "SLOW, BAD, BUT EXPENSIVE," *ZUM REPORTER*, NO 846, BELGRADE, FEBRUARY 10, 1983

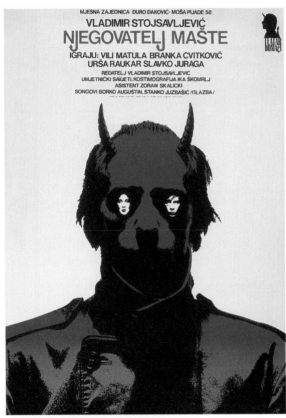

Ulrich Plenzdorf: **The New Sufferings of Young W.**,
SKUC, 1980

Vladimir Stojsavljević:
Caregiver to Imagination,
Teatar Domaći, 1983, SLS,
PHOTO: Luka Mjeda

Georges Feydeau: A Flea in Her Ear,
Satiričko kazalište Jazavac, 1984/5.

Alemka Goljevnček: Under Krležas Head,
Satiričko kazalište Jazavac, 1985

Slawomir Mrozek: The Emigrants,
Theatre MM, 1983

Norberto Avila: Hakim's stories,
Zagreb Youth Theatre, 1982

"I was a regular designer in the Zagreb Youth Theater. I left because the director had a different vision and wanted to treat my poster as if it were a stage, so he was arranging stuff a little to the left, a little to the right. I had to come out and say: I will not do the poster if this character is not cut out, so I did not let him throw things out from my poster."

—MIRKO ILIĆ, *ZUM REPORTER*, NO 846, BELGRADE, FEBRUARY 10, 1983

Erica Jong: Fear of Flying,
monodrama by Rada Đuričin,
Croatian Sociological
Association – Section
Woman and Society, Zagreb
1981

"Despite the fact that there is censorship in China, in my Chinese book they allowed a lot of anti-Communist work, parodies of hammers and sickles, but no sex! But censorship often doesn't translate into the local iconography and the book included a poster I did for the Erica Jong play *Fear of Flying* that showed the middle finger. So you see, censorship can't work; something always falls through the cracks!"

—MIRKO ILIĆ, "THE FIRST MIRKO ILIĆ BOOK WAS NOT PUBLISHED BY AMERICA OR CROATIA BUT—CHINA!,"
VEČERNJI LIST, ZAGREB, APRIL 05, 2001

KO TO TAMO PEVA

uloge:
PAVLE VUISIĆ
DRAGAN NIKOLIĆ
DANILO STOJKOVIĆ
ALEKSANDAR BERČEK
NEDA ARNERIĆ
MILIVOJE TOMIĆ
TAŠKO NAČIĆ
BORISLAV STJEPANOVIĆ
SLAVKO ŠTIMAC
MIODRAG I NENAD KOSTIĆ

režija:
SLOBODAN ŠIJAN
scenario:
DUŠAN KOVAČEVIĆ
scenografija:
VELJKO DESPOTOVIĆ
kostimi:
MIRA ČOHADŽIĆ
zvuk:
MARKO RODIĆ
kompozitor:
VOJISLAV KOSTIĆ
montaža:
LANA VUKOBRATOVIC
direktor fotografije:
BOŽIDAR NIKOLIĆ
direktor filma:
NIKOLA POPOVIĆ
producent:
MILAN ŽMUKIĆ

design by: MIRKO ILIĆ
photo by: RODOLJUB JOVANOVIĆ

Who Sings Over There,
DIR: Slobodan Šijan,
Film Center, Belgrade, 1980

Little Train Robbery, DIR: Dejan Šorak,
Jadran Film, Zagreb / Kinema, 1984,
PHOTO: Luka Mjeda

Life Is Beautiful, DIR: Boro Drašković,
Union Film, Belgrade /
Zvezda film, Novi Sad, 1985
D: Studio TIM, PHOTO: Luka Mjeda

"The vitality of bad taste should not be underestimated. As an example let me state a personal experience—a poster for the film *Ko to tamo peva* (Who sings over there). In now distant 1980, I invited a young designer from Zagreb, Mirko Ilić, to make a poster for the film, which he did—creating a spare, modern poster, which still appears powerful today. At a screening of this film in France, a year later, the director of the festival excitedly ripped the poster out of my hands, and later sent me a postcard of the poster, framed, hanging on the wall of her living room. However, the film producers have never been satisfied with this modern design solution and, twenty years later, while preparing the DVD release of same film, they finally imposed their own "hick" solution to the cover design. Regardless of the fact that the film, wrapped in Ilić's design, earned them an unprecedented amount of money, they couldn't sit still until they'd expressed their kitsch sensibility and shared it with the general audience. Yes, the persistence of bad taste and poor design in our surroundings should not be underestimated."

—SLOBODAN ŠIJAN, SPEECH AT THE OPENING OF THE EXHIBITION *GRIFON* IN 2006, BELGRADE MAY 29, 2006

"The bassist for the band Rage Against the Machine saw my poster in *Graphis* and decided to get a tattoo of it. Then he got a tattoo of an illustration I had done for *The New York Times,* on his back. We were joking that I could take a razor and remove the tattoo because he does not have the copyright. I could demand fees whenever he takes his shirt off on stage. Whenever he seduces a woman I should go into the room and make sure that my work doesn't get scratched or destroyed. He can become my portfolio, and the last idea was, if I am to have a solo exhibition, I'll hang him on the wall."

—MIRKO ILIĆ, "TALENT UNDER THE CARPET,"
VREME NO. 525, BELGRADE, JANUARY 25, 2001

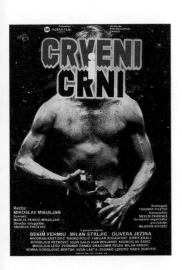

RIGHT: Drawn poster for the film
The Red and The Black,
DIR: Miroslav Mikuljan,
Jadran Film, 1985.
Award at the International Poster
Competition in the category TV and Film,
Los Angeles.
TOP: Photo version of the poster for the
same film, PHOTO: Luka Mjeda

SLS Studio—Slow, Bad, Expensive

UP UNTIL HIS DEPARTURE TO NEW YORK IN 1986, for Ilić the eighties were marked by a period of frantic production where great work was often interspersed with ambitious but quick solutions unsupported by production quality. Ilić's experience during these years prompted his saying that a thing is finished when an idea is born in the head. "After that," he said, "it only gets worse, because my arm is not as good as my head, the print is not as good as my arm, and the money is never as good as all of this put together."

Operating under the name SLS, meaning in English Slow, Bad, Expensive—illustrator and designer Igor Kordej and photographers Zvonimir Atletić and Josip Strmečki formed a collective with Ilić. But the work SLS created was most closely identified with Ilić and Luka Mjeda, notably their series of record covers and the front pages of the weekly news magazine *Danas.*

"Slow, Bad, Expensive was all Mirko Ilić," said Mjeda. "As is the very expression that shows that he was always one to break the rules. If you want to work with someone who is slow, bad, and expensive, there must be something else to it. SLS was his vision. He worked under this name with some other illustrators and photographers as well. Later we started using the name TIM—Tandem Ilić-Mjeda. But everyone remembers the name SLS because it was much more striking."

At SLS Ilić was the lead author, manager, business developer, recruiter, and bill collector. Perhaps most surprising was Ilić's willingness to work within the collective format. Everyone who knows him knows that he has a pronounced ego, which might be why he never wanted to be a one-man band. So even though illustration is a solitary job, he is well aware of the importance of a group for other parts of design. And in doing so, regardless of whether he is collaborating with Milton Glaser or a young designer, his approach is the same—he will seek your input, but fight for his ideas.

He once jokingly said that he likes someone else's input since, if it is good, all the praise will go to him, and if something goes wrong, he can always blame someone else.

"Above all I am a good manager of myself and others," Ilić said. "Because knowing how to work with people is a design in itself. Being a good art director means choosing and getting the best out of people, and then signing your name under their work. When two people are working together, there are always positive results. If it was a nice experience to work with someone, why not do it again? Of course, total crap also occurs. As do arguments, as with any marriage. It does not always work, but I think overall it's terribly positive. It's also important to remember that you are not always the smartest one. Whoever thinks that he is the smartest is wrong; therefore, I'm very happy to get the best from other people, at least what I think is the best. However, I don't think you can be a true designer if you can't work with people. It is very difficult. This is your core job. And because of the Novi kvadrat, and all my other experiences, I think I've learned to work with people. To me it's always a nice experience and I always learn something new. If you pay attention you can always learn something new from everyone, especially from those whose work you appreciate. At the end of the day, the audience, which we often forget, does not care who made it. It must be good; it must satisfy them in one way or another. Whether you worked with your mother, grandmother … it does not matter." ▶

Hot autumn of the third economic reform,

the first cover Ilić made for *Danas*
newsmagazine, *Danas,* no. 15, June 1, 1982

PHOTO: Željko Koprolčec

OPPOSITE PAGE:

New Nationalistic Masks,

Danas, no. 44, December 21, 1982

PHOTO: Luka Mjeda

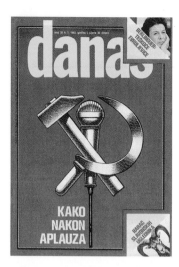

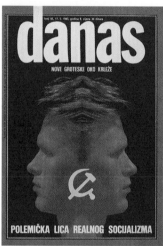

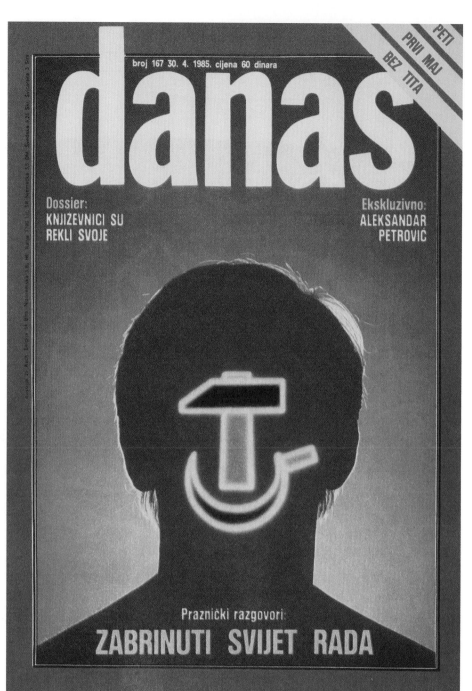

Worried labor force

Danas, no. 167, April 30, 1985, PHOTO: Luka Mjeda

"Here you get paid for lost time, but nobody pays for the idea. I can come up with an idea that takes an hour of work, or I can come up with an idea that takes twenty-four hours of work. It doesn't matter how much time I spend on the job, it's the idea that gets paid for. A good idea can carry the front cover; if it is good enough for that, it is good enough to be paid for."

—MIRKO ILIĆ, "SLOW, BAD, BUT SO EXPENSIVE," *ZUM REPORTER*, NO. 846, BELGRADE FEBRUARY 10, 1983

What after the applause, *Danas*, no. 20, July 6, 1982

Confronted faces of Real Socialism, *Danas*, no. 65, May 17, 1983

New inflation wave threat, *Danas*, no. 126, July 17, 1984

AFTER THE THREE-HUNDREDTH ISSUE OF START, most of the editorial team was replaced by many of the Novi kvadrat members who had been thrown out of *Polet*. *Start* gradually changed its priorities and began focusing more on the worlds of glamour, fashion, and pop culture. It was difficult to replace an illustrator as talented as Ilić, so he did some illustrations for them up until around 1985, but eventually tired of the new format.

"I thought that the new direction would be cool because we had all worked together at *Polet*," said Ilić. "But they were really pushing a new format that included more photography and they soon decided to completely change the whole thing."

The publishing house Vjesnik had long talked of starting a weekly newsmagazine (even though Croatian politicians felt that Vjesnik did not have enough high-quality journalists to pull it off). According to editor Mario Bošnjak: "*Danas* was painstakingly born; entire symposiums were held to discuss what it would be and how we could do it. As much as Vjesnik wanted a political magazine, the circumstances made it difficult and it took some time before *Danas* was successful. But Vjesnik was quite healthy so it could fund the magazine until it found its footing. In the mid-eighties *Danas* became a symbol of the modern, contemporary magazine for all of Yugoslavia."

Ilić started working with *Danas* in the summer of 1982 with SLS often collaborating with photographer Luka Mjeda and the magazine's design department, led by art director Danijel Popović. Ilić and his team designed about 150 covers and illustrations over the next three years. They usually created some kind of photo-illustration, leaving space for headlines to be added by the news editors. "It was a good exercise for the brain," Ilić said. "I had to come up with twenty different cover ideas for topics such as inflation."

Said Mario Bošnjak: "As a newsmagazine, *Danas* with its graphics never reached the quality of its articles. Ilić was investing great efforts in cover pages, but because of the schedule, there was never enough time for more ambitious ideas. Deciding what the cover should be was always put off to the last minute and usually the choice was determined by what could be done the quickest."

Ilić said that his decision to use photographs was a conscious one: "I never thought that illustration was the only way to express an idea. When I got the job, I immediately decided that I would not illustrate the cover of *Danas*, and that there would never be a picture of a politician on it."

"There were attempts to influence us and claims that politicians must be on the cover," Mjeda said. "But we never used a single politician. Even if the editors felt strongly that a politician should be on the cover, we still did not do it. Though sometimes it was done by the graphic department."

"Creatively, Ilić was a great choice for the ambitious newsmagazine, but in the context of the time, his work often rankled the political establishment.

As he said himself, Ilić "was a slap in the face of society" not just with his work, but his entire image. He was among the first to understand and advocate the importance design had in influencing the politics and marketing of ideas.

"The covers really encouraged people to read the articles," Mjeda said. "Of course the success of *Danas* did not depend on them entirely, but they certainly contributed. This idea was confirmed when we spoke to the people at

> **"It is always very important to have a good explanation for your work. Then everything is fine, even if you are politically tied up."**
> —MIRKO ILIĆ

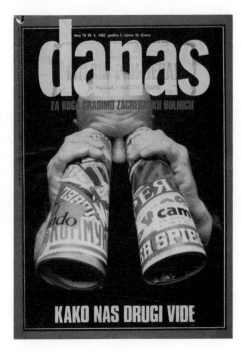

How others see us, *Danas*, no. 19, June 29, 1982, Model is Tomislav Gotovac, well-known experimental filmmaker, artist and performer. Part of his artistic work was created under label "Paranoia View Art".

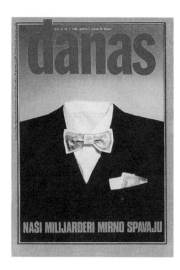

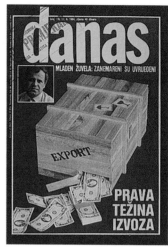

Our dear billionaires,
Danas, no. 21, July 13, 1982
SLS / PHOTO: Hrvoje Knez

Ways to save industry,
Danas, no. 30, September 14, 1982

Inflation is catching up
Danas, no. 51, February 8, 1983
PHOTO: Luka Mjeda

Real weight of imports,
Danas, no. 132, August 28, 1984

Oppened doors to foreign investments
Danas, no. 153, January 22, 1985
Sketch and slide for the cover illustration
PHOTO: Luka Mjeda

Time magazine. What we did with our modest budgets and tight schedules definitely caught their attention. Their comment was: Your front covers are a lot more aggressive and bolder than what we do in America, but that might be what it takes to emphasize a problem so that more attention is dedicated to it.

Journalist and editor Inoslav Bešker said: "We realized while working at the youth newspaper that something might be expressed by an illustration that could not be expressed any other way. We transferred this idea into *Danas* and it was not by chance that Ilić created those powerful covers (for which the editor-in-chief Joža Vlahović was almost skinned alive). One good illustration can more clearly express a story's essence than the seven pages of accompanying text. Ilić never questioned the quality of his work; he was only concerned that what he created helped push the article to a higher level. Of course, this is a debate that has existed since the beginning of time between author and illustrator: Who is really communicating the idea more clearly, the writer or the artist?" ▶

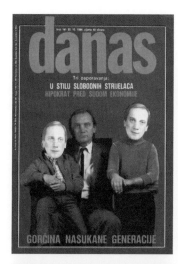

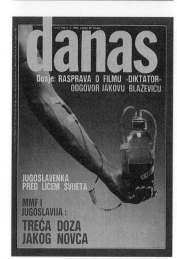

Morality: Greed eats people, *Danas,* no. 85, October 4, 1983, SLS / PHOTO: Luka Mjeda

"I react quickly. This is something nourished by watching everything that is happening around me, from what's on TV and in the movies, to shop windows, to even reading foreign newspapers in the urinals. If you are at all developed intellectually, it can create a new ability within you; like with toy bricks: one person builds a house, another a spacecraft, and someone else an abstract piece of crap. It's important to train yourself to observe each and react differently, not routinely like a hundred other designers in the world would. It makes you special. The big idea will be easily applied later. It's the idea that matters. And that is something that we miss the most now, I think. The skills to come up with that really good idea that shows how you think."

—MIRKO ILIĆ, "SLOW, BAD, BUT SO EXPENSIVE," *ZUM REPORTER*, NO. 846, BELGRADE FEBRUARY 10, 1983

Bitter stranded generation

Danas, no. 141, October 30, 1984, SLS

Connected crime pots,

Danas, no. 90, November 8, 1983

New dosis of fresh cash,

Danas, no. 159, March 5, 1985

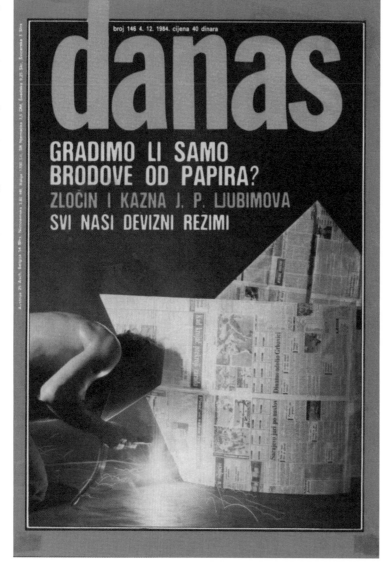

**Terror of
unpaid bills**,
Danas, no. 136,
September 25, 1984

**Writers:
Democracy is
the winning card**,
Danas, no. 164
April 9, 1985

**Are we building
paper ships?**,
Danas, no. 146,
December 4, 1984

"Let me say this straight away: I don't think that Mirko Ilić is a designer at all. I think he's a composer.

Or, to be more precise, a punk rock/New Wave band leader who writes, plays, and conducts various instruments in his imaginary rock band. A rebel. A paradigm breaker. A bit of a scandal maker. And a bit of a loner.

I always thought that being a designer was an activity restricted and reduced to the mechanics of the purely visual. But being a composer means working with more elements than just 'design'. it means having various instruments in your tool kit, with many lines in the score, starting with a STORY—not the obvious starting point for a visual artist. And that's—I think—Mirko's biggest advantage: each of his works could be as easily verbalized as they've been visualized. If it's a magazine cover illustration, it's as if he has placed another headline next to the main, verbal one. Mirko's work makes the accompanying text work in stereo. And if there are no words deployed, the same goes for meaning.

What Mirko does is fight for the dignity of the applied visual arts, which these days is often reduced to mere accompaniment of a product. So whatever turns out to be selling well gets copied. And whatever is copied too much, becomes industrialized. And that's the death of individuality. That's the death of the brand.

All great composers—and I think most of the great designers have been so—they have a way to make you lock in a groove and tap your feet unconsciously. As Frank Zappa once asked of both himself and us, what is the frequency that can make someone clench his fist and hit somebody (if it can make us tap our feet without thinking)? Mirko's work produces the involuntary blockage of eye movements—the visual equivalent of the foot tapping. You look, and look and the smile and the warm brain swelling starts getting bigger and bigger. And you put the player on 'Repeat' immediately."

—LAZAR DŽAMIĆ

"To make the cover we had less than 24 hours from idea to implementation and it was a great exercise in thought. Photographs were made by Luka Mjeda who used to develop them by hand. People who were on the front pages of *Danas* were our friends and random extras in front of the *Kavkaz* café. But the mosto fun was how to come up with a cover page that is provocative, intense, but that will not be prohibited and that's what I was most interested in; how to move that line bit by bit. Editors used to tell me, 'Calm down a little bit,' they criticized me again because of the cover, so we would calm down for an issue or two, and then we would continue as usual."

—MIRKO ILIĆ, "CROATIAN DESIGN IS BETTER THAN AMERICAN,"

NEDELJNA DALMACIJA, SPLIT, APRIL 12, 2002

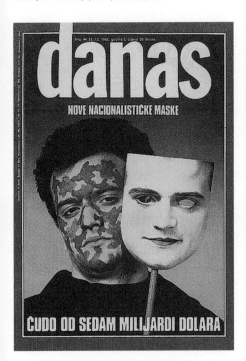

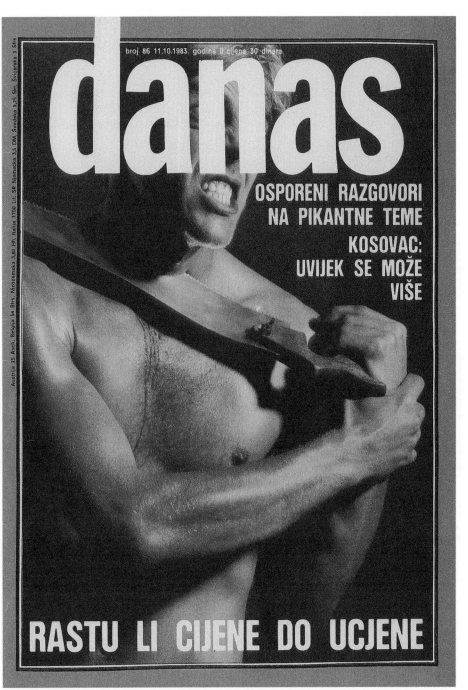

New Nationalistic Masks

Danas, no. 44, December 21, 1982

Are the prices rising to blackmail

Danas, no. 86, October 11, 1983

"The initial idea was quite different. It had already been photographed: the naked human body and the arm cutting itself off with a saw, the blood dripping. It was nationalism—the hand will be separated from the body. The body will be fucked, and the hand will be, too. But it looked too bloody to them, too morbid. So they contacted us at two o'clock in the morning and said: 'Give us a new cover by seven today.' So we had five hours. Car, studio, find a man, paint, take a snapshot fast—and they had their cover. We reused that image for a cover about price hikes."

—MIRKO ILIĆ, "SLOW, BAD, BUT SO EXPENSIVE," *ZUM REPORTER*, NO. 846, BELGRADE FEBRUARY 10, 1983

Covers of *Danas*
newsmagazine
no. 20, August 17, 1982
no. 28, August 31, 1982
no. 33, October 5, 1982
no. 34, October 12, 1982
no. 35, October 19, 1982

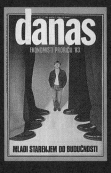
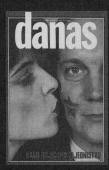

no. 38, November 9, 1982
PHOTO: Zvonimir Atletić
no. 40, November 23, 1982
no. 41, November 30, 1982
no. 42, December 7, 1982
no. 43, December 14, 1982

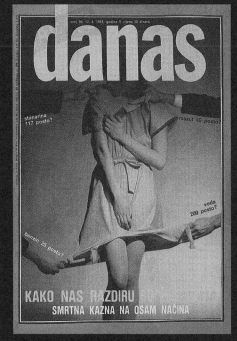

no. 49, January 25, 1983

no. 52, February 15, 1983
PHOTO: Joža Strmečki
no. 53, February 22, 1983
PHOTO: Zvonimir Atletić

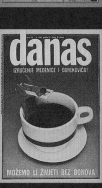

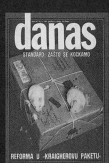

no. 54, March 1, 1983
PHOTO: Zvonimir Atletić
no. 60, April 12, 1983
no. 62, April 26, 1983
no. 64, May 10, 1983

no. 66, May 24, 1983
no. 79, August 23, 1983
no. 82, September 13, 1983
no. 84, September 27, 1983
no. 87, October 18, 1983

no. 92, November 22, 1983
no. 97, December 27, 1983
no. 100, January 17, 1984
no. 130, August 14, 1984
no. 137, October 2, 1984

no. 138, October 9, 1984
no. 145, November 27, 1984
no. 147, December 11, 1984
no. 150, January 1, 1985
no. 151, January 8, 1985

no. 156, February 12, 1985
no. 157, February 19, 1985
no. 160, March 12, 1985
no. 162, March 26, 1985

no. 174, June 18, 1985
no. 176, July 2, 1985
no. 180, July 30, 1985

no. 181, August 6, 1985
no. 185, September 3, 1985
Except where stated
otherwise, all:
PHOTO: Luka Mjeda

"We didn't need to reinvent the wheel, we just needed to do the best with what we had. It was common knowledge that other publications, especially overseas, had a lot more money. We could not compete with them on the production because we had much worse printing and photographic equipment. The only place we could compete was with the idea."

—MIRKO ILIĆ, "SLOW, BAD, BUT SO EXPENSIVE," *ZUM REPORTER*, NO. 846,

BELGRADE FEBRUARY 10, 1983

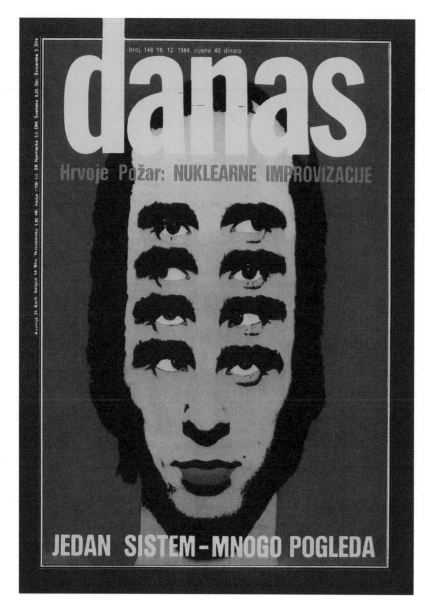

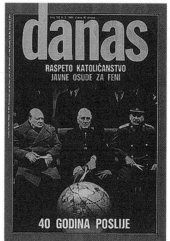

40 years later,
Danas, no. no. 155, February 5, 1985

One system – many views, *Danas*, no. 148, December 18, 1984, MODEL: Luka Mjeda

How to get to the vacations, *Danas*, no. 72, July 5, 1983, MODEL: Sanja Šrekajs

"I don't care what I do in ten years. I might be a director; maybe I'll write books if I discover that I have the talent for writing. I may be a farmer, or maybe I'll be installing solar-energy devices. I do not want to tie myself down. I'm a work in progress. As the saying goes, learn on the job. Everything is tempting to me. I will work on these covers as long as I am interested in it, as long as I see that people are interested in it. I am not interested in designing only one thing, to be a well-known designer of magazine covers. I am interested in them now, but one day I might be interested in doing something else. I hope to do this for a hundred years and I also hope to try at least a thousand professions in those hundred years."

—MIRKO ILIĆ, "SLOW, BAD, BUT SO EXPENSIVE," *ZUM REPORTER*, NO. 846, BELGRADE, FEBRUARY 10, 1983

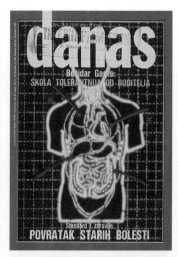

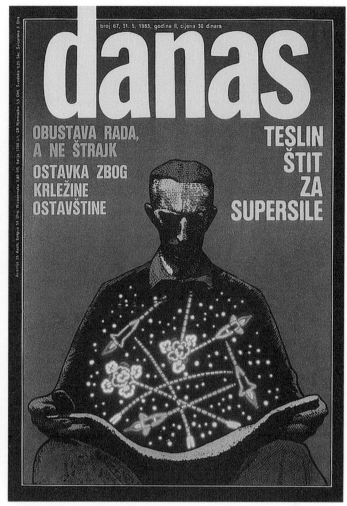

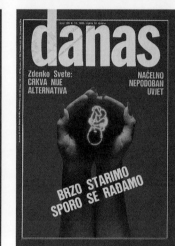

Are we in danger of centralism,
Danas, no. 143, November 13, 1984

Computers at the school doorstep,
Danas, no. 184, August 27, 1985

Return of the old diseases,
Danas, no. 179, July 23, 1985

Faster growing old, and slow at birth,
Danas, no. 190, October 8, 1985

Tesla's shield for superpowers,
Danas, no. 67, May 31, 1983

For the article about favourite subject of conspiracy theories, possible military use of Nikola Tesla's inventions, cover illustration is based on the inventors sculpture created by Ivan Meštrović.

"Since we could not rely on photomontage at pre-press, we had to supply finished artwork that looked perfect. So we invented a technique of work, out of inability, we created neon with no real neon. We could model a person to look like he was made of neon, though we did not have the possibility to model the real piece in neon. Something that is done today with a computer, we did it through photography."

—LUKA MJEDA

"We were kicked out of *Danas* twice," Mjeda said. "The first time we stopped working because the entire editorial board was under attack. This coincided with my trip to America, where I spent four months. During that time, Ilić did not even want to come near *Danas*. Then things quieted down, the editorial board was kept, and they asked for Mirko to keep on working. When I returned, we started work and picked up right where we left off. Our covers were still sharp and critical. Things were back to normal for a while and then a great turmoil occurred; one editor left, his replacement arrived. We did two or three covers that the new editor wanted to change and Mirko got into an argument and said, 'You will not change my covers', and it was a good-bye forever. It was already late 1985 and we simply closed that chapter in our heads. One of the last things we did before we went to America was to collect hundreds of *Danas* covers and give them to Zagrebački salon. In May 1986, my wife called me and said: 'Congratulations on the award.' We were already so far away from *Danas* both physically and emotionally I wondered what award. 'For *Danas*,' she told me. Being in a distant country and getting told that we had received an independent award for something we had worked so hard on (and, not incidentally, been fired for) was wonderful." ▶

Blue Box — a part of a series of photo illustrations that Mjeda and Ilić made when cooperating with *Panorama* magazine as a proposal of possible type of illustration for another magazine of the same publisher, 1985

"**I DID NOT LEAVE YUGOSLAVIA FOR AMERICA** because I had to, but because I wanted to. By that time I was already a well-known designer and illustrator. I had worked on every project I was interested in. When I was twenty-six, I asked myself what I wanted to do in the future. I could have gotten a job at an institution, grabbed an easy seat there and tyrannized some new kids. But I would just be supporting bad designers and rooting out the talented ones to make myself more important. There were no professional challenges left for me there; nothing new to do.

"I had always read *Graphis* and various other books on design," Ilić said. "And no matter which direction you turned, everything pointed to New York. So I concluded that if I had to start all over again professionally, it might as well be with the big boys, peers whose work I respected. I wanted to test my talent and my abilities in a country where I had no friends or family, where I couldn't even charm the ladies because I didn't speak English very well. I knew if I left for New York I wouldn't come back. That's why I didn't go to Germany or any other European country. I knew sooner or later there would come a moment when I would have to leave, so why move twice if I can do it just once."

That he sometimes exuded an attitude of resentment during the time before he left might seem unusual, especially considering the lofty status he enjoyed. Some people registered his discontent with the lack of acknowledgment for his work.

"It had nothing to do with acknowledgments, respect, or disrespect for my work," Ilić said recently. "I just wanted to leave; at that point, I wasn't interested in any credits. I stayed longer than planned, for family reasons. I was terribly bored here."

Ilić was an absolute design star in Yugoslavia long before designers started becoming stars. He had the leading role on the scene. More radical but perhaps less well-known designers remained anonymous, while those who took bigger jobs and had higher fees were not as interesting to the public, and not many people outside of the design world knew them.

Older designers like Arsovski and Bućan never showed an interest in self-promotion and slowly faded away. But Mirko took advantage of the media—he gave interviews, appeared on television, had a radical image, and was always a good PR story. "I guess I'm a design star," Ilić said. "I'm on the front cover of magazines, and on TV. I am having a great time. I think it means more for the promotion of design than anything else. Not that I'm the best designer, but people definitely started noticing the world of design because of all the attention."

In spite of his rebellious image, he was always a professional. When he worked for large socialist companies, like Podravka or Varteks, he never tried to sell them something they didn't want or understand. He fulfilled his assignment, and always tried to achieve high-quality work.

The result of all this work was not always grand or memorable, but served to educate Ilić about the business: how to speak and negotiate and interact with people. This increased awareness of the role and importance of design in business at least partially paved the way for the younger generation of designers in the 1990s.

"Mirko usually did not work in advertising, because it was mostly just a matter of choosing the right photograph and then someone would place some type on top. I worked with the marketing agency in Vjesnik and some others, so we would sometimes work together. Eventually we started working on whole campaigns, Levi's, for example, and this is where his ideas would surface. We managed to push through some new concepts in advertising and propaganda, while working on a new calendar... With Mirko everything always had to have some sort of a catch, an additional accent. He makes up incredible slogans. In *Danas*, we often gave ideas for front cover headlines even though it was the editors' decision in the end. Even in the marketing jobs, it was always important to push the boundaries, but we were always realistic, assuming the clients too know something about their own customers. If we can't convince our client that something is good, we have to work on it some more."

—LUKA MJEDA

Klaus Mann: The Turning Point

GZH, Mirror Editions, Zagreb 1987

ALL COVERS IN MIRROR EDITIONS SERIES:

Mirko Ilić & Luka Mjeda

For the cover of *The Turning Point* Ilić And

Mjedareceived the Award of the Yugoslav

society of publishers and booksellers in 1987

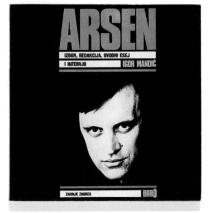

If there was any frustration or displeasure on his part at the time—and perhaps becoming part of the reason for the move to America—it may have been more a reflection of how he felt about his own work than anything else.

"I had a period in Croatia that was, for various reasons, really bad for me. There is no way of saying it nicely and of not offending anyone, but unfortunately, many musicians got the shorter end because of it. I worked with all those folk singers to make money. At that time I had not yet argued and fought with my clients, so I tried to please various managers who wanted this and that, and when it did not work out it was always my fault. I needed the money, Slavenka was sick, we were building a house, and I had a thousand excuses... From this perspective, it was a bad period. However, it was also bad partly because I stayed too long. Change keeps me away from the routine. When you think of an LP it is always the same twelve-inch format, however you look at it—it is always the same square. The year and a half that I worked for *The New York Times* was the longest steady job I have ever held in all my life. Always the same pages and similar assignments. That is when you start thinking: well, why don't I change this or why not that... Illustrating on the side saved me; I also did some side work, doing some of my own things, otherwise I would have died. When you get a job like that, you think you finally got that big break, but to me it feels like a death sentence. I sentence you to fifteen years of hard work in this format and style. I am always interested in changing things within a medium. I really think each of the jobs I did affected my overall work. Comics significantly influenced my work on illustrations—thus I frame my illustrations differently. Illustration influenced my design, LP covers are often like a comic, photographs come in a series, and typography is another influence. I think that's good."

"Mirko was always creating problems and new traps for himself," says Mjeda. "He could really prosper financially if only he would stick within the scope of what he had already accomplished. But he really rebels agains routine. When he does the same thing three times in a row and cannot completely change everything the fourth time—there is no way of continuing, he just leaves. When work becomes automated, for Mirko Ilić it means the end. Even with all the benefits he could have from continuing in that kind of production, he has to leave and find something else. Besides, he doesn't feel like going to meetings where someone else gets to make all the decisions." ▶

Arsen, selected and edited by Igor Mandić, the Bard library, Znanje publishing, Zagreb, 1983

"Zozo (Zoran Pavlović) was always kind of gloomy, but at the same time a lovely person. We worked together really well in the CDD, desinging *Pitanja* and *Polet*. He joked about my earring and I joked about his age, but we worked together just fine. Later, we also worked on some books for the GZH. That work, I think, was quite bad, not not because of him, but because of me. I just tried to be done with it. I completely followed his art direction—i.e., do this with the airbrush. So, I was really just illustrating to his taste."

—MIRKO ILIĆ

H.H. Kirst: 8/15 In the Barracks; 8/15 In the War; 8/15 Until The End,

GZH, Zagreb 1981, AD & D: Zoran Pavlović, ILLUSTRATION: Mirko Ilić

Daniela Gioseffi: The Great American Belly Dance,
GZH, Zagreb 1980

David A. Kauffelt: The Spare Parts,
GZH, Zagreb 1980

Thomas Gifford: The Wind Chill Factor,
GZH, Zagreb 1981

AD & D: Zoran Pavlović,
ILLUSTRATION: Mirko Ilić

MIRKO ILIĆ

EXHIBITION OPEN FROM DECEMBER 9 – 30, 1987

YUGOSLAV PRESS AND CULTURAL CENTER GALLERY 767 THIRD AVE NYC 838·2306

PRINTED BY : NENAD   DESIGN BY : MIRKO ILIĆ & NICKY LINDEMAN © 1987

Looking for America

Illustrations and design from 1986 to today

IN MARCH 1986, AT THE AGE OF THIRTY, after ten years as an artist, illustrator, and designer in Yugoslavia, Ilić moved to the United States, to New York City to be exact, which is "a wonderful mix of America and Europe, a blend of different cultures and ways of thinking," Ilić said. "It has a good relationship with people, and does not care if you're a foreigner or even a *gastarbeiter*. Before leaving for America, I traveled a lot around Europe, and especially dear to me were three countries: Italy, the Netherlands, and the United Kingdom. I occasionally worked in Italy. Wonderful country, especially the food, but you could never count on money or women there."

The Netherlands was dear to him because of the quality of graphic design and the liberal atmosphere, but it seemed too small, while the United Kingdom was economically unattractive. "It was a time of great economic depression. Margaret Thatcher had destroyed everything; they did not have jobs for themselves and I was the last thing they needed in such a situation."

Since, according to him, he would be only a *gastarbeiter* in any other country in Europe despite his success, he opted for the United States, and on March 25, 1986, accompanied by Luka Mjeda, he arrived in New York "with two suitcases and two-thousand dollars in my pocket."

As Ilić said, "This was my first trip to America, and I did not know anyone personally. In one suitcase, I had my work and in other, clothes. I came in the spring, which meant that my wardrobe was only good until the end of summer. So I had to start earning money before autumn."

A few days after his arrival, with only his portfolio and a recommendation from the Italian magazine *Panorama* in hand, he visited *Time* magazine. After a week, based on art director Rudy Hoglund's commission, he created a sketch for a cover on the subject of the oil industry. It was rejected, and he was ready to return to Yugoslavia. But he decided to stay. Soon, a few other commissions trickled in, and then things started to roll.

Asked if it was bravery or foolishness to knock on the door of the *Time* news desk, Ilić simply replied: "It was not courage; I had nothing to lose. No one gave me a job for a song, but they soon realized that every dollar they gave me would earn them a thousand. They had seen my portfolio and I guess they thought I had something worth showing."

OPPOSITE PAGE:

Poster for the exhibition at the Yugoslav Press and Cultural Center, New York, 1987
AD: Nicky Lindeman
silkscreen print: Nenad Božić

Glasnost: Between Hope & History,
New York Times Book Review, 1987, AD: Steven Heller

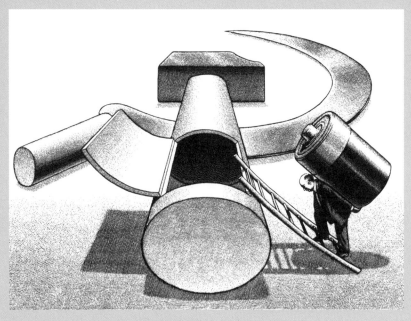

Gorbachev's Gambit,
The New York Times – Week in Review, 1988
AD: John Cayea

BELOW: **In Trouble in Black and White**,
cover, *The New York Times Book Review*, 1987
AD: Steven Heller

"For decades the *Times* op-ed page and book review sections published numerous foreign artists, from Roland Topor to Eugene Mihaesco to Mirko Ilić. The joke was that all one needed to gain entry was an unpronounceable name. But in fact, the surrealist visual language that these artists employed to circumvent censorious regimes was a perfect fit at the *Times*."

—STEVEN HELLER: "WHO'S ZOOMING WHOM?" *EYE 41*, AUTUMN 2001

MILTON GLASER: Unfortunately I can't remember how it all started, except for the fact that Mirko had a ponytail when he came to see me, along with his bristling personality. I also assumed that that was part of his entry experience into American life. When was that?

MIRKO ILIĆ: I think it was April 2, 1986. It was at this table.

GLASER: I'm glad that one of us still remembers. I don't recall why you came here anyway, whether somebody had called me about you.

ILIĆ: Yes, somebody had called you, it was Gloria Steinem.

GLASER: You had met Gloria under some kind of women's group association via your first wife, correct?

ILIĆ: You were on my "must-see" list. I did not know the protocol, the appropriate etiquette here in the States. Do you call? Do you knock on the door? Gloria asked me one evening, at a party she had thrown, what I was up to. I told her I was trying to meet this guy Milton Glaser. And she said, "Oh, I know Milton." So she called you and Walter [Bernard] for me. And that's how I came here.

GLASER: Gloria was an old friend. In this very same building that we are now sitting in, we launched *Ms.*, within *New York* magazine. Gloria started *New York* magazine with us; she was one of the very first editors who worked on the magazine from its inception, and later when the opportunity came to launch *Ms.*, she was passionately committed to the project. But at any rate, when Mirko came to see me I was enormously impressed by the quality of his work and the intelligence behind it. Mirko's portfolio had a vocabulary that was fundamentally editorial. It was driven by narrative, and by the idea that there was a subject and a story to tell, and not by the decorative qualities of illustration. I've always been interested in the role of illustration as a storytelling device as opposed to simply a stylistic form. But what continues to be interesting in Mirko's work is the fact that everything originates with the core objective of communicating something to an audience. And since I think that is both illustration and design's essential purpose, whenever the work expresses that idea, I find that I'm more drawn to it than pure virtuoso, formal means. When you came here your work was largely scratchboard and illustration, very European in its orientation. It was often linked to political ideas or ideas about culture and society. I have to say that in the States, that interest has not been a significant part of the development of illustration.

"MIRKO ILIĆ & MILTON GLASER: THE KING AND THE JESTER," EDITED BY LAETITIA WOLFF, *GRAPHIS* ISSUE #350, MARCH/APRIL 2004

Asked about the role of chance, Ilić responded readily: "I do not know if all of it happened by chance. Remember that old joke that says that you can't win the lottery if you don't buy the ticket? Before going to New York—as always—I had made a list of my desires and goals. I always start from the top, thinking that life will take me down, so why do it to myself. Because these plans are actually some of my dreams, they are always set very high, so it is easier for me not to fulfill them than to do more than I expected."

The well-known designer and illustrator Milton Glaser occupies a special place in Mirko Ilić's American experience. "The first week, maybe ten days after I came to America, I knocked on his door. I brought my work. I did not even know at that time how a real portfolio should look, and my English was nothing special, so I simply placed everything on the table. And he surveyed my stuff thoroughly. Then he asked me where I lived, and I told him that I was still at my friend's place. 'Where will you draw if you get a job?' he asked. I said: 'In the kitchen, on the table.' Then he said: 'The studio is here, so you can always come and use a desk.' He asked me if I personally knew any designers or art directors in New York and since I did not, two days later he gave me a list with names and the ones he'd already called to recommend me were noted. Afterward, I found out what he told them. It was something like, 'someone will call you and he speaks poor English, but don't worry, his work is much better than his English'."

Soon Ilić repeated his success in New York. Very quickly he established himself as one of the most interesting political illustrators.

"Once you're in the system in America, as long as you don't mess up, or start taking drugs, or start disrespecting deadlines, you will keep moving forward. At first I was producing about twenty illustrations per month, which meant that I did not sleep much."

From the very beginning Ilić insisted that the letter *ć* always have the accent over the last letter instead of the typical Americanized way of *Ilic* or *Ilich*. "It was pure spite. I explained to them that my name simply sounds different. However, I cannot put *ć* in an e-mail address, and it gets thrown out frequently, so I do not insist on it that much anymore."

And so begun the first phase of his career in the U.S. where he was profiled in the new market as a political illustrator, i.e. an illustrator-commentator.

Damage Control — Reagan's Lonely Defense of a Deal with Iran,
The New York Times, 1986
AD: John Caeya

Uneasy Partners — Learning to Live with a Coalition Government,
The New York Times, November 22, 1987
AD: John Caeya

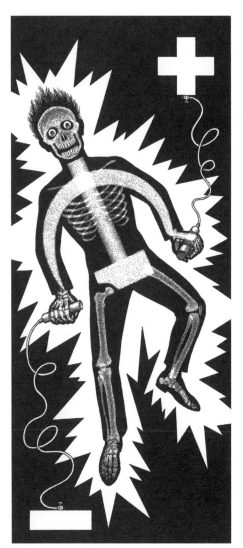

His visually sharp black-and-white illustrations were published in a number of newspapers and magazines—*Time, US News & World Report, Money, The New York Times, The New York Times Book Review, The Boston Globe, Wall Street Journal, The Washington Post, Los Angeles Times,* and so on.

In an interview he commented, "I'm very sorry that I never drew for *Playboy* that was sixth on my list; I never got there because of the work load, and they have never asked me, probbably thinking I was different kind of illustrator." One *Playboy* editor read his statement, so eventually they called him and commissioned an illustration. First of his illustrations for *Playboy* was published in January 2006, twenty years after his arrival to the USA.

Ilić characterizes the American design scene as follows: "If they realize that you draw apples well, you will forever draw apples as they already have someone who draws pears and they do not want to take risk." But he quickly noticed a weaknesses in such labeling. "I realized that most editors in the U.S. did not want my brains, they only wanted my hand. They liked my scratchboard illustrations and didn't want me to change."

In an interview for *Graphis*, Glaser said: "Usually people hire for style. When an art director or a designer looks for someone, their choice is made on the basis of style, not on the basis of intelligence. So if you want something lighthearted, or something black-and-white, or a baby, you go to a specific person. This idea of typecasting by style or by ability is the inevitable consequence of the structure of art direction in the United States and, I suspect, elsewhere."

A few months after arriving in America, Ilić met Nicky Lindeman (he and his first wife had divorced years earlier). She was a painter who occasionally did illustrations as well. They moved in together and were soon married. "She was a painter and designer, I was an illustrator and designer. She knew all the tricks to making a phone call in New York, I was still figuring that out; her mother tongue was English, mine was not; she was a freelancer, I was a freelancer; she was handsome, I was not; the combination seemed ideal."

They worked on a series of projects together including posters for local theater and designs for a series of books by Herman Hesse. Later on, Nicky got a

Shock Therapy and Its Victims

The New York Times, 1992. AD: Michael Valenti

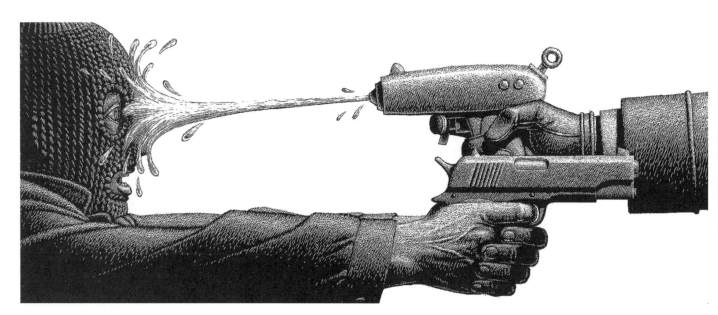

Terrorists, Tourists, and New Refugees, Los Angeles Times 1987, AD: Tom Trapnell

New Role of NATO,
The New York Times
Op-Ed, 1991,
AD: Michael Valenti

GF Tries the Old Restructure Ploy,
Business Month, 1987
AD: Cynthia Friedman

job as an art director at Sony, and together they collaborated on the design of a few CDs. In the early nineties, they bought a loft in the (at the time) sketchy meatpacking district of Manhattan. By the time *Sex and the City* rolled around, the area had become one of New York's most prized locations. At the end of 1995 their son Ivo was born, and in 1999, they welcomed their daughter, Zoe.

Ilić's first major breakthrough in the States occurred in 1991 when he accepted the position of art director for the international edition of *Time* magazine. "It was worth having it on the résumé," Ilić said.

"I had been doing illustrations for years here, but it was very difficult to do any actual design. To do design, you had to show design, and I did not have most of my work from Zagreb, so I thought it was a nifty thing to be the art director of *Time* magazine, put it on my résumé and then move on.

"It was the first full-time employment of my life. And I had never designed a magazine before. They offered me the job not so much because of my technical and design skills, but because of my understanding of foreign policy."

After only six months, he left *Time* and was soon was offered a position as art director of *The New York Times*' op-ed page. Both jobs offered Ilić the opportunity to work with many illustrators and designers he admired. "It gave me a good reason to call them and talk to them. It also gave me a chance to offer jobs to young illustrators. For many of them it was their first big job." ▶

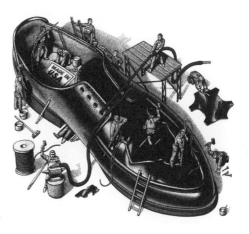

U.S. Shoe Firms Step into High Tech,
Washington Post, 1987
AD: Marty Barrick

Elusive Images-Reagan's Top Aides Paint Conflicting Presidential Portraits, *The New York Times*, 1987, AD: Margaret O'Connor

He arrived at my door unannounced. I was busy, not in the mood to see an artist's work. To this day I don't recall how he got there. Black shoes, black socks, black pants, black shirt, and black jacket draped straight down from wide, hard shoulders. The tieless, buttoned shirt collar abruptly ended the outfit and announced the beginning of a fair-skinned head draped with straight blond hair and deep-set,

Where the Reagan Revolution Went Awry,

The New York Times 1987, AD: John Cayea

terrifying eyes. He was either an artist or a murderer. Since he carried a small portfolio, I was safe. Mirko Ilić sat down. He introduced himself and gave away immediately the fact that he was foreign born. His accent was a strong reminder of a comedy routine on *Saturday Night Live* featuring Steve Martin as a nutty Slav in New York.

An illustrator's worth is something he usually carries with him... his portfolio. I did not intend to spend much time with this one. I was preparing my usual statement: "I'm going to look at this very fast, but I'll see everything I have to, so don't be offended." The speech never made its way from my mouth. The first illustrations were so compelling and well drawn that all the other responsibilities of the day started leaving my mind. Here was a brain at work! Here was talent to put the ideas down clearly and precisely. Here was a superb craftsman. The range was staggering: line, tone, photography, posters, scratchboard, cartooning. But most important, the strength of the ideas was overpowering. As I commented about his individual illustrations, Mirko would fill in occasionally with stories behind the pieces, most of them anecdotes about inhuman deadlines, nights without sleep, and editors whose opinions have been the bane of our existence since publishing began. But through these stories came further, more personal insight: devotion to craft, humility, love of life, trust. I

wanted to work with this person. Actually, I told him I wanted him chained to a desk so he wouldn't get away from me. We talked for perhaps forty-five minutes. I usually spend about fifteen minutes with artists. We talked about his past in Yugoslavia, about his varied assignments there and in Italy. Mirko came to New York just over a year ago carrying little more than his talent. Shortly after arriving he met his wife, Nicky, and settled in the West Village.

While I was art director of *Discover*, Mirko illustrated columns and stories, and on one occasion conceptualized and art-directed one of the magazine's most powerful covers. Recently he was honored by a feature in *Graphis*, the internationally acclaimed publication for graphic artists. In the past year alone, he has produced over two-hundred illustrations for such publications as the *The New York Times* and *U.S. News & World Report*.

A huge calendar on his studio wall reveals what appear to be deadlines for every day of next month. But I have a part in Mirko's future every bit as rewarding as his professional career: I have been declared his friend. Yes, that's right—"declared." It just happened one day. He said I was his friend, and that was that. I'm very glad I accepted.

ERIC SEIDMAN, ART DIRECTOR OF THE MAGAZINES *DISCOVER* AND *MONEY*, FROM THE CATALOG OF AN EXHIBITION AT THE YUGOSLAV PRESS AND CULTURAL CENTER GALLERY, NEW YORK CITY, 1987

The cover of the catalog from Ilić's exhibition at the Yugoslav Press and Cultural Center Gallery, New York City, 1987
D: Nicky Lindeman

"I must say that I could have worked and lived a normal life in Yugoslavia with the money I earned. I did not come to America for economic reasons; I did not come for political reasons. I came on a whim. It was a challenge. A challenge to leave all the things I did in Yugoslavia and to say 'let's start from the beginning.'"

"THE CAPRICE OF THE NEW BEGINNING," *NEDELJNA BORBA*, BELGRADE, MARCH 14–15, 1987

"I love working for newspapers because I have to adhere to a deadline. Otherwise, I would keep on working, redoing, and at the end would probably destroy it all. When I read the text to be illustrated, if I do not get the idea by the first half of the page, I have a problem. If read the text and do not know what to do, I wait until the last five minutes. Everything gets boiled down; what now, what now. These quick ideas are simple. It is fun for me to sweat over my work. I do not have to, but I love to create challenges for myself."

—MIRKO ILIĆ

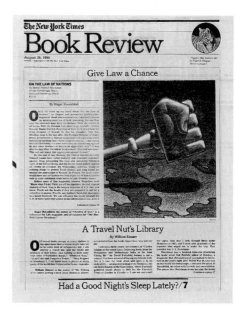

Tales of Terror and the 1040,
The NYT Book Review, February 11, 1990

RIGHT COLUMN: **Give Law a Chance**,
The NYT Book Review, August 26, 1990

Rising Sun—Is Japan Really Out to Get Us?,
The New York Times Book Review,
February 9, 1992;

Should War Be Left to the Generals,
The NYT Book Review, July 5, 1992

AD: Steven Heller

> "It's very important to introduce new ideas into your design. When you're listening to music, going out to the theater, visiting museums, socializing with friends, and so forth, you will accumulate additional ideas, and from some place other than looking at other designers' work or at the design annuals. The best ideas come from cross-pollination. Not from just recycling the same crap again and again."

—MIRKO ILIĆ INTERVIEW ON WILL SHERWOOD'S SUCCES SECRETS AND TIPS BLOG

The New York Times
Book Review

August 16, 1987
Section 7 © The New York Times

"Little Eden," a war memoir by Eva Figes, reviewed by Lore Segal. Page 14.

Of Moles and Men

Cloak & Gown
Yale University has always been a great nursery for spooks, according to Robin Winks, who takes a scholarly machete to the jungle of myth about the Ivy League heroes of the O.S.S. and the C.I.A. A portrait of dining-club idealists, champions of a sentimental imperialism, missionaries bent on improving the world. **7**

Conspiracy of Silence
The eminent art historian Sir Anthony Blunt was in truth part of the infamous ring of spies laced through upper levels of British society and government. A traitor's life story, told by Barrie Penrose and Simon Freeman. **11**

Spycatcher
Britain's hottest banned book, Peter Wright's memoirs recount his career bugging phones, cracking codes and feverishly pursuing supposed moles in Her Majesty's secret service. **13**

The Heirs of Calvino and the Eco Effect
By Sergio Perosa

ON his sudden death two years ago, Italo Calvino left no true literary children, only *nipotini*, little nephews (as we call them in Italy, half affectionately, half disparagingly), and some quarrels. Calvino, the only Italian novelist who could have been a suitable candidate for the Nobel Prize, died at a relatively early age

Sergio Perosa is the author of "American Theories of the Novel, 1793-1903" and of "Henry James and the Experimental Novel."

and in the full enjoyment of his powers: "He became his admirers," as W. H. Auden sang of W. B. Yeats in his elegy, he survived in his books, but not as a source of literary inspiration. The sheer variety of his forms and interests — narrative, ideological and otherwise, ranging from poetic to social realism, from allegorical fables to science fiction, from the "sea of objectivity" he celebrated in an essay to self-reflective, artificially constructed fiction, from political engagement to literature as a puzzle or a game of chess — prevented it, and caused uneasi-

ness and embarrassment, even resentment.

Two well-publicized conferences mounted to solemnize his demise, as seems to be customary in Italy in such cases — who would grudge a dead writer his right to a post-mortem reputation? — ended in very significant partial failures. Critics of different schools, on learning of each other's presence, failed to appear; others, in sympathy or in protest, withdrew. The assessment of Calvino's varied claims to literary achievement and fame was even

Continued on page 24

'You Must Remember This' by Joyce Carol Oates/3

LEFT:

On Moles and Men,
The NYT Book Review,
August 16, 1987

Below:

A Savage and Demeaning Ritual,
The NYT Book Review, October 14, 1990

In the Name of the President,
The NYT Book Review, May 26, 1991

Thrills and Chills,
The NYT Book Review, July 28, 1991

Close to Home,

The New York Times Book Review, August 23, 1992

Close to Home,

The New York Times Book Review, August 23, 1992

The Worst Is Yet to Come,

The New York Times Book Review, February 14, 1993

The Struggle for Memory,

The New York Times Book Review, May 30, 1993

OPPOSITE PAGE

An American Feast: You Are What You Buy,

The Wall Street Journal, 1988

A New World,

The Wall Street Journal, July 9, 1990

When The Patient Takes Charge,

The Wall Street Journal, 1987

Early Retirement— Bailing Out Early,

The Wall Street Journal Reports, 1989

AD: Greg Leeds

Pay for Performance,

The Wall Street Journal, 1990

AD: Joe Dizney

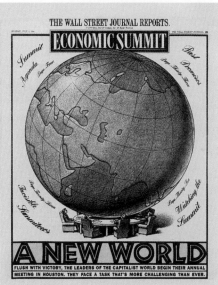

Warrant for Murder: How Florida Almost Killed an Innocent Man, *Amnesty Action* 1989

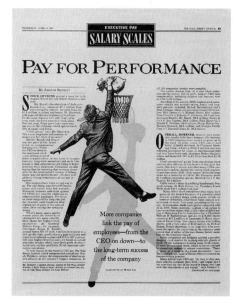

Self Portraits

FROM THE VERY BEGINNING, ILIĆ had a habit of using his own image in his work. He appears in his comics and illustrations, sometimes as a model in the photo-illustrations he created for *Danas*, and he can also be easily recognized in some more recent computer illustrations.

Writing about Stefan Sagmeister, Rick Poynor said: "Many designers have exploited photogenic good looks in their publicity photos, but few have put a high degree of emphasis on their personal appearance."[01]

Sagmeister is an example of a designer who uses his body in almost an exhibitionistic manner. He famously carved letters into his skin with a razor blade for an AIGA poster as a sort of designer's tribute to Vienna actionists. Although Ilić's critics often claim that he is an egomaniac, self-portraiture has a completely different meaning and purpose for him than merely showing off in public. Placing your own face in awkward social themes which are predominant in his illustrations—nationalism, racism, violence, terrorism, government and media manipulation—has important political significance. Self-portraiture in politically charged situations shows that the author is not isolated from the world; that he observes from a lofty distance, but is included in its tensions. What Walter Benjamin says of Baudelaire can also be applied to Ilić: "When describing the corruption and vice, he always includes himself. He does not know the gesture of satirist."[02]

Ilić is a fighter, always directly involved in the ideological struggle against all the forces of conservatism, nationalism, racism, sexism, or any official policy that seeks only to maintain power, and does not contribute to the improvement of living conditions for citizens.

In an interview he said: "Content is very important to me. I am not interested in pure design that much, it is a little bit boring to me. I've always felt that my design has to antagonize someone." ▶

01 | Rick Poynor: Baring it all —Stefan Sagmeister and the return of idea-based design, in *Handarbeit*, MAK, Vienna, 2002, pp. 62

02 | Walter Benjamin: Central Park, *New German Critique*, No. 34 (Winter, 1985), p. 54

Free Your Mind – Start with Your Mouth,
MTV ad published in *Colors Magazine*, 1993
AD: Jefferey Keyton, ILLUSTRATION: Mirko Ilić

Mafia, *Il Venerdi di La Republica*,
Milano 1992, AD: Franco Lefévre

Our Times — The Illustrated History of the 20ᵗʰ Century, Overstock
Unlimited Inc. 1995, AD: Linda Root, Milton Glaser & Walter Bernard

"Leonardo Da Vinci said only bad artists draw themselves. But I draw myself very often. Uusally as a bad guy because I noticed that's who the girls always end up with."

—MIRKO ILIĆ, "A SLOTH WITH CREATIVE SPIRIT,"
POPBOKS, APRIL 1, 2005

"Of course, with Mirko it is hard to separate the work from the man, but I'll try. His illustration and design have extraordinary intelligence. Far more is going on beneath the surface than meets the eye. The work is witty. And though Mirko is quick to point out nuances that may have escaped me, I sense other depths of subtlety and humor that he is keeping in reserve. So perhaps it is impossible to speak differently about the work and the man after all."

—JULIE LASKY

Mirko Ilić: The Eye.

by **Laetitia WOLFF**

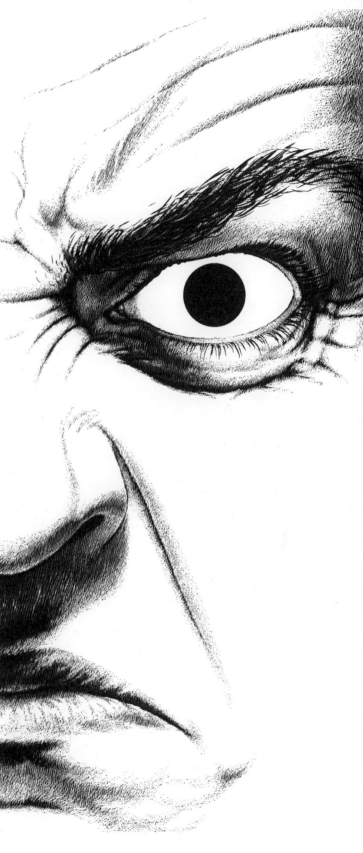

MIRKO IS AN EYE—SHARP AND PLAYFUL—that looks, observes, and remembers images and icons. Whether he deals with socio- or geopolitics, scandals related to financial, governmental, or medical issues, Ilić manages to throw the concept right at the reader's face, somewhat brutally, however never losing a distant sense of humor, and always with the utmost relevance to and intelligence about f the subject. Milton Glaser has said about Mirko: "He is a designer that draws and an illustrator that thinks."

Playing with visual analogies, Ilić's work questions the limit of what can be done in design, bypassing the established design rules while making new use of them. Analogy, juxtaposition, and comparison are recurring techniques used to visually reinforce the editorial content he is given to work with. His book layouts are often built on thought-provoking diptychs, which in essence convey a mental link between two images, i.e., two concepts. His art of provocation is not limited to gratuitous visual puns or juggling concepts, it also redefines the relationship between type and illustration. Typography seems to completely invade design while being shaken, toyed with, objectified with imaginative details, as if the designer wanted to disrupt both the body of text and the overall meaning of design. ✖

"THE EYE, PART I*" WAS ORIGINALLY PUBLISHED IN *MIRKO ILIĆ*, EDITED BY LAETITIA WOLFF IN THE DESIGN FOCUS SERIES, PUBLISHED BY CHINA YOUTH PRESS (2000), DISTRIBUTED BY GINGKO PRESS.

A member of the band Rage Against the Machine has a copy of the *Red and Black* movie poster tattooed on his arm and the illustration "Rising Sun" from *The New York Times*, on his back. Above spread from *Spin* magazine.

Rising Sun—Is Japan Really Out to Get Us?, *The New York Times Book Review*, February 9, 1992; AD: Steven Heller

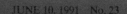

JUNE 10, 1991   No. 23

TIME
INTERNATIONAL

Does it exist — or
do bad things just happen?

AUSTRIA	S 30	FRANCE	F 17.00	IRELAND (incl. tax)	IR£1.50	NORWAY	Kr 17.00	SWITZERLAND	F 4.00
BELGIUM	F 100	GERMANY	DM 4.80	ISRAEL (incl. tax)	NS 5.90	POLAND	PLZ 18000.00	TURKEY (incl. tax)	TL 6000
CZECHOSLOVAKIA	CZC 35.00	GIBRALTAR	£1.50	ITALY	Lit 3300	PORTUGAL	Esc 350	UNITED KINGDOM	£1.30
CYPRUS	CP 1.30	GREECE	Dr 400	LUXEMBOURG	F 100	ROMANIA	ROL 50.00	U.S. ARMED FORCES	$2.35
DENMARK	Kr 18.00	HUNGARY	HUF 120.00	MALTA	80c	SPAIN	Pta 325	U.S.S.R.	SUR 4.00
FINLAND	Mk 12.00	ICELAND (incl. tax)	Kr 160.00	NETHERLANDS	F15.00	SWEDEN (incl. tax)	Kr 17.00	YUGOSLAVIA	ND 55.00

WEEKLY

"When I got the chance to do my first cover for *Time*, it was less exciting than meeting Mario Bošnjak on the street in Zagreb and him inviting me to do illustrations for *Start*."

—MIRKO ILIĆ

Evil,
Time International, June 10, 1991
AD & D: Mirko Ilić

"The 1992 cover that received an award for exceptional creativity sums up Ilić's thinking about evil: four black letters on a black background. Something that's known in the history of modern art, but which was never done on the pages of a major magazine. All the injustice of the system in which Ilić has lived and worked, he has commented on over the years in a unique way, which was brought to simple perfection by the use of those four letters."

SANDRA KRIŽIĆ ROBAN, MIRKO ILIĆ EXHIBITION CATALOG: GRAPHIC DESIGN, ILLUSTRATION, ART PAVILION, ZAGREB 1992

"In one week, this cover has transformed the look of *Time* magazine," said William Drenttel on the front page edition of June 10, 1992. "It has truly surprised people and it is a good example of the power of design." All the jury members praised the subtleties and boldness of the simple, two-tone design. "As far as I can remember, this is the only case that *Time* magazine has taken such a risk," said Carol Carson. "For them it is quite an unusual design." Apart from the deviation from the usual magazine practice, according to Louise Fili, the Evil cover stands out for its "stunning use of *Time*'s otherwise extremely restrictive typographical formula".

38TH *I.D.* ANNUAL DESIGN REVIEW, JULY / AUGUST 1992

A WEEK AFTER LANDING in the United States Ilić was commissioned to offer design ideas for the cover of *Time* magazine. He was elated. A few days later, he hit rock bottom. The practice at *Time* in the late eighties was to get proposals from four authors whose articles were competing for the cover. His illustration was not accepted (the winner was Seymour Chwast). "I was ready to pick up my things and go back home. I thought it was the biggest failure of my career."

However, other jobs followed and in the coming years many of his ideas were accepted by the magazine's American and international editions.

"The opportunity to do the cover of *Time* did not surprise me because I came to America with the intention of doing just that. It was much more exciting when they offered me a full-time job. It's nice to write in the biography that my first full-time job was as art director of the international edition of *Time*."

His first few covers are in the recognizable style of colored scratchboard illustrations, but soon Ilić began to use different approaches, including photography and collage.

"When I bought my first computer, I used it to scan drawings and add color," Ilić said. "The best example of this was the cover with Germany. The first illustration I ever made in Illustrator was published in *Time*. And the first illustration that I made using Photoshop was the cover of *Time* magazine. But I feel a lot of stress using these new programs, so if I don't have a good reason to use them, I won't do it."

As an illustrator, designer, and art director Ilić managed to publish many bold ideas. In one example, the main cover story had no headlines; in another the main headline was printed in black against a black background. According to Ilić, one of his biggest successes was a story about the conflict between English- and French-speaking Canadians. There was no text at all, not a single headline on the cover of *Time*. At first the editors were confused, but eventually they had to accept the argument that using an English title suggested favoritism for one side, which of course, *Time* magazine could not allow.

Illustrations for *Time*, especially for the cover, are created in close collaboration among artists, illustrators, art directors, and editors. Within that creative chain Ilić frequently changed roles from one to the other—sometimes as an illustrator, sometimes as a designer, and when he was employed as an art director, he asked other designers and illustrators to work with him. When asked how he so easily moved from one position to another, he replied: "It can be frustrating, especially when you work with a designer who is not as good or is less experienced. You know immediately what will happen. You are working on a story that is

Gridlock, *Time*, September 12, 1988
AD: Rudolph Hoglund, PHOTO: Roberto Brosan

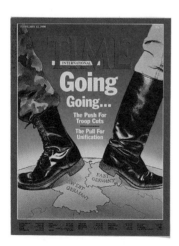

The Spectre of Stalin,

Time, June 20, 1988, d: Ina Saltz

Going, Going...,

Time International, February 12, 1990

AD: Rudolph Hoglund

highly political and the other guy doesn't understand what the story is about and says to you, No, no, it should be like this. I even told one man at one point, *I wrote the book.* I always joke that the only difference between a good art director and a bad art director is that the good one gets the best out of you and gets the credit and fame, and the bad one brings out only the worst."

Sometimes editors and art directors had a clear idea of what they wanted and what they considered important in the story, and sometimes they gave illustrators free rein and hoped for the best. According to Ilić, there were three ways that he came up with cover ideas: by reading the first half of a story; by listening to what the editors said; or by having no clue until the last half hour before a deadline. He often stressed that he was inspired by the relentless rhythm of the production cycle. "On Thursday I get called for a meeting, by Saturday the cover is complete, and two days later distributed throughout the world. And after a week it's all gone and a new image takes its place."

Because Ilić often added much more thinking to a story than just the imagery he was eventually offered a permanent position. In editor Robert L. Miller's "From the publisher" piece, he unveiled his new art director and how they had found him. Miller mentioned to *Time* art director Rudy Hoglund that he was looking for a new art director for the international edition and Hoglund recommended Ilić. "I can call on him at any time of day or night and be sure he will come up with something very quickly," he said. They also concluded that the new art director should be someone who is interested in international politics, has good contacts with illustrators and photographers around the world, and knows his way around the *Time* newsroom. When Ilić mentioned this to his wife, Nicky, she said: "Well that's you." When Hoglund recommended Ilić, editors did not need much persuading.

"I like to change things, and many people don't. Why take a risk? So I do not like to stay in one place for long because constant repetition lulls you to sleep.

But being art director of a world-renowned magazine gives you endless possibilities. You get to work with the best artists and photographers, you can call anyone and they will answer. If I said that I wanted Naomi Campbell for the cover page, we would photograph Naomi Campbell. *Time* International has not had until then an African-American model on the cover."

During his time as the art director, a much more dynamic version of the design layout was being introduced. This was due to the fact that the columns were of different widths, drew up in each other, and started at different heights; for the theme of Switzerland, he arranged the text and photos into shapes that suggested the cross from the flag, and in a special issue on France, his interest in figurative typography is obvious. He would later develop the interest further in the *Times*' op-ed pages and for the book *Elvis + Marilyn*.

Despite numerous accomplishments and accolades, Ilić left *Time* after just six months.

"They told me that I had to rearrange the whole magazine," Ilić said. "I was not interested in that. I always find it amusing when Americans tell me that I must do something. I must nothing. I came from a country that has had much more powerful instruments of repression. I didn't have to do it there and I don't have to do it here, either. So I left." ▶

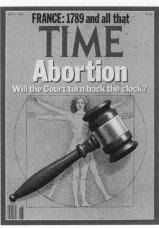

Germany: Toward Unity,

Time International, June 25, 1990

Abortion,

Time, May 1, 1989

Canada,

Time International, June 18, 1990

ALL AD: Rudolph Hoglund

"**My greatest success is that there are no headlines on the cover of the *Time* magazine about the English-French conflict in Canada. They first placed the headline on the cover in English, but I told them, 'Hold on, if you put it in English, it will seem as if you are taking the English side.' So they replied that they will put the headine in both languages, but I told them that next time, when we had Chinese on the cover, we also need to put the headline in both languages, and they just said 'Forget the headline.' So, only the illustration remained on the cover, and my greatest success is in what was not on it.**"

—MIRKO ILIĆ

Germany One Year Later,

Time International, July 1, 1991

AD & ILLUSTRATION: Mirko Ilić

Cup Magic,

Time International, July 9, 1990

What is Kuwait?,

Time, December 24, 1990

200th Anniversary W.A. Mozart, *Time International*, July 22, 1991, illustration: Mark Sommers, d: Louise Fili

Mirko and I were art directors at *Time* magazine in New York during the eighties. It was exciting to work with him in the same place, because you never knew what he was going to do next. He always pushed the limits that other artistic directors did not dare touch. In fact, he cared neither for limits nor for the way that we as art directors should behave. He made a stunning range of covers for the international edition of the magazine. His departure was a great loss for the magazine—we missed the creative and ironic way he represented his position. But in the end, he was too big a personality for *Time*'s rooted and scrupulous traditions. He had no ladder left to climb. If he was in charge—art director of the whole magazine—he would have in time no doubt insulted a politician at a high post so that the graphic and photographic departments for years would have been banned from any contact with the White House or something like that, though it might have been good for us to get a healthy shaking.

After I left *Time*, I stayed in touch with Mirko. I'm proud of it and I'm glad. When I was invited to work on some simple charts for his book about the Olympics, I learned what other illustrators already knew: that he will take care of me. Because he was in this position before, he knows what illustrators and designers need: clearly defined job, sufficient time, and an appropriate fee. And then they are to be left alone in order to do their job. As for me, I knew that whatever I made for him would be beautifully designed and I'd be happy with the result. To have confidence and respect for a person in this way means that for that person you will work as hard as you can. Some illustrators will strive to do better work for some art directors and designers more than for others. Usually they will enjoy the work more and the final results will be better.

—NIGEL HOLMES

"At the time, Mark Sommers was my competition, working in a similar style. And then, as an art director for one of the first covers, I decided to hire him. His first cover for *Time* magazine was the illustration of Mozart. To make sure that I did not screw up his drawing, I hired Louise Fili to be the designer, because they had already worked together, so the two of them would have a blast, doing whatever they wanted. This is my personal justice system and my reason to hire someone else. I could have done a very similar job, but I found it easier and fairer to give it to him."

—MIRKO ILIĆ

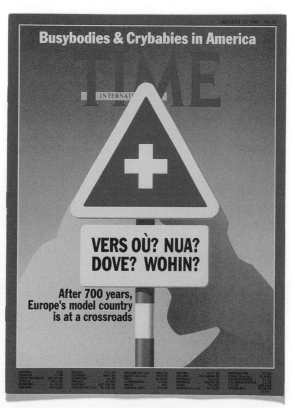

Busybodies & Crybabies in America

TIME
INTERNATIONAL

VERS OÙ? NUA?
DOVE? WOHIN?

After 700 years,
Europe's model country
is at a crossroads

Vers Où? Nua? Dove? Wohin?,

ILLUSTRATION: Mirko Ilić

Angst in the Swiss Alps,

Time International, August 12, 1991

D: Jamie Elsis

ALL AD: Mirko Ilić

EUROPE: Cocaine's New Target

TIME
INTERNATIONAL

GLOBO
COP

COMING SOON TO
YOUR COUNTRY?

When Volcanoes Blow

TIME

UNWANTED

Europe

COVER STORIES

Angst in the Swiss Alps

After 700 years of confederation, Switzerland frets that it may be left behind in splendid isolation

Europe

Neutrality's Payoff

Down the years, Switzerland has struggled heroically to stay aloof from foreign entanglements

> "I started to fool around a bit with the articles and then they told me that it's not a *Time* standard, the text does not read so and so. In my very bad English, I tried to explain to them that the English copy represents 30 percent gray area to me and thus I act accordingly. If I didn't have an accent in America, I would have to invent one, because in this way they never know if I really thought what I said or they just didn't understand me all that well."
>
> —MIRKO ILIĆ

Globo Cop,

Time International,
April 1, 1991,

ILLUSTRATION: Nicholas
Fasciano,

PHOTO: Matthew Klein,

D: Jamie Elsis

The Unwanted,

Time International,
June 24, 1991,

AD&D: Mirko Ilić,

ORIGINAL PHOTO BY
Anthony Suau [Black Star]

RE-SHOT BY Tom Arma

> "Every Saturday, in the early morning hours, when we were finishing up *Time,* the editor-in-chief would come to us and thank us for a job well done. It did not matter if it was just a courtesy, it meant a lot to us at three o'clock in the morning."
>
> —MIRKO ILIĆ, "A KID THAT'S DOODLING SOMETHING," *NEDELJNA DALMACIJA,* JUNE 01, 1992

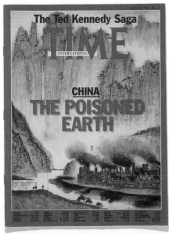

Euro Blues,

Time International, April 22, 1991

PHOTO: Tom Arma

China: The Poisoned Earth,

Time International, April 29, 1991

ILLUSTRATION: Wenhua Xu

Hong Kong — The Year of Living Anxiously,

Time, May 13, 1991

PHOTO: Ian Berry

The New France,

Time International, July 15, 1991

ILLUSTRATION: Albert Uderzo

Supermodels, Beauty & Bucks,

Time International, September 16, 1991

PHOTO: Brigitte Lacombe

Stolen — The Fine Art of Thievery Time,

International, November 25, 1991

ILLUSTRATION: Mirko Ilić

ALL: D: Jamie Elsis, AD: Mirko Ilić

A State That Deserved to Die, *Time*, December 30, 1991

AD: Rudolf Hoglund, D: Nomi Silverman

"I made those letters and the page layout on the disintegration of the USSR, but they killed the text. But they really liked the solution, so they kept it for another occasion and printed it two or three weeks after I left *Time*, so someone else was signed as the art director, a woman who succeeded me…"

—MIRKO ILIĆ

New Europe,

Time International,
December 9, 1991

AD: Irene Ramp

Europe 1993,

Time, December 28, 1992

ILLUSTRATION: Mirko Ilić /
Oko & Mano

AD: Rudolf Hoglund

Stock stampede,

Time, April 27, 1998

AD: Paul Lussier

Reading Europe's Future,

Time, September 21, 1992

AD: Rudolf Hoglund

Where's the Beef,

Time, February 26, 2001

AD: Paul Lussier

Which Way Will France Go,

Time, May 30, 2005

AD: Paul Lussier

ALL ILLUSTRATIONS: Mirko Ilić

"They faxed me an article published in Croatia where I was mentioned as a successful American illustrator who earns tons of money, wears Armani suits, and has a platinum American Express card. If they think that this is my biggest success, I don't know what to say. And by the way, I do not have a platinum credit card, it's a fabrication by the magazine. I think that my biggest success is that I am still looking forward to what I do. What makes me happy is that I don't know what I will do tomorrow, what in five days—something will come, someone will knock at the door, the phone will ring, and something different will be on my desk."

—MIRKO ILIĆ, *TRANSFER NO.* 81, HTV, JULY 9, 1998

"A month after I accepted the job at *Time,* the war started in Slovenia and then in Croatia and war photographs from my former homeland began to arrive at my desk. I had a terrible sense of powerlessness. I had no illusions that I could have done something if I had been there, but watching the war in Croatia from the U.S. was like watching a nightmare, but displaced.

I experienced a terrible shock when I traveled with my wife to London. We entered the hotel room, I turned on the TV, and on CNN I saw a picture of my elementary school in Bijeljina and in front of it members of Arkan's Tigers, the Serbian paramilitary formations of Željko Ražnatović. The newscaster was talking about a large massacre in the town where I was born and where I attended fourth grade. When I came to New York, hardly anyone knew of Yugoslavia, and now everyone was watching massacres in Bijeljina and knows this Bosnian town. I was safe, but part of that despair, anger, and stupidity still got to me." ▶

The Maze of Nationalism, *Time International,* September 9, 1991,
D: Jamie Elsis; AD: M. I.

About Serbian and Croatian nationalism
The New York Times Op-Ed,
1994, AD: Michael Valenti

The Havoc in Yugoslavia,
The New York Times Book Review,
January 21, 1996
AD: Steven Heller; ILLUSTRATION: Mirko Ilić

"It is difficult to create a fantastically good thing, not everybody can do it. But for some reason violence and crime come easy to a majority of people who want to do it."

—MIRKO ILIĆ, SATURDAY NIGHT, *RTZ* JUNE 12, 1979

"What shocked me more than the cruelty to another religion or a nation was the cruelty that the 'democratically elected governments' inflicted on their own people."

—MIRKO ILIĆ, HOMELAND FROM A NIGHTMARE, *FERAL TRIBUNE*, SPLIT, SEPTEMBER 21, 1998

For Belgrade and Sarajevo exhibitions in 2005, Mirko tore the illustration made for *Danas* in 1985 and presented one half in Belgrade and the other half in Sarajevo.

OPPOSITE PAGE:

You Can't Judge a Book by Its Cover,
MTV, 1993,
AD: Jeffrey Keyton,
ILLUSTRATION: Mirko Ilić

"I come from a generation that first got to know Mirko as a legend, and then through his works. And when I saw his works for the first time, I realized that I had a role model for life. The power that was produced by a combination of his reputation and the quality of his illustrations had left an indelible mark on my entire generation. We all wanted to be like him. We followed his career in America wide-eyed, certainly more critically than any American would. Each of his successes gave us new strength to continue to do this job in very difficult times. Mirko is the only one from this region who has achieved the most difficult: to easily move from the domain of local star to that of globally influential creative figure. In June 2000, I was fortunate enough, after fifteen years of waiting, to see him for the first time in person, and at his best, at a lecture in Ljubljana. All the humor and lucidity of his illustrations appeared embodied in his figure. When I extended my hand to meet him, my knees were weak as a teenage girl's at a Rolling Stones concert. He selflessly opened all the doors of this business to me, offered advice that I never dreamed I'd get, and thus saved me at least ten years of breaking through into the West. My generation is slowly entering the mature phase, achieving global recognition on many levels, awards, festivals, better life, but there's one thing I am sure of: We wouldn't have been here if it wasn't for an idol like Mirko Ilić."

—SLAVIMIR STOJANOVIĆ

Drip, Drip, Drip... — Boutros-Ghali, Arhitect of UN Failure,

The New Republic, 1994, AD: Eric Baker, IL: Oko & Mano – Mirko Ilić

"I watch as huge amounts of energy get lost in the wrong direction. I watch people who I've never even heard of, or have heard very little of, or only bad things—blast in the newspapers to pieces some other people who are considered to be living, walking monuments of culture and a great value to this land. People are being stoned, newspapers bad-mouth their relatives, their private lives. At the same time, this same crowd is horrified when Serbian bombs blast cultural monuments to pieces. I do not see any difference, because the scars that they leave on these people are the same as those of Dubrovnik. It is unacceptable that people look the other way and don't react or even laugh. Silence means approval."

—MIRKO ILIĆ, "A KID THAT DOODLES SOMETHING," *NEDELJNA DALMACIJA*, JULY 1ST, 1992

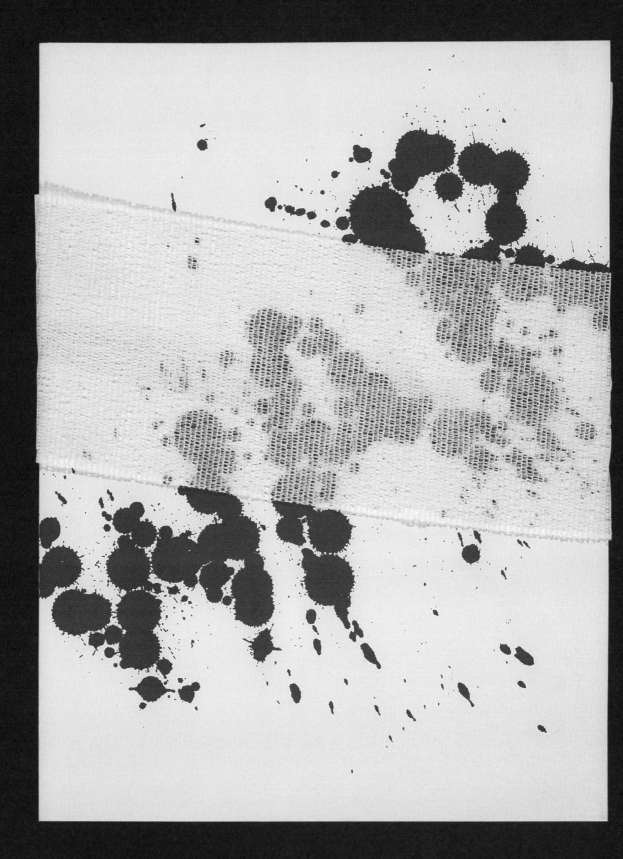

WAR,
The folder with information
on a charitable activity.
CLIENT: Toni Mandić, 1991,
AD & D: Mirko Ilić

"Toni Mandić, who was vice-president of Atlantic Records, had organized in Los Angeles a campaign to collect aid for victims of the war in Croatia. The cover was silkscreen printed by Nenad Božić, originally from Belgrade. The bandage is real, hand-glued ..." —MIRKO ILIĆ

Russia Comes Apart, *The New York Times* Op-Ed, January 10, 1993 AD & D & ILLUSTRATION: Mirko Ilić

"I told the *Times* that I would not work for more than a year. Also, I was making less money than before, so I had a lot of freedom. I could always say 'if you don't like the work and you don't want it, good-bye!' And slam the door. They could not blackmail me by threatening to fire me. So, the deal was I would work there only if I could do what I wanted, which was to have fun with typography, text shapes, and so on."

—MIRKO ILIĆ

"One of the problems with *The New York Times* was that it was printed very poorly on horrible paper stock," said Ilić. "So all that was left was art and typography. I needed to come up with something unique and different."

For inspiration, Ilić turned to sixteenth century German designs that arranged figurative poems into various shapes, as well as an illuminated page from the tenth century "Aratus" manuscript. "These kinds of things have existed for centuries; I personally like to stretch the territory," Ilić said.

He used these ancient works as the basis for a series of *Times* op-ed pages that literally turn type into art. For an article titled "One Strange Bird," he added subtle illustrations of a beak and eye to lend life to a typographic turkey.

For the editorial piece "You're Out," Ilić created a typographic baseball soaring over the flags of the stadium and off the page.

Like the unknown German designers, Ilić created a visual solution that illustrates without pictures, blending playful imagery with sober words. And it overcomes the constraints of low-quality printing and paper.

Ilić also had to overcome the constraints of a cranky editor: "My editor noted that his pages were looking very different from the rest of *The New York Times*," Ilić recalls, "The wild combinations of people and subject matter were amazing."

The paper received mixed reviews on Ilić's designs. "You have a lot of people who have nothing to do but write to *The New York Times* and complain," he said. "Some people saw my designs and thought the rest of the paper was going to look like that. But people who read op-ed pages will read them anyway."

"My goal was to catch the eye of the person who was turning from the front page to the sports page," he continued. "If I could catch their eye for just a second and make them ask 'What is this?' Then maybe he would read the story. I wanted something bold, strong, and shocking."

—BRYN M. MOOTH: INSPIRING TYPE, *HOW* MAGAZINE, FEBRUARY 1996, PS. 95–96

Op-Ed Pages

The New York Times • before and after 1992

ILIĆ AND *THE NEW YORK TIMES* seemed to have been made for each other. For one thing, when he arrived in the United States, it was a bountiful time for illustrators. For another, it was the era of Gorbachev and perestroika, so articles about the Soviet Union and Eastern Bloc countries were in demand, and with his background, there was hardly anyone who knew these topics better.

"During the first three or four years in the U.S., I worked on a lot of political illustrations. Since I came from Eastern Europe, editors assumed that I knew more about it than the average American illustrator. When they did not fully understand a piece, they would say: 'Ah, well, you will think of something.' It was very good for my career. I was labeled as an 'Eastern European political illustrator,' and they loved it.

When he became the art director of the *Times*' op-ed page, Ilić was not satisfied with merely commissioning and drawing witty and smart illustrations. He quickly began integrating the illustration with the page layout to its maximum potential.

The op-ed pages required that designers and art directors be directly involved in the editorial process. If original art director of Op-Ed pages Louis Silverstein did not want the layout to be predictable, Ilić took full advantage of that mandate and began to explore a range of graphic possibilities. While always adhering to the basic *Times* structure, Ilić broke boundaries, experimenting with various forms and formats of illustration. It helped that the diversity of the op-ed content invited more design freedom by allowing for unusually large white spaces. Before Ilić, type treatment on the pages was mainly restricted to playing with headlines. Ilić immediately seized the opportunity to create illustrations with the text itself. Figurative typography has been used for years in many constructs, but never for one of the world's leading daily newspapers, that is, graphic format which is considered a most conventional and conservative.

It was a bustling and prolific time for illustration and illustrators. And Ilić had successfully created a signature look for the op-ed section. Alas, it wasn't to last. Over the following years, the power of editors—at the *Times* and other publications—began to increase, while that of the art directors decreased. Several magazines, like *The New Yorker,* have remained faithful to the form of illustration, but steadily photography and pop culture portraiture began to dominate majority of magazine pages. After a decade marked by innovative illustrative and typographic experimentation, even the most avant-garde and edgy magazines in the early twenty-first century retreated to a more conservative design approach.

These are the days of Photoshop and stock photography. Illustration is too costly and complicated. Abstract is out.

"Illustration has so many expressive possibilities," Ilić said. "A photograph is worth a thousand words, and it's also easily understood by those who cannot read. That's really the crux of the problem and why there are so few illustrations in publications these days. Editors and publishers have no power over their message. Photographs are easier to control. The problem is political as well. Imagine that the all the horrible photos of politicians sitting at a table in front of a plant with a glass of water were drawn instead. It would introduce a whole new insightful layer to their character."

A decade ago illustrators were expected to offer sharp commentary about

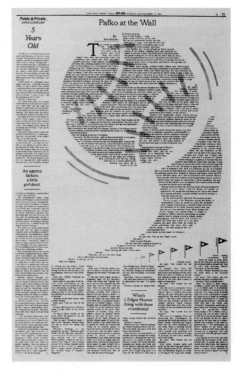

Pafko at the Wall,
Op-Ed, September 13, 1992
ILLUSTRATION: Alejandro Arce,
AD & D: Mirko Ilić

A Brief Version of Time,
Op-Ed, February 18, 1993
AD & D: Mirko Ilić

Dining In/Out,
Logos for *The New York Times* columns, 2001

the state of American society. It was their job to criticize the president and mock the politicians. But in today's political climate, on one hand obsessed with political correctness and so called "culture of complaint", and on the other hand with fear of terrorism, it is becoming more difficult to run the edgy illustrations that were so common in newspapers only a few decades ago, especially in *The New York Times*. That does not mean that good illustration never appears, but generally speaking the position and the selection of illustrations today are dictated by editors who are guided by differing criteria. Milton Glaser believes this reflects a general lack of understanding and appreciation for the importance of details, vital "shades of difference," and that commercial media these days is controlled by large corporately controlled conglomerates, all of which has led to the destruction of abstract thinking. "Corporations are all cautious when it comes to individual expression," Glaser said. "Editors are increasingly looking to control that voice and to submit it to a previously agreed methodology," he added. According to Glaser, photography has one basic feature that illustration is missing—an inborn sense of recording "real" moments in time, of showing what really exists. Because we can see it and therefore "believe it," the photo has become the best tool to induce consumer desires. "The imaginative potential of illustrations have become irrelevant today. The illustration is far too specific, too personal."

The result is that magazines are becoming repetitive and overly similar. These predictable formulas are used because the circle of those who decide the content and design is becoming smaller, and the possibility of influential creative people coming in from the outside is narrowing.

Citing Brad Holland and Roland Topor as role models who encouraged him to work professionally with the illustrated form, Ilić believes that illustrators today do not have the courage and boldness to revitalize the discipline. "Illustrators need to be more ambitious, to deeply reflect on ideas and not be shy when it comes to fighting for the professional financial satisfaction or job be damned," Ilić said. He also said that more art directors need to promote high-quality illustration.

"I think that the attitude toward illustration is getting worse by the day," Ilić said. "Newspaper and magazine editors are gaining more power. I often say in lectures that nowadays art directors are the highest-paid couriers in American corporations. Give them the work, and they will carry it to someone who actually makes the decision.

"I once sent a piece to an art director and I got no response, so I asked him what was going on, and he said, 'I don't know yet, I haven't shown it to the editor.' Why? If the art director says that he likes it and the editor does not like it, then he would have to fight for the piece. If he doesn't show it to him at all, then he won't be told what to think by the editor."

Ilić's observation that art directors are more accurately described as *art secretaries* follows the famous thesis of feminist analysis. Feminization of an occupation occurs when a profession begins to lose its social reputation, i.e., certain occupations open up to women only when they start to lose the position of power. All the great art directors of the fifties and sixties—except for Cipe Pineles—were male.[01] That's changed a bit lately as many women have become art directors,

01 | Alexey Brodovitch [*Harper's Bazaar*, 1934–58], Bradbury Thompson [*Mademoiselle*, 1945–59]; Allen Hurlburt [*Look*, 1953–68], Henry Wolff [*Esquire*, 1953–58; *Harper's Bazaar*, 1958–51; *Show*, 1961–64], Thomas Cleland and Leo Lionni [*Fortune* 1948–62], Milton Glaser & Walter Bernard [*New York*], Richard Gangel [*Sports Illustrated*], Herb Lubalin [*Fact*, 1967, *Avant-Garde*, 1968], Roger Black [*Rolling Stone* 1976–78]... The first member of the New York Art Directors Club was Cipe Pineles, and from 1941 until 1945 she was the art director of *Glamour*, while in late 40's she formed a new teenage market through the *Seventeen* magazine, and then in the period from 1950 to 1958 through *Charm* magazine she created a prototype of a magazine for a new target group, young employed woman. Martha Scotford published a book about her work: *Cipe Pineles – A Life of Design* [WW Northon & Co., 1999], see also Martha Scotford: *The Tenth Pioneer*, Eye 18, autumn 1995; Steven Heller: *Big Ideas That Built America*, Eye 22, autumn 1996.

but the position no longer holds the importance it did decades ago. Major design decisions are made by publishers, editors, and marketing departments.

"Art directors are more or less anonymous today," Ilić said. "There are several big art directors, but for the most part they are an endangered species. Great art directors are way too expensive and they usually argue with the editors. Then they get fired and for half the price the editors can get someone younger who listens. So in America today, very few of them have creative freedom. Someone like Sagmeister likes to take jobs where he has total creative freedom, but loses the money. People see his book and think, Wow, he must be earning a lot of money. But in what he does, there is not a whole lot of money. The real big money is in a good corporate identity, but he does not do that, not because he would not be given such a job, but because he knows what compromises need to be made and what it is that you can do there. Maybe one day he will become so great that he will be able to do whatever he wants and he would not be picked at, but for now, sometimes you have to say: We do not do this and that's it, because it is a *no-win situation*. There are art directors who argue with editors, fight for their ideas and for you as an illustrator, and they do very good things, but in most cases they are engaged for smaller projects. Of course the design and illustrations in *Rolling Stone* are better than in the *Financial Times,* and of course *Rolling Stone* will be the first to take a good gimmick from a good independent magazine because it can afford it. On the one hand, you cannot make *Ray Gun* from *Time* magazine, and you must not. Accordingly, the editor of *Time* magazine has more influence, because the magazine is editorially driven, more driven by the content, text. On the other hand, *Ray Gun* has no content, so the editor does not have anything to say. Since there is no content, *let's have a look!*"

These changes are connected to a new phenomenon that *stock* agencies are becoming the largest clients and distributors of illustrations. There are some benefits that come out of it—readers get quality illustrations, and magazines are saving money by publishing illustrations that are not made exclusively for them, but the problem is that art directors are not raising new illustrators.

In the article "Where Credit Is Due," Ilić has—using the example of one edition of *Time*—pointed out the increasing common practice of magazines not signing illustrators, just the agency from which they have purchased the right to publish the illustration.

"In the midst of Bill Gate's monopoly problems with our government, it's appropriate to observe that he has begun to monopolize our visual history. He owns both Corbis and Bettmann and who knows what else. If this trend of crediting only stock houses continues, people of the future will read these magazines and assume our most prolific and versatile painter and illustrator was Corbis Bettmann." [02] ▶

02 | Mirko Ilić, *Where Credit is Due,* AIGA Magazine, vol 18 no. 1, 2000

ILIĆ: Up to then, the op-ed page design depended solely on the quality of illustrations. The only real hurdle was to not to screw up the illustration.

Michael Valenti, who worked on the op-ed pages at that time, was going on vacation, so they said: Why don't you take over for the summer? They were setting me up, because Steve Heller said that if they offered me a job, I might not accept it. So I did this for a while and they asked me if I liked it, and I said: Well, there are some possibilities. And there was some of the *Polet* atmosphere in me; I could have called anyone I wanted, young illustrators, old ones, people who were my idols and people who became famous later on. I've heard people saying that that position made them illustrators—once they published an illustration in *The New York Times*, others began to take them much more seriously.

To make a long story short, they finally offered me a job, and I told them: Yes, but I do not want to work there for long. But according to the law, you have to be on probation for half a year and then work for a year... So they asked and said that it would be nice if I worked for a year and a half. OK, I said, but after that, I'm gone. I am not staying more than a year and a half. And that move made a big difference for me. For two reasons. I proved to them that *The New York Times* salary was a lot less money for me than I could earn as a freelancer. As a freelancer in *The New York Times*, I was earning more than the employed art director! Therefore, the money was not an issue. One should not forget that these years were important because of all that was happening here. It seemed to me a moral obligation, to do something that I could, to push something in one of the world's most important newspapers. And if the case was that editors were giving me a hard time, I'd say, You know, I'm going home. They could not blackmail me. Then they would give in: Let's talk. So I still managed to sell them a lot of things.

How To Lose The Cold War,
The New York Times, 1992, AD: Michael Valenti

Beds of Nails,

The New York Times Op-Ed June 13, 1992

IL: Seymour Chwast

After the Geldkrieg,

The New York Times Op-Ed, September 20, 1992

ILLUSTRATION: Milan Trenc

Time Out. It's Almost Summer,

The New York Times Op-Ed, June 20, 1992

ILLUSTRATION: Milton Glaser

Failure by Design,

The New York Times Op-Ed, May 2, 1993

ILLUSTRATION: Paul Rand

ILIĆ: During the LA riots we ran a piece that had an image of a drop of blood. This was the first page that I started experimenting with. Because there was panic. The text was coming from Los Angeles and as things developed, the text was being changed. I had to have a closed page even if I did not get enough of the text and so I had to leave it open for more text. That's why those blood drops were invented; I sprayed it on the spot and pasted in between the text. Something arose out of pure necessity that came out pretty good. It was at this point that they realized that something different could be done than just *grid grid grid*.

The things that I did for them were mostly mechanically assembled. At that time, there was a single Macintosh on the entire floor and mostly charts were being made on it. *Sandglass* was the first page that was made with a computer and there were a lot of problems with the graphic union because, according to their rules, I could not touch the letters. Before that, when the art director or designer came to the printing office and wanted to arrange or to change something by himself, a strike of graphic workers would break out immediately—they would leave their metal rulers and go out. This push me-pull me situation lasted for about two or three months, until they got some additional paid time off due to the introduction of computers.

It is interesting that around that time— *Ray Gun* started in 1992—David Carson was doing something similar to some of these things with typography. However, what seemed to me an essential difference was that it was much harder to move the wall for five centimeters in the *The New York Times* than two kilometers in *Ray Gun*. This made it interesting. It was also interesting because they probably would not accept it had it not been most positively assessed by the audience— the pages became more interesting. Of course, someone is always complaining about something. And not all of them were revolutionary; occasionally something unusual would happen. Sometimes it would all come together just in the last minute, sometimes we had a good classical illustration, and sometimes there was no reason to do anything unusual.

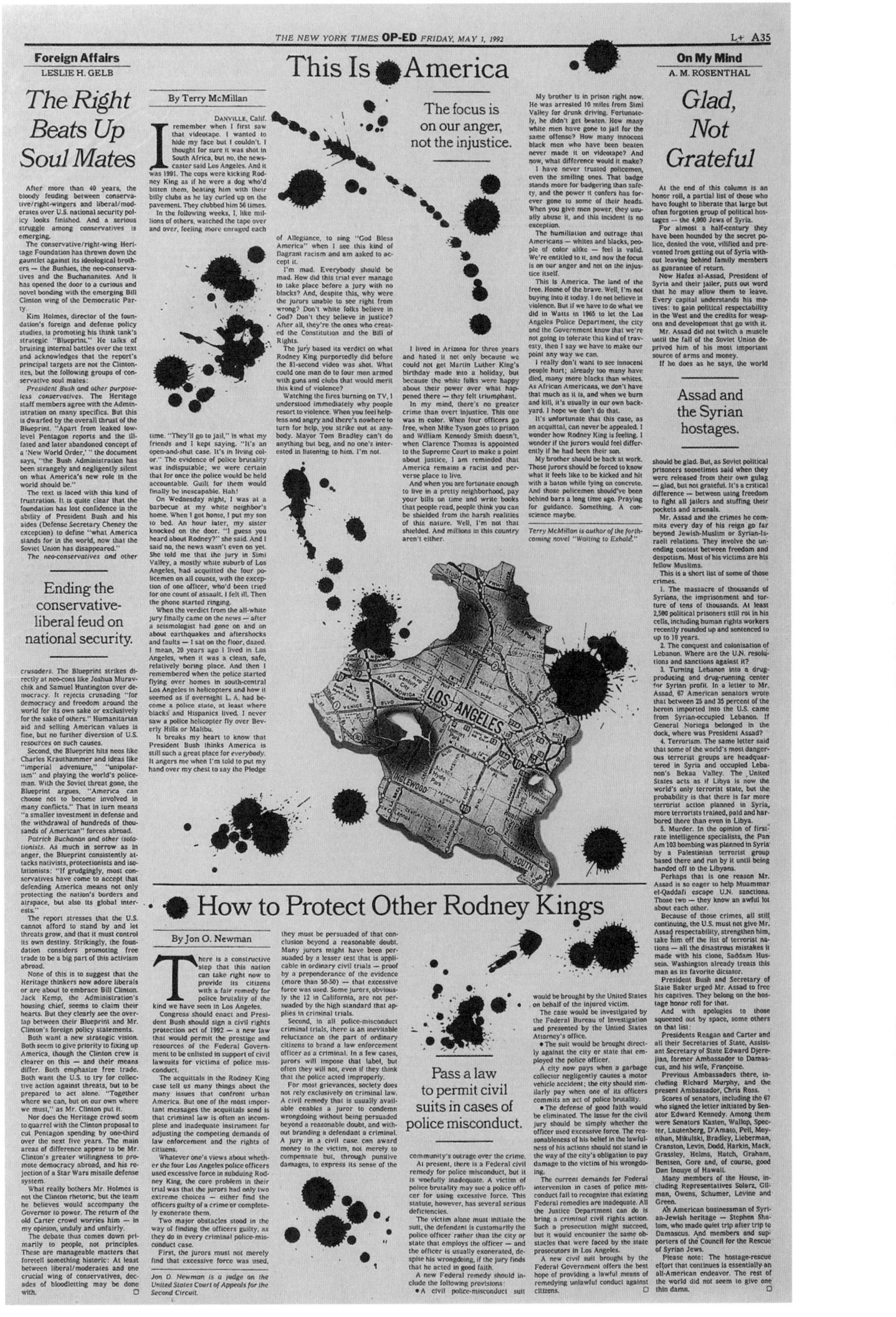

THE NEW YORK TIMES **OP-ED** FRIDAY, MAY 1, 1992 L+ A35

Foreign Affairs

LESLIE H. GELB

The Right Beats Up Soul Mates

After more than 40 years, the bloody feuding between conservative/right-wingers and liberal/moderates over U.S. national security policy looks finished. And a serious struggle among conservatives is emerging.

The conservative/right-wing Heritage Foundation has thrown down the gauntlet against its ideological brothers — the Bushies, the neo-conservatives and the Buchananites. And it has opened the door to a curious and novel bonding with the emerging Bill Clinton wing of the Democratic Party.

Kim Holmes, director of the foundation's foreign and defense policy studies, is promoting his think tank's strategic "Blueprint." He talks of bruising internal battles over the text and acknowledges that the report's principal targets are not the Clintonites, but the following groups of conservative soul mates:

President Bush and other purposeless conservatives. The Heritage staff members agree with the Administration on many specifics. But this is dwarfed by the overall thrust of the Blueprint. "Apart from leaked low-level Pentagon reports and the ill-fated and later abandoned concept of a 'New World Order,' " the document says, "the Bush Administration has been strangely and negligently silent on what America's new role in the world should be."

The text is laced with this kind of frustration. It is quite clear that the foundation has lost confidence in the ability of President Bush and his aides (Defense Secretary Cheney the exception) to define "what America stands for in the world, now that the Soviet Union has disappeared."

The neo-conservatives and other crusaders. The Blueprint strikes directly at neo-cons like Joshua Muravchik and Samuel Huntington over democracy. It rejects crusading "for democracy and freedom around the world for its own sake or exclusively for the sake of others." Humanitarian aid and selling American values is fine, but no further diversion of U.S. resources on such causes.

Ending the conservative-liberal feud on national security.

Second, the Blueprint hits neos like Charles Krauthammer and ideas like "imperial adventure," "unipolarism" and playing the world's policeman. With the Soviet threat gone, the Blueprint argues, "America can choose not to become involved in many conflicts." That in turn means "a smaller investment in defense and the withdrawal of hundreds of thousands of American" forces abroad.

Patrick Buchanan and other isolationists. As much in sorrow as in anger, the Blueprint consistently attacks nativists, protectionists and isolationists: "If grudgingly, most conservatives have come to accept that defending America means not only protecting the nation's borders and airspace, but also its global interests."

The report stresses that the U.S. cannot afford to stand by and let threats grow, and that it must control its own destiny. Strikingly, the foundation considers promoting free trade to be a big part of this activism abroad.

None of this is to suggest that the Heritage thinkers now adore liberals or are about to embrace Bill Clinton. Jack Kemp, the Administration's housing chief, seems to claim their hearts. But they clearly see the overlap between their Blueprint and Mr. Clinton's foreign policy statements.

Both want a new strategic vision. Both seem to give priority to fixing up America, though the Clinton crew is clearer on this — and their means differ. Both emphasize free trade. Both want the U.S. to try for collective action against threats, but to be prepared to act alone. "Together where we can, but on our own where we must," as Mr. Clinton put it.

Nor does the Heritage crowd seem to quarrel with the Clinton proposal to cut Pentagon spending by one-third over the next five years. The main areas of difference appear to be Mr. Clinton's greater willingness to promote democracy abroad, and his rejection of a Star Wars missile defense system.

What really bothers Mr. Holmes is not the Clinton rhetoric, but the team he believes would accompany the Governor to power. The return of the old Carter crowd worries him — in my opinion, unduly and unfairly.

The debate thus comes down primarily to people, not principles. These are manageable matters that foretell something historic: At least between liberal/moderates and one crucial wing of conservatives, decades of bloodletting may be done with. □

This Is America

By Terry McMillan

The focus is on our anger, not the injustice.

DANVILLE, Calif.

I remember when I first saw that videotape. I wanted to hide my face but I couldn't. I thought for sure it was shot in South Africa, but no, the newscaster said Los Angeles. And it was 1991. The cops were kicking Rodney King as if he were a dog who'd bitten them, beating him with their billy clubs as he lay curled up on the pavement. They clubbed him 56 times.

In the following weeks, I, like millions of others, watched the tape over and over, feeling more enraged each time. "They'll go to jail," is what my friends and I kept saying. "It's an open-and-shut case. It's in living color." The evidence of police brutality was indisputable; we were certain that for once the police would be held accountable. Guilt for them would finally be inescapable. Hah!

On Wednesday night, I was at a barbecue at my white neighbor's home. When I got home, I put my son to bed. An hour later, my sister knocked on the door. "I guess you heard about Rodney?" she said. And I said no, the news wasn't even on yet. She told me that the jury in Simi Valley, a mostly white suburb of Los Angeles, had acquitted the four policemen on all counts, with the exception of one officer, who'd been tried for one count of assault. I felt ill. Then the phone started ringing.

When the verdict from the all-white jury finally came on the news — after a seismologist had gone on and on about earthquakes and aftershocks and faults — I sat on the floor, dazed. I mean, 20 years ago I lived in Los Angeles, when it was a clean, safe, relatively boring place. And then I remembered when the police started flying over homes in south-central Los Angeles in helicopters and how it seemed as if overnight L. A. had become a police state, at least where blacks and Hispanics lived. I never saw a police helicopter fly over Beverly Hills or Malibu.

It breaks my heart to know that President Bush thinks America is still such a great place for *everybody.* It angers me when I'm told to put my hand over my chest to say the Pledge of Allegiance, to sing "God Bless America" when I see this kind of flagrant racism and am asked to accept it.

I'm mad. Everybody should be mad. How did this trial ever manage to take place before a jury with no blacks? And, despite this, why were the jurors unable to see right from wrong? Don't white folks believe in God? Don't they believe in justice? After all, they're the ones who created the Constitution and the Bill of Rights.

The jury based its verdict on what Rodney King purportedly did before the 81-second video was shot. What could one man do to four men armed with guns and clubs that would merit this kind of violence?

Watching the fires burning on TV, I understood immediately why people resort to violence. When you feel helpless and angry and there's nowhere to turn for help, you strike out at anybody. Mayor Tom Bradley can't do anything but beg, and no one's interested in listening to him. I'm not.

I lived in Arizona for three years and hated it not only because we could not get Martin Luther King's birthday made into a holiday, but because the white folks were happy about their power over what happened there — they felt triumphant.

In my mind, there's no greater crime than overt injustice. This one was in color. When four officers go free, when Mike Tyson goes to prison and William Kennedy Smith doesn't, when Clarence Thomas is appointed to the Supreme Court to make a point about justice, I am reminded that America remains a racist and perverse place to live.

And when you are fortunate enough to live in a pretty neighborhood, pay your bills on time and write books that people read, people think you can be shielded from the harsh realities of this nature. Well, I'm not that shielded. And millions in this country aren't either.

My brother is in prison right now. He was arrested 10 miles from Simi Valley for drunk driving. Fortunately, he didn't get beaten. How many white men have gone to jail for the same offense? How many innocent black men who have been beaten never made it on videotape? And now, what difference would it make?

I have never trusted policemen, even the smiling ones. That badge stands more for badgering than safety, and the power it confers has forever gone to some of their heads. When you give men power, they usually abuse it, and this incident is no exception.

The humiliation and outrage that Americans — whites and blacks, people of color alike — feel is valid. We're entitled to it, and now the focus is on our anger and not on the injustice itself.

This is America. The land of the free. Home of the brave. Well, I'm not buying into it today. I do not believe in violence. But if we have to do what we did in Watts in 1965 to let the Los Angeles Police Department, the city and the Government know that we're not going to tolerate this kind of travesty, then I say we have to make our point any way we can.

I really don't want to see innocent people hurt; already too many have died, many more blacks than whites. As African Americans, we don't have that much as it is, and when we burn and kill, it's usually in our own backyard. I hope we don't do that.

It's unfortunate that this case, as an acquittal, can never be appealed. I wonder how Rodney King is feeling. I wonder if the jurors would feel differently if he had been their son.

My brother should be back at work. Those jurors should be forced to know what it feels like to be kicked and hit with a baton while lying on concrete. And those policemen should've been behind bars a long time ago. Praying for guidance. Something. A conscience maybe.

Terry McMillan is author of the forthcoming novel "Waiting to Exhale."

How to Protect Other Rodney Kings

By Jon O. Newman

Pass a law to permit civil suits in cases of police misconduct.

There is a constructive step that this nation can take right now to provide its citizens with a fair remedy for police brutality of the kind we have seen in Los Angeles.

Congress should enact and President Bush should sign a civil rights protection act of 1992 — a new law that would permit the prestige and resources of the Federal Government to be enlisted in support of civil lawsuits for victims of police misconduct.

The acquittals in the Rodney King case tell us many things about the many issues that confront urban America. But one of the most important messages the acquittals send is that criminal law is often an incomplete and inadequate instrument for adjusting the competing demands of law enforcement and the rights of citizens.

Whatever one's views about whether the four Los Angeles police officers used excessive force in subduing Rodney King, the core problem in their trial was that the jurors had only two extreme choices — either find the officers guilty of a crime or completely exonerate them.

Two major obstacles stood in the way of finding the officers guilty, as they do in every criminal police-misconduct case.

First, the jurors must not merely find that excessive force was used, they must be persuaded of that conclusion beyond a reasonable doubt. Many jurors might have been persuaded by a lesser test that is applicable in ordinary civil trials — proof by a preponderance of the evidence (more than 50-50) — that excessive force was used. Some jurors, obviously the 12 in California, are not persuaded by the high standard that applies in criminal trials.

Second, in all police-misconduct criminal trials, there is an inevitable reluctance on the part of ordinary citizens to brand a law enforcement officer as a criminal. In a few cases, jurors will impose that label, but often they will not, even if they think that the police acted improperly.

For most grievances, society does not rely exclusively on criminal law. A civil remedy that is usually available enables a juror to condemn wrongdoing without being persuaded beyond a reasonable doubt, and without branding a defendant a criminal. A jury in a civil case can award money to the victim, not merely to compensate but, through punitive damages, to express its sense of the community's outrage over the crime.

At present, there is a Federal civil remedy for police misconduct, but it is woefully inadequate. A victim of police brutality may sue a police officer for using excessive force. This statute, however, has several serious deficiencies.

The victim alone must initiate the suit, the defendant is customarily the police officer rather than the city or state that employs the officer — and the officer is usually exonerated, despite his wrongdoing, if the jury finds that he acted in good faith.

A new Federal remedy should include the following provisions:

- A civil police-misconduct suit would be brought by the United States on behalf of the injured victim.

The case would be investigated by the Federal Bureau of Investigation and presented by the United States Attorney's office.

- The suit would be brought directly against the city or state that employed the police officer.

A city now pays when a garbage collector negligently causes a motor vehicle accident; the city should similarly pay when one of its officers commits an act of police brutality.

- The defense of good faith would be eliminated. The issue for the civil jury should be simply whether the officer used excessive force. The reasonableness of his belief in the lawfulness of his actions should not stand in the way of the city's obligation to pay damage to the victim of his wrongdoing.

The current demands for Federal intervention in cases of police misconduct fail to recognize that existing Federal remedies are inadequate. All the Justice Department can do is bring a *criminal* civil rights action. Such a prosecution might succeed, but it would encounter the same obstacles that were faced by the state prosecutors in Los Angeles.

A new *civil* suit brought by the Federal Government offers the best hope of providing a lawful means of remedying unlawful conduct against citizens. □

Jon O. Newman is a judge on the United States Court of Appeals for the Second Circuit.

On My Mind

A. M. ROSENTHAL

Glad, Not Grateful

At the end of this column is an honor roll, a partial list of those who have fought to liberate that large but often forgotten group of political hostages — the 4,000 Jews of Syria.

For almost a half-century they have been hounded by the secret police, denied the vote, vilified and prevented from getting out of Syria without leaving behind family members as guarantee of return.

Now Hafez al-Assad, President of Syria and their jailer, puts out word that he may allow them to leave. Every capital understands his motives: to gain political respectability in the West and the credits for weapons and development that go with it.

Mr. Assad did not twitch a muscle until the fall of the Soviet Union deprived him of his most important source of arms and money.

Assad and the Syrian hostages.

If he does as he says, the world should be glad. But, as Soviet political prisoners sometimes said when they were released from their own gulag — glad, but not grateful. It's a critical difference — between using freedom to fight all jailers and stuffing their pockets and arsenals.

Mr. Assad and the crimes he commits every day of his reign go far beyond Jewish-Muslim or Syrian-Israeli relations. They involve the unending contest between freedom and despotism. Most of his victims are his fellow Muslims.

This is a short list of some of those crimes.

1. The massacre of thousands of Syrians, the imprisonment and torture of tens of thousands. At least 2,500 political prisoners still rot in his cells, including human rights workers recently rounded up and sentenced to up to 10 years.

2. The conquest and colonization of Lebanon. Where are the U.N. resolutions and sanctions against it?

3. Turning Lebanon into a drug-producing and drug-running center for Syrian profit. In a letter to Mr. Assad, 67 American senators wrote that between 25 and 35 percent of the heroin imported into the U.S. came from Syrian-occupied Lebanon. If General Noriega belonged in the dock, where was President Assad?

4. Terrorism. The same letter said that some of the world's most dangerous terrorist groups are headquartered in Syria and occupied Lebanon's Bekaa Valley. The United States acts as if Libya is now the world's only terrorist state, but the probability is that there is far more terrorist action planned in Syria, more terrorists trained, paid and harbored there than even in Libya.

5. Murder. In the opinion of first-rate intelligence specialists, the Pan Am 103 bombing was planned in Syria by a Palestinian terrorist group based there and run by it until being handed off to the Libyans.

Perhaps that is one reason Mr. Assad is so eager to help Muammar el-Qaddafi escape U.N. sanctions. Those two — they know an awful lot about each other.

Because of those crimes, all still continuing, the U.S. must not give Mr. Assad respectability, strengthen him, take him off the list of terrorist nations — all the disastrous mistakes it made with his clone, Saddam Hussein. Washington already treats this man as its favorite dictator.

President Bush and Secretary of State Baker urged Mr. Assad to free his captives. They belong on the hostage honor roll for that.

And with apologies to those squeezed out by space, some others on that list:

Presidents Reagan and Carter and all their Secretaries of State, Assistant Secretary of State Edward Djerejian, former Ambassador to Damascus, and his wife, Françoise.

Previous Ambassadors there, including Richard Murphy, and the present Ambassador, Chris Ross.

Scores of senators, including the 67 who signed the letter initiated by Senator Edward Kennedy. Among them were Senators Kasten, Wallop, Specter, Lautenberg, D'Amato, Pell, Moynihan, Mikulski, Bradley, Lieberman, Cranston, Levin, Dodd, Harkin, Mack, Grassley, Helms, Hatch, Graham, Bentsen, Gore and, of course, good Dan Inouye of Hawaii.

Many members of the House, including Representatives Solarz, Gilman, Owens, Schumer, Levine and Green.

An American businessman of Syrian-Jewish heritage — Stephen Shalom, who made quiet trip after trip to Damascus. And members and supporters of the Council for the Rescue of Syrian Jews.

Please note: The hostage-rescue effort that continues is essentially an all-American endeavor. The rest of the world did not seem to give one thin damn. □

This Is America, *The New York Times* Op-Ed, May 1, 1992

AD & D & ILLUSTRATION: Mirko Ilić

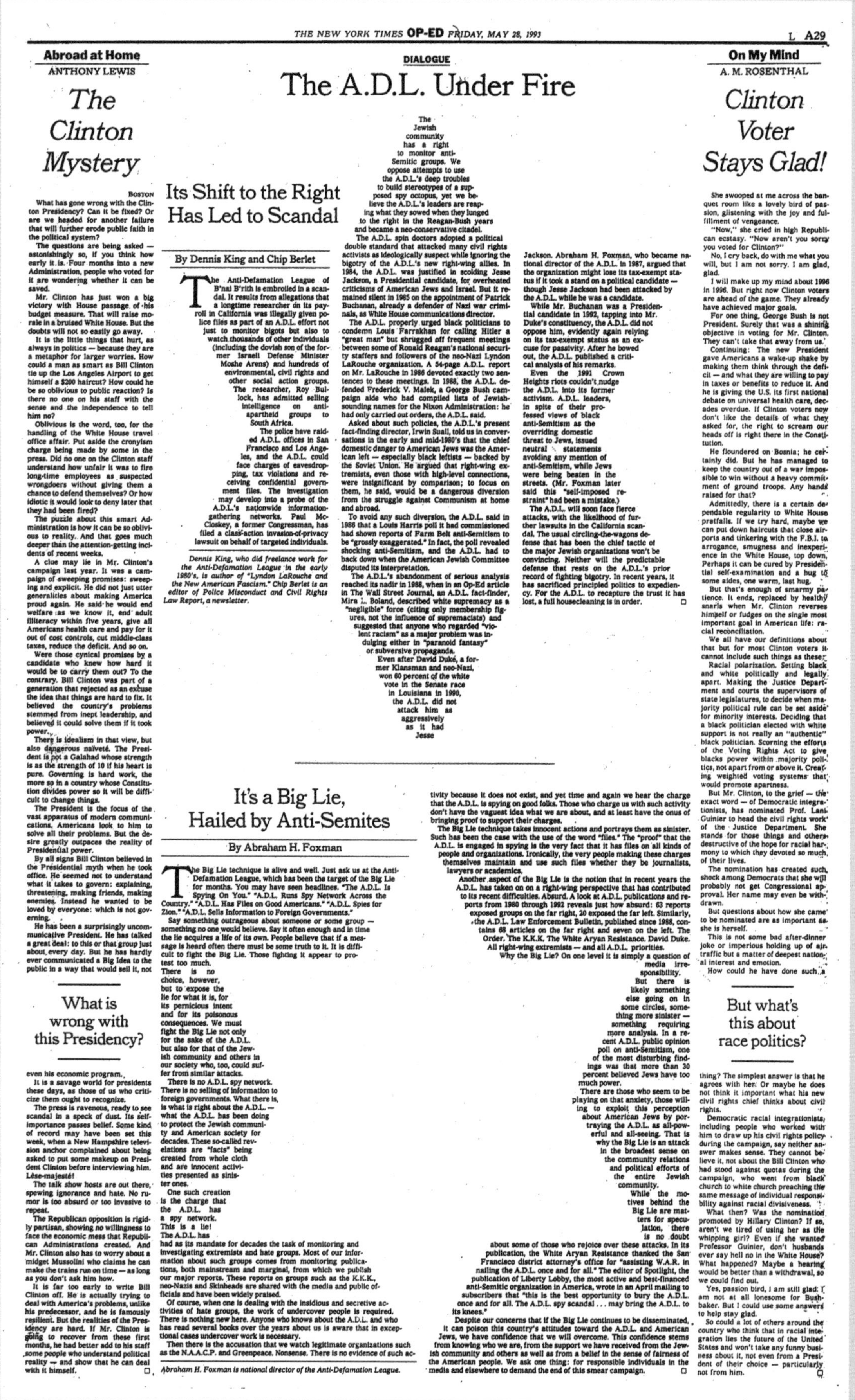

THE NEW YORK TIMES **OP-ED** FRIDAY, MAY 28, 1993 — L A29

Abroad at Home

ANTHONY LEWIS

The Clinton Mystery

BOSTON

What has gone wrong with the Clinton Presidency? Can it be fixed? Or are we headed for another failure that will further erode public faith in the political system?

The questions are being asked — astonishingly so, if you think how early it is. Four months into a new Administration, people who voted for it are wondering whether it can be saved.

Mr. Clinton has just won a big victory with House passage of his budget measure. That will raise morale in a bruised White House. But the doubts will not so easily go away.

It is the little things that hurt, as always in politics — because they are a metaphor for larger worries. How could a man as smart as Bill Clinton tie up the Los Angeles Airport to get himself a $200 haircut? How could he be so oblivious to public reaction? Is there no one on his staff with the sense and the independence to tell him no?

Oblivious is the word, too, for the handling of the White House travel office affair. Put aside the cronyism charge being made by some in the press. Did no one on the Clinton staff understand how unfair it was to fire long-time employees as suspected wrongdoers without giving them a chance to defend themselves? Or how idiotic it would look to deny later that they had been fired?

The puzzle about this smart Administration is how it can be so oblivious to reality. And that goes much deeper than the attention-getting incidents of recent weeks.

A clue may lie in Mr. Clinton's campaign last year. It was a campaign of sweeping promises: sweeping and explicit. He did not just utter generalities about making America proud again. He said he would end welfare as we know it, end adult illiteracy within five years, give all Americans health care and pay for it out of cost controls, cut middle-class taxes, reduce the deficit. And so on.

Were those cynical promises by a candidate who knew how hard it would be to carry them out? To the contrary. Bill Clinton was part of a generation that rejected as an excuse the idea that things are hard to fix. It believed the country's problems stemmed from inept leadership, and believed it could solve them if it took power.

There is idealism in that view, but also dangerous naïveté. The President is not a Galahad whose strength is as the strength of 10 if his heart is pure. Governing is hard work, the more so in a country whose Constitution divides power so it will be difficult to change things.

The President is the focus of the vast apparatus of modern communications. Americans look to him to solve all their problems. But the desire greatly outpaces the reality of Presidential power.

By all signs Bill Clinton believed in the Presidential myth when he took office. He seemed not to understand what it takes to govern: explaining, threatening, making friends, making enemies. Instead he wanted to be loved by everyone: which is not governing.

He has been a surprisingly uncommunicative President. He has talked a great deal: to this or that group just about every day. But he has hardly ever communicated a Big Idea to the public in a way that would sell it, not

What is wrong with this Presidency?

even his economic program.

It is a savage world for presidents these days, as those of us who criticize them ought to recognize.

The press is ravenous, ready to see scandal in a speck of dust. Its self-importance passes belief. Some kind of record may have been set this week, when a New Hampshire television anchor complained about being asked to put some makeup on President Clinton before interviewing him. Lèse-majesté!

The talk show hosts are out there, spewing ignorance and hate. No rumor is too absurd or too invasive to repeat.

The Republican opposition is rigidly partisan, showing no willingness to face the economic mess that Republican Administrations created. And Mr. Clinton also has to worry about a midget Mussolini who claims he can make the trains run on time — as long as you don't ask him how.

It is far too early to write Bill Clinton off. He is actually trying to deal with America's problems, unlike his predecessor, and he is famously resilient. But the realities of the Presidency are hard. If Mr. Clinton is going to recover from these first months, he had better add to his staff some people who understand political reality — and show that he can deal with it himself. □

DIALOGUE

The A.D.L. Under Fire

The Jewish community has a right to monitor anti-Semitic groups. We oppose attempts to use the A.D.L.'s deep troubles to build stereotypes of a supposed spy octopus, yet we believe the A.D.L.'s leaders are reaping what they sowed when they lunged to the right in the Reagan-Bush years and became a neo-conservative citadel.

Its Shift to the Right Has Led to Scandal

By Dennis King and Chip Berlet

The Anti-Defamation League of B'nai B'rith is embroiled in a scandal. It results from allegations that a longtime researcher on its payroll in California was illegally given police files as part of an A.D.L. effort not just to monitor bigots but also to watch thousands of other individuals (including the dovish son of the former Israeli Defense Minister Moshe Arens) and hundreds of environmental, civil rights and other social action groups. The researcher, Roy Bullock, has admitted selling intelligence on anti-apartheid groups to South Africa.

The police have raided A.D.L. offices in San Francisco and Los Angeles, and the A.D.L. could face charges of eavesdropping, tax violations and receiving confidential government files. The investigation may develop into a probe of the A.D.L.'s nationwide information-gathering networks. Paul McCloskey, a former Congressman, has filed a class-action invasion-of-privacy lawsuit on behalf of targeted individuals.

Dennis King, who did freelance work for the Anti-Defamation League in the early 1980's, is author of "Lyndon LaRouche and the New American Fascism." Chip Berlet is an editor of Police Misconduct and Civil Rights Law Report, a newsletter.

The A.D.L. spin doctors adopted a political double standard that attacked many civil rights activists as ideologically suspect while ignoring the bigotry of the A.D.L.'s new right-wing allies. In 1984, the A.D.L. was justified in scolding Jesse Jackson, a Presidential candidate, for overheated criticisms of American Jews and Israel. But it remained silent in 1985 on the appointment of Patrick Buchanan, already a defender of Nazi war criminals, as White House communications director.

The A.D.L. properly urged black politicians to condemn Louis Farrakhan for calling Hitler a "great man" but shrugged off frequent meetings between some of Ronald Reagan's national security staffers and followers of the neo-Nazi Lyndon LaRouche organization. A 54-page A.D.L. report on Mr. LaRouche in 1986 devoted exactly two sentences to these meetings. In 1988, the A.D.L. defended Frederick V. Malek, a George Bush campaign aide who had compiled lists of Jewish-sounding names for the Nixon Administration: he had only carried out orders, the A.D.L. said.

Asked about such policies, the A.D.L.'s present fact-finding director, Irwin Suall, told us in conversations in the early and mid-1980's that the chief domestic danger to American Jews was the American left — especially black leftists — backed by the Soviet Union. He argued that right-wing extremists, even those with high-level connections, were insignificant by comparison; to focus on them, he said, would be a dangerous diversion from the struggle against Communism at home and abroad.

To avoid any such diversion, the A.D.L. said in 1986 that a Louis Harris poll it had commissioned had shown reports of Farm Belt anti-Semitism to be "grossly exaggerated." In fact, the poll revealed shocking anti-Semitism, and the A.D.L. had to back down when the American Jewish Committee disputed its interpretation.

The A.D.L.'s abandonment of serious analysis reached its nadir in 1988, when in an Op-Ed article in The Wall Street Journal, an A.D.L. fact-finder, Mira L. Boland, described white supremacy as a "negligible" force (citing only membership figures, not the influence of supremacists) and suggested that anyone who regarded "violent racism" as a major problem was indulging either in "paranoid fantasy" or subversive propaganda.

Even after David Duke, a former Klansman and neo-Nazi, won 60 percent of the white vote in the Senate race in Louisiana in 1990, the A.D.L. did not attack him as aggressively as it had Jesse Jackson. Abraham H. Foxman, who became national director of the A.D.L. in 1987, argued that the organization might lose its tax-exempt status if it took a stand on a political candidate — though Jesse Jackson had been attacked by the A.D.L. while he was a candidate.

While Mr. Buchanan was a Presidential candidate in 1992, tapping into Mr. Duke's constituency, the A.D.L. did not oppose him, evidently again relying on its tax-exempt status as an excuse for passivity. After he bowed out, the A.D.L. published a critical analysis of his remarks.

Even the 1991 Crown Heights riots couldn't nudge the A.D.L. into its former activism. A.D.L. leaders, in spite of their professed views of black anti-Semitism as the overriding domestic threat to Jews, issued neutral statements avoiding any mention of anti-Semitism, while Jews were being beaten in the streets. (Mr. Foxman later said this "self-imposed restraint" had been a mistake.)

The A.D.L. will soon face fierce attacks, with the likelihood of further lawsuits in the California scandal. The usual circling-the-wagons defense that has been the chief tactic of the major Jewish organizations won't be convincing. Neither will the predictable defense that rests on the A.D.L.'s prior record of fighting bigotry. In recent years, it has sacrificed principled politics to expediency. For the A.D.L. to recapture the trust it has lost, a full housecleaning is in order. □

It's a Big Lie, Hailed by Anti-Semites

By Abraham H. Foxman

The Big Lie technique is alive and well. Just ask us at the Anti-Defamation League, which has been the target of the Big Lie for months. You may have seen headlines. "The A.D.L. Is Spying On You." "A.D.L. Runs Spy Network Across the Country." "A.D.L. Has Files on Good Americans." "A.D.L. Spies for Zion." "A.D.L. Sells Information to Foreign Governments."

Say something outrageous about someone or some group — something no one would believe. Say it often enough and in time the lie acquires a life of its own. People believe that if a message is heard often there must be some truth to it. It is difficult to fight the Big Lie. Those fighting it appear to protest too much.

There is no choice, however, but to expose the lie for what it is, for its pernicious intent and for its poisonous consequences. We must fight the Big Lie not only for the sake of the A.D.L. but also for that of the Jewish community and others in our society who, too, could suffer from similar attacks.

There is no A.D.L. spy network. There is no selling of information to foreign governments. What there is, is what is right about the A.D.L. — what the A.D.L. has been doing to protect the Jewish community and American society for decades. These so-called revelations are "facts" being created from whole cloth and are innocent activities presented as sinister ones.

One such creation is the charge that the A.D.L. has a spy network. This is a lie! The A.D.L. has had as its mandate for decades the task of monitoring and investigating extremists and hate groups. Most of our information about such groups comes from monitoring publications, both mainstream and marginal, from which we publish our major reports. These reports on groups such as the K.K.K., neo-Nazis and Skinheads are shared with the media and public officials and have been widely praised.

Of course, when one is dealing with the insidious and secretive activities of hate groups, the work of undercover people is required. There is nothing new here. Anyone who knows about the A.D.L. and who has read several books over the years about us is aware that in exceptional cases undercover work is necessary.

Then there is the accusation that we watch legitimate organizations such as the N.A.A.C.P. and Greenpeace. Nonsense. There is no evidence of such activity because it does not exist, and yet time and again we hear the charge that the A.D.L. is spying on good folks. Those who charge us with such activity don't have the vaguest idea what we are about, and at least have the onus of bringing proof to support their charges.

The Big Lie technique takes innocent actions and portrays them as sinister. Such has been the case with the use of the word "files." The "proof" that the A.D.L. is engaged in spying is the very fact that it has files on all kinds of people and organizations. Ironically, the very people making these charges themselves maintain and use such files whether they be journalists, lawyers or academics.

Another aspect of the Big Lie is the notion that in recent years the A.D.L. has taken on on a right-wing perspective that has contributed to its recent difficulties. Absurd. A look at A.D.L. publications and reports from 1980 through 1992 reveals just how absurd: 63 reports exposed groups on the far right, 20 exposed the far left. Similarly, the A.D.L. Law Enforcement Bulletin, published since 1988, contains 68 articles on the far right and seven on the left. The Order. The K.K.K. The White Aryan Resistance. David Duke. All right-wing extremists — and all A.D.L. priorities.

Why the Big Lie? On one level it is simply a question of media irresponsibility.

But there is likely something else going on in some circles, something more sinister — something requiring more analysis. In a recent A.D.L. public opinion poll on anti-Semitism, one of the most disturbing findings was that more than 30 percent believed Jews have too much power.

There are those who seem to be playing on that anxiety, those willing to exploit this perception about American Jews by portraying the A.D.L. as all-powerful and all-seeing. That is why the Big Lie is an attack in the broadest sense on the community relations and political efforts of the entire Jewish community.

While the motives behind the Big Lie are matters for speculation, there is no doubt about some of those who rejoice over these attacks. In its publication, the White Aryan Resistance thanked the San Francisco district attorney's office for "assisting W.A.R. in nailing the A.D.L. once and for all." The editor of Spotlight, the publication of Liberty Lobby, the most active and best-financed anti-Semitic organization in America, wrote in an April mailing to subscribers that "this is the best opportunity to bury the A.D.L. once and for all. The A.D.L. spy scandal . . . may bring the A.D.L. to its knees."

Despite our concerns that if the Big Lie continues to be disseminated, it can poison this country's attitudes toward the A.D.L. and American Jews, we have confidence that we will overcome. This confidence stems from knowing who we are, from the support we have received from the Jewish community and others as well as from a belief in the sense of fairness of the American people. We ask one thing: for responsible individuals in the media and elsewhere to demand the end of this smear campaign. □

Abraham H. Foxman is national director of the Anti-Defamation League.

On My Mind

A. M. ROSENTHAL

Clinton Voter Stays Glad!

She swooped at me across the banquet room like a lovely bird of passion, glistening with the joy and fulfillment of vengeance.

"Now," she cried in high Republican ecstasy. "Now aren't you sorry you voted for Clinton?"

No, I cry back, do with me what you will, but I am not sorry. I am glad, glad.

I will make up my mind about 1996 in 1996. But right now Clinton voters are ahead of the game. They already have achieved major goals.

For one thing, George Bush is not President. Surely that was a shining objective in voting for Mr. Clinton. They can't take that away from us.

Continuing: The new President gave Americans a wake-up shake by making them think through the deficit — and what they are willing to pay in taxes or benefits to reduce it. And he is giving the U.S. its first national debate on universal health care, decades overdue. If Clinton voters now don't like the details of what they asked for, the right to scream our heads off is right there in the Constitution.

He floundered on Bosnia; he certainly did. But he has managed to keep the country out of a war impossible to win without a heavy commitment of ground troops. Any hands raised for that?

Admittedly, there is a certain dependable regularity to White House pratfalls. If we try hard, maybe we can put down haircuts that close airports and tinkering with the F.B.I. to arrogance, smugness and inexperience in the White House, top down. Perhaps it can be cured by Presidential self-examination and a hug to some aides, one warm, last hug.

But that's enough of smarmy patience. It ends, replaced by healthy snarls when Mr. Clinton reverses himself or fudges on the single most important goal in American life: racial reconciliation.

We all have our definitions about that but for most Clinton voters it cannot include such things as these:

Racial polarization. Setting black and white politically and legally apart. Making the Justice Department and courts the supervisors of state legislatures, to decide when majority political rule can be set aside for minority interests. Deciding that a black politician elected with white support is not really an "authentic" black politician. Scorning the efforts of the Voting Rights Act to give blacks power within majority politics, not apart from or above it. Creating weighted voting systems that would promote apartness.

But Mr. Clinton, to the grief — the exact word — of Democratic integrationists, has nominated Prof. Lani Guinier to head the civil rights work of the Justice Department. She stands for those things and others destructive of the hope for racial harmony to which they devoted so much of their lives.

The nomination has created such shock among Democrats that she will probably not get Congressional approval. Her name may even be withdrawn.

But questions about how she came to be nominated are as important as she is herself.

This is not some bad after-dinner joke or imperious holding up of air traffic but a matter of deepest national interest and emotion.

How could he have done such a

But what's this about race politics?

thing? The simplest answer is that he agrees with her. Or maybe he does not think it important what his new civil rights chief thinks about civil rights.

Democratic racial integrationists, including people who worked with him to draw up his civil rights policy during the campaign, say neither answer makes sense. They cannot believe it, not about the Bill Clinton who had stood against quotas during the campaign, who went from black church to white church preaching the same message of individual responsibility against racial divisiveness.

What then? Was the nomination promoted by Hillary Clinton? If so, aren't we tired of using her as the whipping girl? Even if she wanted Professor Guinier, don't husbands ever say hell no in the White House? What happened? Maybe a hearing would be better than a withdrawal, so we could find out.

Yes, passion bird, I am still glad. I am not at all lonesome for Bushbaker. But I could use some answers to help stay glad.

So could a lot of others around the country who think that in racial integration lies the future of the United States and won't take any funny business about it, not even from a President of their choice — particularly not from him. □

The A.D.L. Under Fire, *The New York Times* Op-Ed, May 28, 1993

Observer

RUSSELL BAKER

Joining Up For Glory

Here is another country-club problem. They are always the same. Someone political is found to be a member of or to have played golf at a racially segregated country club. After the discovery, the fat is in the fire, as we used to say back when we still had clichés fit for children's ears.

This week's case involves Webster L. Hubbell, a Little Rock lawyer nominated to become Associate Attorney General. The usual minuet is now in progress.

Hubbell, who joined the club in the mid-1980's, is said to have worked to get blacks admitted to membership. If so, says the chairman of the Arkansas Legislature's black caucus, Hubbell never asked any of the caucus's 13 members to recommend candidates for admission.

And so on.

Joining country clubs, segregated or not, has always seemed foolish to me, but so does the game of golf, which is closely associated with country clubs, and I know a few sensible people for whom life without golf would not be worth living.

For this reason I always refuse to picket the Capitol demanding the abolition of country clubs. "Let a thousand bizarre tastes flourish," as Chairman Mao should have said.

What is baffling, however, is why segregation is necessary to country-club culture. The aim of segregation is to put distance between yourself and people who are unworthy to enjoy the splendor of your company. This is precisely what a golf course affords: plenty of distance between the parties.

True, a golfer with keen vision may identify a player as black even from a distance of 100 yards, but at basketball, baseball and football games white people are positioned much closer than that to blacks playing games, yet do not seem affronted by the sight.

Since country-club members can't possibly need the segregation for their golf, other explanations must be sought. My knowledge of country clubs comes entirely from John O'Hara's "Appointment in Samarra." It is about an unpleasant group of people, all of them white, who spend most of their time getting drunk and insulting each other at dance parties at a country club.

Reading this book at an impressionable age probably warped my view of country clubs, but to this day I cleave to my youthful suspicion of country clubs as places full of ill-mannered clods who drink to excess and are liable to insult people whose fox trot is the least bit presumptuous.

I am sure Webster Hubbell's coun-

> Here is another country-club problem.

try club is not like that at all. The papers say the initiation fee is $25,000. For that kind of money, even a lawyer is surely entitled to a little respect from the other members.

Groucho Marx's refusal to pay good money to belong to a club that lets in "people like me" really goes to the heart of the matter. Groucho may have been able to see through the fraud of clubby exclusivity, but most of us do not see so clearly. The appeal of being accepted into exclusive clubs lies, just as Groucho saw, in the absurd suggestion that you are not just another person like you, but somebody fancier.

I speak from experience, having yielded many years ago to the urge to move up several floors above myself by joining a campus fraternity. Like all such operations, it excluded practically everybody. Included among the excluded were practically all the people whose company I most enjoyed.

These people were very patient with me. It was right after World War II and most of them were veterans and grown-up and knew that preaching didn't work when a man was determined to make a fool of himself. You let him learn for himself about the folly of taking the country-club route.

I was 21, tuxedoed, kneeling in a candlelit room and listening to ritualistic mumbo-jumbo suitable only for 17-year-olds when the wisdom of Groucho Marx overwhelmed me with a sense of my own silliness. I was engaged in a silly, childish project not to be somebody like me.

Nowadays whenever tempted to sneer at politicians trapped in the country-club problem, I grant them absolution after reflecting what a tough investigator could do with my own past. That fraternity excluded people for their sex, race and religion and once, so help me, debated excluding an otherwise flawlessly orthodox young man because his father did not wear a jacket at the dinner table. □

Campaign Spending: Despised but Addictive

By Peter Kostmayer

WASHINGTON

In 1976, at the age of 29, I ran for an open seat in Congress and was elected. In a crowded five-way Democratic primary, and in a tough general election campaign, I spent a total of $67,000 to win the seat.

In 1980, I lost the seat in the Reagan sweep. My opponent had personal resources to spend on the campaign that I didn't. This was the first time TV was used in a campaign for my Congressional seat. I raised and spent $250,000; he spent twice that. In 1982, I ran again. I decided I would never again be outspent in a campaign. I wasn't.

Television played an even larger role in that campaign. Three of every four of the half-million dollars I raised paid for TV commercials.

Fund-raising became the dominant part of my campaigns — and campaigning came to dominate my life.

I was barely re-elected in 1984; in 1986, I won by a more comfortable margin. The money increased each time. In 1988, while George Bush was defeating Michael Dukakis by 60 percent to 40 percent in my district, I beat a well-known local official 57 percent to 42 percent. In that race, I raised and spent more money than I ever had before, $1.1 million.

The campaign of 1990 was easier, and I spent less money but still more than six times the amount my opponent spent. In 1992, the toughest campaign I ever faced, I raised and spent even more than in 1988, over $1.2 million. I lost.

My story is typical. In 1980, total spending by all candidates for Congress in the general election was $101.5 million. By 1992, that total had grown to $503.9 million. The amount required to run a campaign we routinely describe as obscene.

Obviously, concentrating on raising money has a bad influence. It distracts members of Congress from doing what they're sent to do and forces them to consider how a vote will affect not only their constituents and the country but also their donors.

> Clinton's reforms don't go far enough.

They'll tell you it doesn't, but it does. You don't look a constituent in the eye when the question gets asked. You lower your voice and look away.

If I run again and the law governing campaign financing is not changed, I will propose to my opponent the following: first, no political-action committee money; second, no independent expenditures by outside groups or political parties on behalf of either candidate; third, a maximum contribution from individuals of $100 or perhaps $250; finally, an overall cap on the amount spent.

I'm open to criticism on this plan, since I rejected voluntary spending limits every time I ran because they were then unenforceable.

The latest Clinton Administration proposal does two important things: it sets overall limits and provides free TV and radio time. Here's what's wrong with it: In 1992, a man raised nearly $100,00 for me. Under the current proposal, he could do it again by getting 100 friends to give $1,000 each. That makes voters think he has more influence than they do. They're right. A person who comes to me with an envelope filled with his friends' $1,000 checks has a lot more impact than most other people.

The second flaw in the Clinton proposal is the $200,000 in vouchers which can be used in TV ads. That amount still represents a lot of stupid political commercials — children running through fields and candidates romping with rented dogs.

Scrap the $200,000. Instead, compel radio and TV to give candidates ample free debating time. Real people, real issues, no meadows, no dogs.

When I think of the time I spent raising what I raised — the dinners, receptions, phone calls, visits — it adds up to time wasted. My time and my constituents' time. How stupid!

Members of Congress despise the process but are addicted to it, terrified that change means defeat. They are wrong. Change will place a premium on well-informed candidates. With the time formerly spent on raising money, members could spend some time reading and preparing for debates. The lessening of pressure to raise money could even revive the finest traditions of American political discourse and oratory. □

Peter Kostmayer represented Pennsylvania's Eighth Congressional District for 14 years.

Broadway Book War — A Reader's Guide

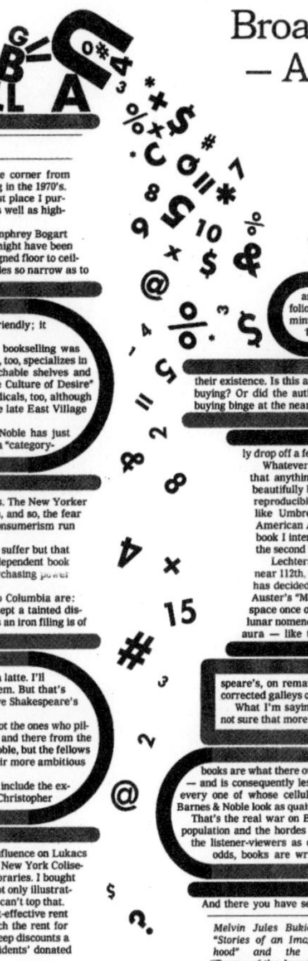

By Melvin Jules Bukiet

The New Yorker Bookstore, on 89th Street around the corner from Broadway, reflected an individual style of book-selling in the 1970's. The ground floor was essentially a newsstand, the first place I purchased the gloriously lubricious East Village Other as well as high-toned works like Paul Krassner's Realist.

Behind the cash register, a rickety staircase led past a poster of Humphrey Bogart holding a gun that seemed to follow customers in a manner that might have been meant to deter shoplifting. At the top, a haphazard collection reigned floor to ceiling in two tiny rooms and in a few alcoves connected by aisles so narrow as to compel one-way traffic. The store was not user-friendly but book-friendly; it died in 1982.

A further step on the evolutionary ladder of Upper West Side bookselling was Shakespeare & Company, at Broadway and 81st, founded in 1981. It, too, specializes in new books, and has wider aisles than the New Yorker did, reachable shelves and posters provided by publishers to advertise their tomes like "The Culture of Desire" that get noticed in this establishment. Shakespeare's stocks periodicals, too, although they are more likely to be the Times Literary Supplement than the late East Village Other.

At the current peak of this great chain of being, a Barnes & Noble has just opened, spanning Broadway from 82d to 83d. Stock analysts call this a "category-killer" — a carnivorous monster that feeds on lesser entities. The New Yorker Bookstore would have been a mere appetizer for this behemoth, and so, the fear is, will Shakespeare's. Hearing cries of unfair competition and consumerism run amok in the hallowed precincts of the text, I wonder.

The helpful flacks at Barnes & Noble say that not only will no one suffer but that their new store will encourage book-buying in the neighborhood. Independent book stores worry that it will drive them under by virtue of superior purchasing power and lower prices.

The questions asked in literary society from Lincoln Center to Columbia are: "Shall I go? Should a moral person drink a cappuccino and accept a tainted discount?" Since I'm as incapable of not entering a bookstore as an iron filing is of eluding an electromagnet, I will go. Guiltless, I may even sip a mocha latte. I'll certainly buy remainders, because Shakespeare's doesn't carry them. But that's avoiding the issue. The more pointed question is whether I will give Shakespeare's $2.12 more than Barnes & Noble charges for "Rameau's Niece."

There is, of course, another option, the street book sellers — not the ones who pilfer from book shops and lift a carton from warehouses and here and there from the trucks delivering merchandise to Shakespeare's and Barnes & Noble, but the fellows with the gray blankets spread with rain-sodden paperbacks or their more ambitious peers with folding tables set up and deconstructed daily.

Most writers prefer little guys to big guns. My favorite vendors include the ex-academic at Columbia's 115th Street gate who will on request whip Christopher Caudwell out from under Truman Capote and discuss his influence on Lukacs as well as the fellow, long since evicted from the sidewalk at the New York Coliseum, who specialized in children's books deaccessioned by public libraries. I bought a broken-spined copy of Robert Graves's "The Green Book" there, not only illustrated but signed by Maurice Sendak. Barnes & Noble's children's corner can't top that.

These new marketeers can compete financially, too. Whatever cost-effective rent Barnes & Noble negotiated for its 32,000 square feet still can't match the rent for nine square feet of sidewalk at 111th and Broadway. And whatever deep discounts a category-killer can demand from publishers still don't match residents' donated duplicate editions of Conrad's "Secret Sharer."

There are three tables staffed by three different homeless men between 72d and 73d Streets, each of which has, in addition to a folio of magazines with titles like Babes in Arms, two mint copies of Eric Van Lustbader's meretricious best-seller "Zero." I won't buy any, but appreciate their existence. Is this an example of collective buying? Or did the author, en route to a CD-buying binge at the nearby HMV, spontaneously drop off a few copies to the less-fortunate?

Whatever the reason, this is precisely the thrill I want — that anything may come my way. I bought, for example, a beautifully bound anthology of selections of The Journal of Irreproducible Results — mock scientific exercises with titles like Umbrella Disappearance, Exchange and Loss Rates in American Academic Libraries. I love the serendipity — not the book I intended to buy but the book I realize I can't live without the second I see it.

Lechters, the houseware chain's emporium on Broadway near 112th, offers idiosyncratic bookselling at its best. The store has decided to stock one novel among its pots and pans: Paul Auster's "Moon Palace." This is because the store inhabits the space once occupied by the Chinese restaurant of that poetic, lunar nomenclature. The dumplings are no longer, but their aura — like that of better books in paper at Shakespeare's, on remainder at Barnes & Noble and in uncorrected galleys on the sidewalk — remains.

What I'm saying about Barnes & Noble is that I'm not sure that more is better. Better is better, and better books are what there ought to be more of. We live in a society that does not read — and is consequently less likely to write — books, at least. Blockbuster Video, every one of whose celluloid products presumably originated in print, makes Barnes & Noble look as quaint as the newsstand entry in the New Yorker Bookshop.

That's the real war on Broadway, between the tattered remnants of a literate population and the hordes of Cynthia Ozick's sadly ascendant "aural culture" — the listener-viewers as opposed to the readers. Nevertheless, and despite the odds, books are written and occasionally published, purchased and read.

And there you have several miracles, first among them the wonder of a three-dimensional volume where black squiggles on white paper create worlds. □

Melvin Jules Bukiet, author of "Stories of an Imaginary Childhood" and the forthcoming "Tongue of the Jews," is fiction editor of Tikkun magazine.

Mirko Ilić

My Hopes, My Fears, My Disease

By Dennis deLeon

For four years, I have been torn about when and how to say publicly that I carry H.I.V., the virus that causes AIDS.

There were always too many compelling reasons not to say anything. Every such excuse started with the word "fear" — fear of employment discrimination, fear of the politics of AIDS, fear of becoming a pariah.

When I contemplated disclosure, I felt that my hope to continue contributing to society as a lawyer and human rights activist was threatened. Would I be evaluated on my merits if I sought to be a judge, a law professor, a law firm member or a governmental appointee?

Mayor David N. Dinkins has known of my H.I.V. for two years and has remained supportive of me and committed to my abilities. But what about my next employer? As Commissioner of Human Rights, I have overseen hundreds of cases in which H.I.V.-positive New Yorkers and their families have been shunned by colleagues and employers. Often, the person is transferred into a meaningless position, passed over for advancement or fired. Such treatment is often made to appear superficially legitimate but is frequently revealed through investigation to be based on discrimination. Why should I put up with this?

Another reason for not discussing my status was the crazy quilt of social activist roles I am given to play as a Latino, a gay man and a person with H.I.V. These are not easy paths to simultaneously follow. New York's Puerto Rican and Latino political agenda has never recognized the needs of the thousands of us who are gay and lesbian.

Conversely, gay and lesbian leaders rarely speak to the needs of the racial and ethnic minorities. A cursory glance at the boards of most gay organizations reveals only token recognition of the city's Latino homosexual presence. The unspoken rule is that you can exist only as one thing at a time — a Latino or a gay man — with no recognition of reality's complexity.

> With each H.I.V. self-disclosure, we fight bigotry.

Add an H.I.V. diagnosis to this mix and it gets complicated. A few Latino leaders seek to portray AIDS organizations as a powerful white presence that takes things away from women, families and racial minorities with H.I.V. These leaders often want to redirect state AIDS funds away from mainstream gay groups to Latino-run organizations with little experience in dealing with gays and lesbians. On the other hand, some gay and lesbian service providers, such as the Gay Men's Health Crisis, have tried to cover all the city's ethnic groups when Latinos may be better served through developing our own H.I.V. service organizations.

I have been concerned about what the words "person with H.I.V." would do to my self-image. But I now know that I will not let a phrase control my potential. If I don't feel sick, why should I tell myself I am? I avoid the crêpe hangers and knowing looks of pity. Why become the prisoner of uninformed beliefs about the productive potential of persons living with H.I.V.?

Given all of these reasons for not being public about the disease, why come out? Why put my professional and economic life in jeopardy? Why subject my partner of 15 years (who is H.I.V. negative) to possible reprisals just for living with me?

The simple answer is hope. If more people proclaim their H.I.V. status, we will change the way society treats persons with the virus. My hope is not based on any expectation that discrimination will end tomorrow but on a sense that it is good to show society that people with H.I.V. are leading productive lives and will tenaciously resist attempts at exclusion.

We need more role models like Thomas K. Duane, the New York City Council member; Ronald Johnson, the Mayor's AIDS services coordinator, and the hundreds of others who have disclosed their H.I.V. status. Every time the public sees one more person with the virus leading a productive life, the possibility of eliminating AIDS-based bigotry becomes more tangible.

Ultimately, the decision to disclose rests with every individual. But it's time for more of us with the virus to begin thinking about crossing the threshold. For me, hope lies on the other side of fear. □

Dennis deLeon is New York City Human Rights Commissioner.

Broadway Book War – A Reader's Guide, *The New York Times* Op-Ed, May 28, 1993

> "I am a designer. I observe how the picture is arranged with the copy and what their relation is. A bad illustrator does not look at the copy at all. Even though the copy is actually the subtext of an illustration, it is the thing existing between her words. Vice versa, the illustration exists in between the lines of the text. The illustration is a separate room for your comment on the topic. You would have to take the liberty of thinking differently from the guy who wrote the text. Illustrations must not be 'illustrative' in terms of if you have a guy with a green tie and black suit—you draw him. No, the illustration must be a supplement to the text."

—MIRKO ILIĆ, "THE ARROGANCE OF THE NEW BEGINNING," *NEDELJNA BORBA*, BELGRADE, MARCH 14–15, 1987

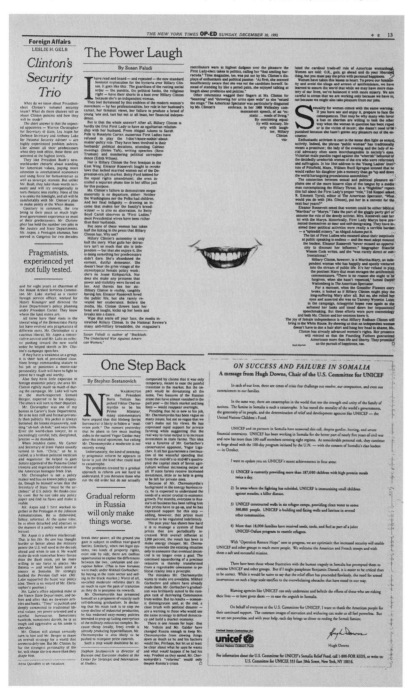

The Power Laugh, *The New York Times* Op-Ed, December 20, 1992, ILLUSTRATION: Ruth Marten, AD & D: Mirko Ilić

The Elements Defy Hungry Zimbabwe, *The New York Times* Op-Ed, August 3, 1992

ILLUSTRATION: Ruth Marten

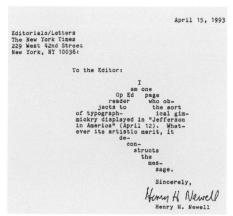

Jefferson Is America –

And America Is Jefferson,

The New York Times

Op-Ed, April 12, 1993

AD & D: Mirko Ilić

A letter from an irate reader dated April 15, 1993,

sent on the occasion of the layout of the page

with a text on Jefferson.

Conservative's Faith, Liberals' Disdain,

The New York Times Op-Ed, August 15, 1993

ILLUSTRATION: Milton Glaser

AD & D: Mirko Ilić

"I love to play with the media, to see what the limits are, and push it as much as I can. Of course the boundaries within *The New York Times* and *Emigre* are two different things, but to move the boundaries within the *Times* means much more than to move them within *Emigre*. Within *Emigre* you can actually do what you want, and in fact as far as wide audience is concerned, you did not do anything since designers are buying *Emigre* and after selling its milder version around. It reaches the general public after a number of transformations. About a year later. If you make a move in *The New York Times*—you will get a response tomorrow! The moves were not that dramatic, but were just as important."

—MIRKO ILIĆ, "DESIGN IS NOT FOREVER," *ARKZIN* NO. 53, ZAGREB, DECEMBER 8, 1995

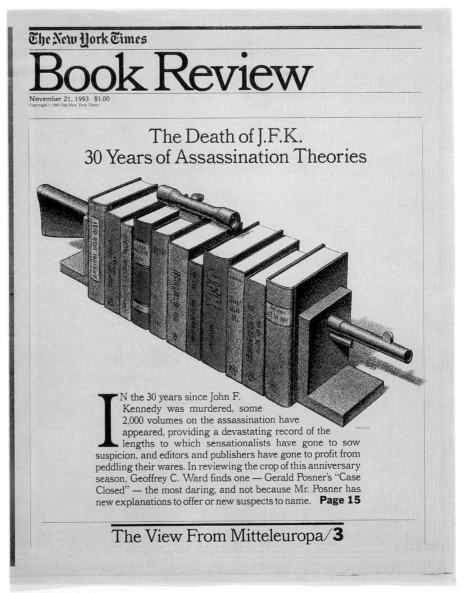

"As for success, all success in the world looks much bigger than here in Croatia. From my perspective in America, I can say that I work hard and that I became successful as a result. Here in Croatia it looks as if someone gave me that success. Most often in Croatia the only success you get is the one that you steal or the one that is given to you by someone else. In America you have to work for success while in Croatia work does guarantee success. My work at *The New York Times*, glorified here in Croatia, is the result of some everyday work, no better or worse in comparison to what I did in *Danas*. If I did the same work for a daily newspaper here, no one would have noticed anything, just the same as designers creating amazing work here before were not noticed."

—MIRKO ILIĆ, "IMMATURE AND INSECURE ARTISTS LOVE TO SNUGGLE NEXT TO THE GOVERNMENT,"

NOVI LIST, MEDITERAN, RIJEKA, JULY 7, 2003

Caustic iconoclast

by **Steven HELLER**

AS A TRADITIONAL ILLUSTRATOR AND DESIGNER, Mirko Ilić routinely seeks out new tools. He once noted, "something new and dramatic only comes along every ten or fifteen years." The Macintosh was one of those revelations, and Ilić bought his first computer in 1990 determined that it would enable him to be a studio and remain an individual.

Mirko Ilić Corp is a studio that makes distinctly individual marks on paper and the screen. But marks are only part of the calculus. Ilić the person creates profound ideas that reduce complexity to accessibility without sacrificing intelligence or wit.

I have worked with him for almost two decades and his mind has contributed incalculable value to the pages that I design and art direct. Indeed there are times when I am so stymied by conceptual roadblocks that the only savior is Ilić. Like a Sherpa guide,[01] he has led me out of a conceptual wilderness. Sure, this may sound like hyperbole, but I assure you that conceiving a visual that speaks the proverbial thousand words—and much more—is not easy, especially when the theme has already been hashed and rehashed in media. Ilić, however, appears to have an endless supply of image/ideas that unlock and comment on issues of import.

Despite his keen ability to save the day, Ilić is not without his share of problems. Perhaps this is endemic to any iconoclast working in a commercial art, but his ideas when powerful are sometimes too powerful for prevailing proprieties, and when caustic are too caustic for the reticent art director and editor who are so nervous about offending the amorphous reader that they pre-censor the best ideas. Ilić has little patience for such obstruction and it takes its toll on his output.

Therefore, the work that Ilić shows is that which passed through the gauntlet unfettered by interference. What remains is pure thought produced by strong will. Indeed Ilić's art is his will. ✖

01 | The Sherpa are an ethnic group from the most mountainous region of Nepal, high in the Himalayas. The term Sherpa is also used to refer to local people, typically men, who are employed as guides for mountaineering expeditions in the Himalayas, particularly Mt. Everest. They are highly regarded as elite mountaineers and experts in their local terrain.

OPPOSITE PAGE:

**Hyperfiction: Novels
for the Computer**,
August 29, 1993,
ILLUSTRATION: Oko & Mano

Does Democracy Have a Future?,
January 22, 1995,
ILLUSTRATION: Oko & Mano

Free Market Dreams,
January 26, 1997

Kennedy Assasination Theories,
November 21, 1993

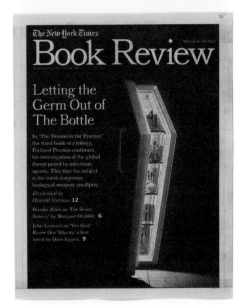

100 Percent, All the Time,
July 15, 1997

Letting the Germ Out of the Bottle,
November 10, 2002

ALL ILLUSTRATIONS:
The New York Times Book Review
AD: Steven Heller

"I do not do advertising because I do not want to lie to people to buy crappy products. I'll maybe do advertising for the things that I think are important and good, where I can find an interesting angle. I am doing a lot of things at the moment, which are fun for me and extremely bad for business. In America, you find the key to one door and then you go only through that door. I am interested in all doors, so now we do a lot of illustrations that I no longer draw by hand; they are exclusively either 3-D computer illustrations or Photoshop. We design a lot of books, a great number of CDs, the majority of which are classical music CDs; we do very little rock music. And we design hotels, and restaurants. In addition to this we are doing computer animations, from MTV to movie credits."

—MIRKO ILIĆ, "ANTIWALL ORIGINATED FROM THE GALLERY WALLS," *VIKEND*, BELGRADE, JANUARY 27, 2001

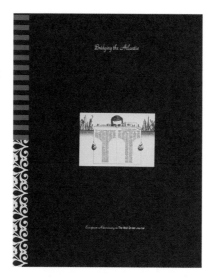

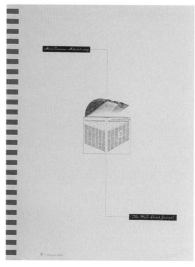
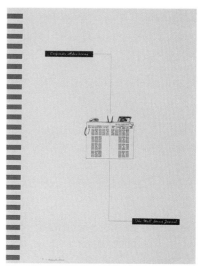
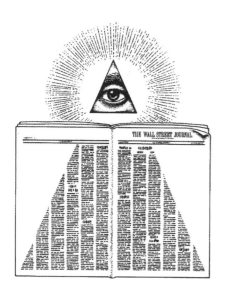
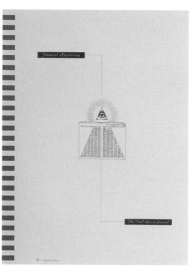
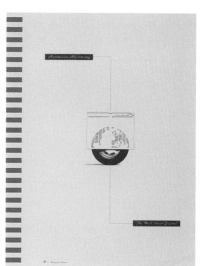

Illustration for the title page of
Financial Advertising section, 1992

Bridging the Pacific and Bridging the Atlantic,
Publications for advertisers in *The Wall Street Journal*.
Dow Jones & Co. Inc., 1992

Promotional publication for Champion Paper Mystique

AD: Mike Gerike/Pentagram

Cooper-Hewitt National Design Museum,
Designing Time: America's
Graphic Designers Celebrate 1998,
Universe 1997, calendar page for November
DESIGN & ILLUSTRATION: Mirko Ilić

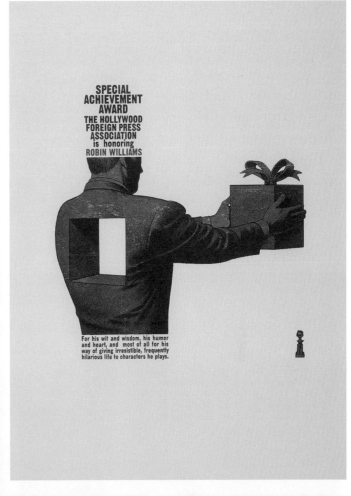

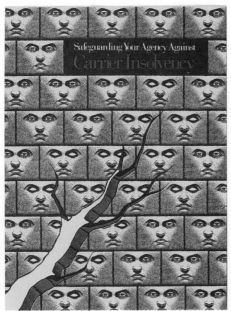

Safeguarding Your Agency Against Carrier Insolvency, *Insurance Review* 1989.
AD: Sara Burris

Special Achievement Award, The Hollywood Foreign Press Association, 1992.

Graphic Artist Guild Directory of Illustration #5, Madison Square Press, 1987.
AD: Walter Bernard, Milton Glaser
IL: Nicky Lindeman, M.I.

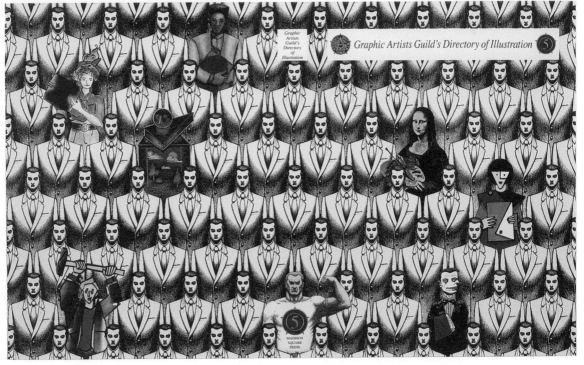

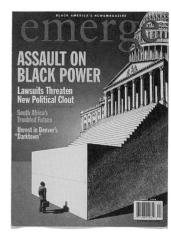

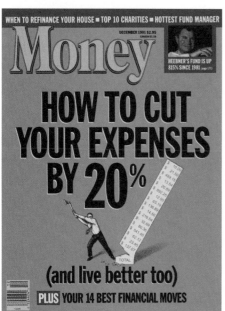

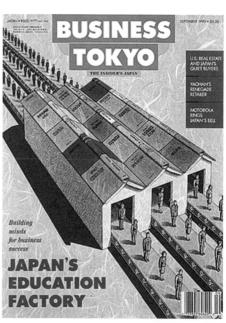

Power Brokers, *Manhattan, Inc.*, September 1989, AD: Nancy Butkus • **The New American Establishment**, *U.S. News & World Report*, February 8, 1988 • **Are We Loosing It?**, *U.S. News & World Report*, February 8, 1988 • **Assault on Black Power**, *Emerge*, March 1994, AD: Wayne N. Fitzpatrick • **How to Cut Your Expenses**, *Money*, December 1991 • **Inside Japan's M&A**, *Business Tokyo*, November 1989, AD: Collen McCudden • **Japan's Education Factory**, *Business Tokyo*, September 1990, AD: Collen McCudden • *Management*, August 1988 • *Macintosh*, January 1989 • *Personnel*, March 1988 • *Sports Inc*, February 1989

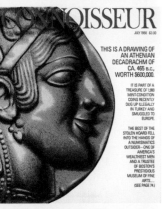

Restaurant Business, December 10, 1988

This is a drawing of an Athenian Decadrachm of CA – 465 B.C., worth $600,000, Connoisseur, July 1988
AD: Sandra DiPasqua

The enviroment at risk,
National Issues Forum, 1987
Public Agenda

"**When you're an illustrator and designer, sometimes you find yourself working on an illustration for Milton Glaser at the same time he is working on an illustration for you. It is a weird thing, when you are simultaneously someone's boss and are also working for him. I'm looking forward to it.**"

—MIRKO ILIĆ, "GIVE ME A DEADLINE AND MONEY," INTERVJU, *ORIS* NO. 2, ZAGREB 1999

Livres d'occasion,
Lire, 1989,
AD: Milton Glaser &
Walter Bernard

A New Revolution, *U.S. News & World Report*, October 19, 1987, AD: Milton Glaser & Walter Bernard

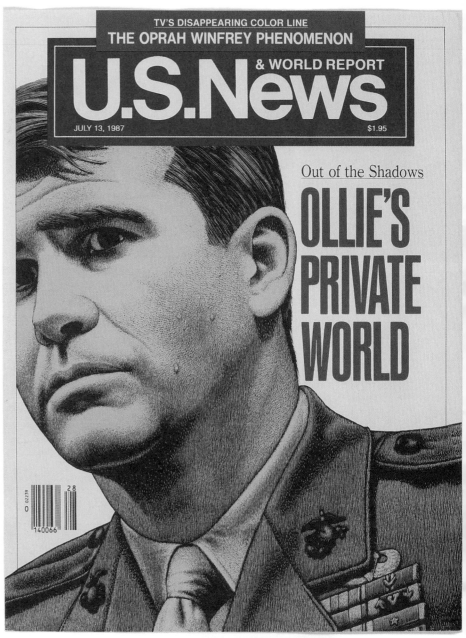

Ollie's Private World, *U.S. News & World Report*, July 13, 1987 AD: Milton Glaser & Walter Bernard

Will the Real Thomas Jefferson Please Stand Up?, *Regardie's*, November 1989, AD: John Korpics

What, Messe Worry?, *Manhattan Inc.*, August 1987, AD: Nancy Butkus

Malcolm X, *Emerge*, April 1995, AD: Wayne N. Fitzpatrick

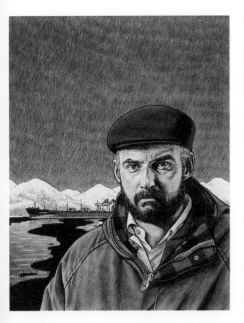

Exxon Valdez,
Time, 1989 [unpublished]
AD: Rudolf Hoglund

Sting and the Rainforest,
Time for Kids, 1990
AD: Milton Glaser &
Walter Bernard

"All I care about is what is good and what is bad design, and not where it comes from. It is obvious that almost every good designer and illustrator from Europe is generally trying to make it in America. The fact is that more designers are still going in this direction than vice versa. The only thing I do not know is whether this says more about America or Europe."
—MIRKO ILIĆ, "WHEN GASTARBEITER BECOMES THE ART DIRECTOR OF *TIME* MAGAZINE," *VEČER*, MARIBOR, JUNE 8, 2000

Donald Trump,
Business Month, January 1988
AD: Cynthia Friedman

Elisabeth Claiborne Ortenberg,
Working Woman, 1989
AD: Caroline Bowyer

"It is very difficult to find a client who understands the aesthetic part of design. It is much easier to push design by saying: this solution costs so much, but if you take this one, which I prefer, it will cost you 40 percent less! Most of them will decide to take a 40 percent lower price. Their bottom line is the price. It is very difficult to find a client who can see the value in aesthetic qualities and realize that it will bring him more money because it looks better."
—MIRKO ILIĆ

"Ilić is a visual satirist. His works naturally follow texts, but their primary function is not only to compress ideas presented in texts, but to synthesize them. To be truly effective, such a synthesis must be visually and conceptually fully purified, to the point where works can function entirely independently. Although we do not know those texts that he illustrated, we understand their main ideas in a split second—probably sometimes even more clearly than if we actually read the texts."

—LEV MENAŠE, "NOT AN ILLUSTRATOR, BUT A VISUAL SATIRIST,"
DELO, LJUBLJANA, JUNE 24, 2000

The First Amendment:

Friend and Sometimes Foe,

Emerge, 1994, AD: Wayne N. Fitzptrick

What's Right With America?,

New Choices Magazine, 1989, AD: Richard Boddy

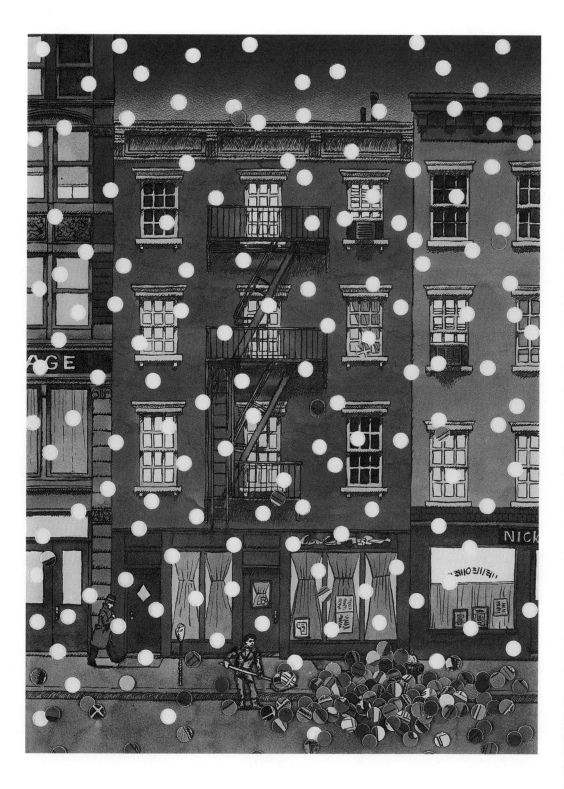

Human Guinea Pig,

Emerge 1994,

AD: Wayne N. Fitzpatrick

Winter in New York,

Unpublished illustration for

the *New Yorker* cover, 1991

Photoshop and Digital Illustration

Oko & Mano (1993–95) and after

"I BOUGHT MY FIRST COMPUTER IN 1990" ILIĆ SAID. "It was an Apple Macintosh IIfx. First I fooled around with Photoshop a bit, then I began to scan black-and-white illustrations and to color them, and it then went a little further, and further yet, and I slowed down by drawing illustrations by hand. I have gained more freedom and started to work on collages, montages, and things like that.

That was the simplest for me. It was much easier for me to design with Mac and to work alone than to hire a lot of people. I do not think that my approach changed significantly. The only thing now is that when I think about something, I do not need to draw everything by myself. I can make something on the computer, I can take photographs, and scan, so the possibilities are wider."

He started to work with digital and computer-mediated 3-D graphics and animations more seriously in 1993 after he established the studio Oko & Mano with Alejandro Arce.

"Arce used to come to the *Time* magazine and help them set up the computer system, and he used to give them some advice. We met there, he helped me with my first computer, and we started talking to each other, had fun. We listened to the same music, for example Shonen Knife ... I was interested in 3-D, which he started to work in as well, but he did not have a computer. Then I said, Well why don't we buy a computer together, which was a bit stupid, because at that time a good machine that you could work on with additional equipment was $150,000. We split the costs in half, and it was such an investment that we had to establish a firm because of that computer that became out of date in three years. We would mix drawing, Photoshop and 3-D in our work at that time. One of the first rendered front pages for the *Time* was the one made of the European stars building the fortress, the wall.

We soon started doing some animations, for example for Sony. The first animations were some chips that travel, binary numbers, we did a video for a DJ and the like. In the meantime, fortunately for Arce, my wife got pregnant, so I was devoting less and less time to my work, and he had just got married to a young girl who also wanted to do what we did. When I told them that I wanted to pause a bit, she realized that perhaps the time came for them to take over the firm and its clients, so they first changed the lock on the door. My computer stayed on the other side of the locked door.

For a while I worked at home, but there was no 3-D at home! At that time, you needed to have a Silicon Graphic the size of a refrigerator in order to be able to do it well, so I started to make illustrations in Photoshop again. Sometime starting from 1995, I stopped drawing my works by hand, except for sketches. Then at one point in 1996 or '97, I decided to buy a new machine and restart the 3D work. One of the first illustrations was the magnetophone for the topic of wiretapping in the White House. That one was actually made on a Macintosh, and not on the Silicon Graphics." ▶

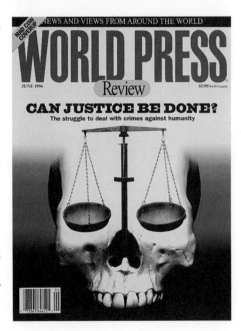

Hiroshima's Legacy,

cover and article illustration,

The New York Times Book Review,

July 30, 1995

AD: Steven Heller

Can Justice Be Done?,

World Press Review, 1996.

AD: Hopkins/Bauman

OPPOSITE PAGE:

Arguing Affirmative Action,

The New York Times Book Review,

April 14, 1996,

AD: Steven Heller

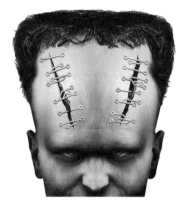

"When Nicky got pregnant, she left her job at CBS, I closed down the Oko & Mano, and I stopped working at night. These moments were too important for me to be missed. When my son Ivo started to crawl, I realized that I would not be able to work at home anymore. At that time, Milton Glaser offered me the fourth floor of the house where his studio was"

—MIRKO ILIĆ

Today's Shakespeare,
New York Times Book Review

Creating a Monster,
New York Times Book Review,
January 1999

RIGHT:
What Fairy Tales Mean,
New York Times Book Review,
November 5, 1995

"This was the story about how fairy tales were made, stories told by the fire to scare the kids. I found a CD-ROM, with figures from the tops of buildings in Chicago. I was joking that it was Hieronymus Bosch meets Walt Disney."

ALL:
AD: Steven Heller
ILLUSTRATION: Mirko Ilić

Ireland Pattern of Violence
The New York Times Op-Ed, 1997
AD: Nicholas Blechman

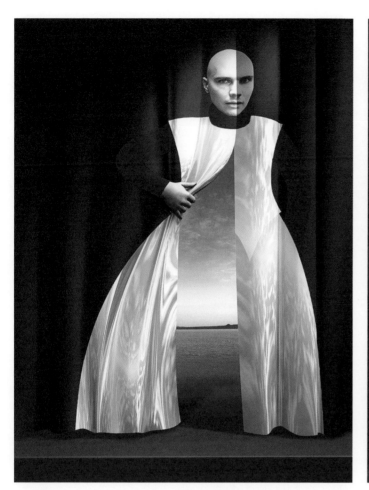

Billy Corgan /

Smashing Pumpkins

Rolling Stone,

January 18, 2001

AD: Fred Woodward

In Spin We Trust

Print 1997,

AD: Andrew P. Kner

Ilić's Illustration for *Rolling Stone*'s article about the band Smashing Pumpkins' farewell tour was to show that the future of singer Billy Corgan was undefined and rather uncertain. The curtain had fallen. *Rolling Stone* sent a black-and-white portrait of Corgan. The desert in the background was from a Corel stock image. In collaboration with Lauren DeNapoli at Maya, curtains were shaped. The bright redness of the drapes dramatically contrasts with Corgan's black-and-white face. The individual elements—rendered drapes, the picture of the desert, and the photo of the face—were finally assembled in Photoshop.

This illustration received several awards and attracted the attention of the organizers of 27th Annual Humana Festival of New American Plays in 2003.

So The Actors Theater called Ilić, mentioning the Corgan illustration published in *Rolling Stone* and asked him to create "something in that direction." Within the given limitations—including the red curtain—he created a picture of the hand which pulls a heavy theatrical curtain and reveals a face, surreally constructed of two hands.

The upper hand holds a mirror—made of silver foil—facing the viewer. Ilić said that he decided to use hands, because many people act with their hands. Hands are important in acting, hands are important in writing, and of course, there are theater stage "hands". The mirror symbolizes the aret of theater—a play is an act of reflection in which viewers recognize themselves, they see their reflection and recognize the states of their lives.

27th Annual Humana

Festival of New American

Plays, Poster, Actors

Theatre, 2003

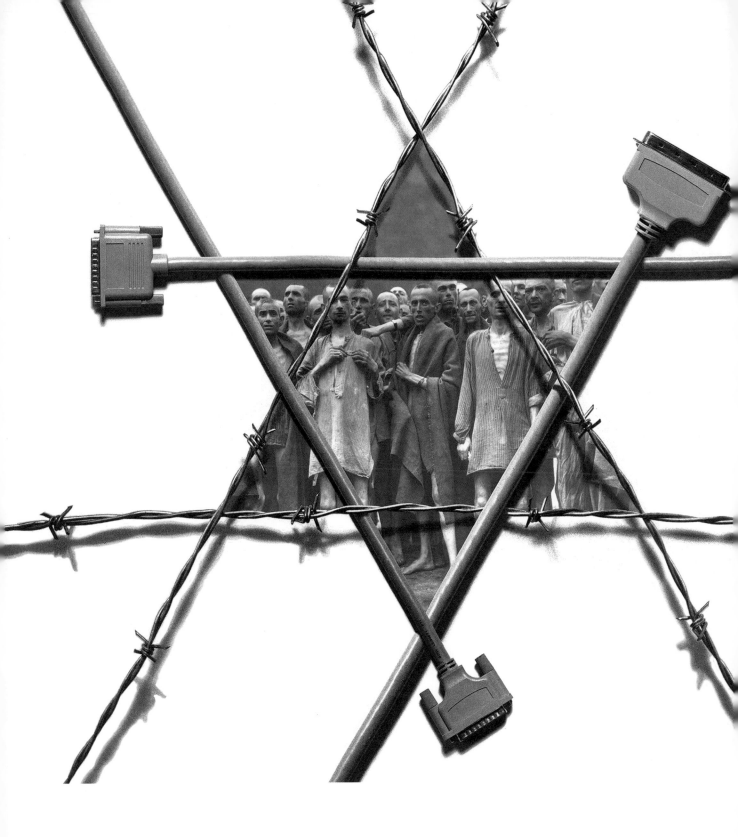

"Mirko Ilić is one of those rare illustrators who understand the meaning of his profession very well. You are the illustrator with your entire body. You do not have only hands and you are not a Cyclops, the contents of the texts require a head. Because the head is thinking."

—MAJA B. JANČIČ, DEPILIJAN GALERIJA AVLA, LJUBLJANA, 2000

The First Interactive Holocaust Museum, *Swing* magazine, 1995
AD: David Lauren

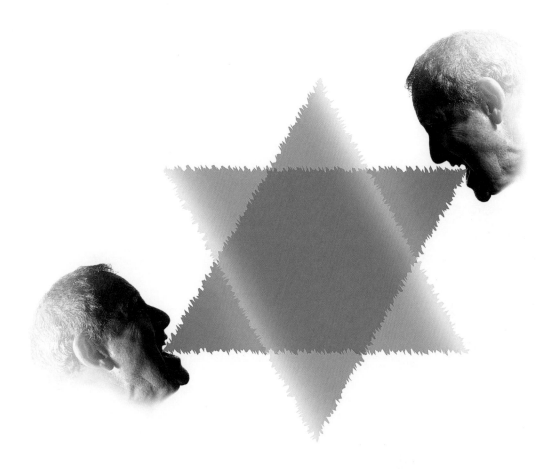

"Of course, technology should introduce some new things. It's wrong to just sit in front of the computer for hours trying things until something happens. Then you may get lost. Knowing what a computer can do, I would always first draw a sketch and develop the idea on paper. When the idea was totally finalized, I would move to the computer. If something happened in the computer that could help the idea, that's great. I like to control things very much, and to sit in front of the computer and let it lead the way doesn't interest me. At this moment, thousands of designers are sitting in front of the same computer, with the same programs and are, most likely, going down a similar path usinge the same computer tricks. They just press the button and whatever happens happens!"

—MIRKO ILIĆ, "DESIGN IS NOT FOREVER," *ARKZIN* NO. 53, ZAGREB, DECEMBER 8, 1995

Cries and Whispers,
The Washington Post Magazine,
May 26, 1996, AD: Kelly Doe

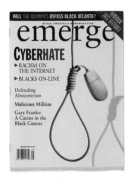

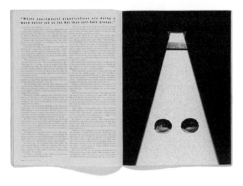

Cyberhate,

Emerge, August 1996

AD: Wayne Fitzpatric

"Especially striking is the cycle *Cyberhater*, which successfully illustrates, in a devastating, ironic manner, how the Internet as a medium represents not only a means of free communication, but also a means for the dispersal of a racist messages; how primitivism survives despite advances in technology. Ilić captures and communicates these problems through an excellent combination of the iconography of the computer and of the Ku Klux Klan."

—SANDI VIDULIĆ: "WORLD CURRENT TOPICS," SLOBODNA DALMACIJA, SPLIT, JUNE 1, 1999

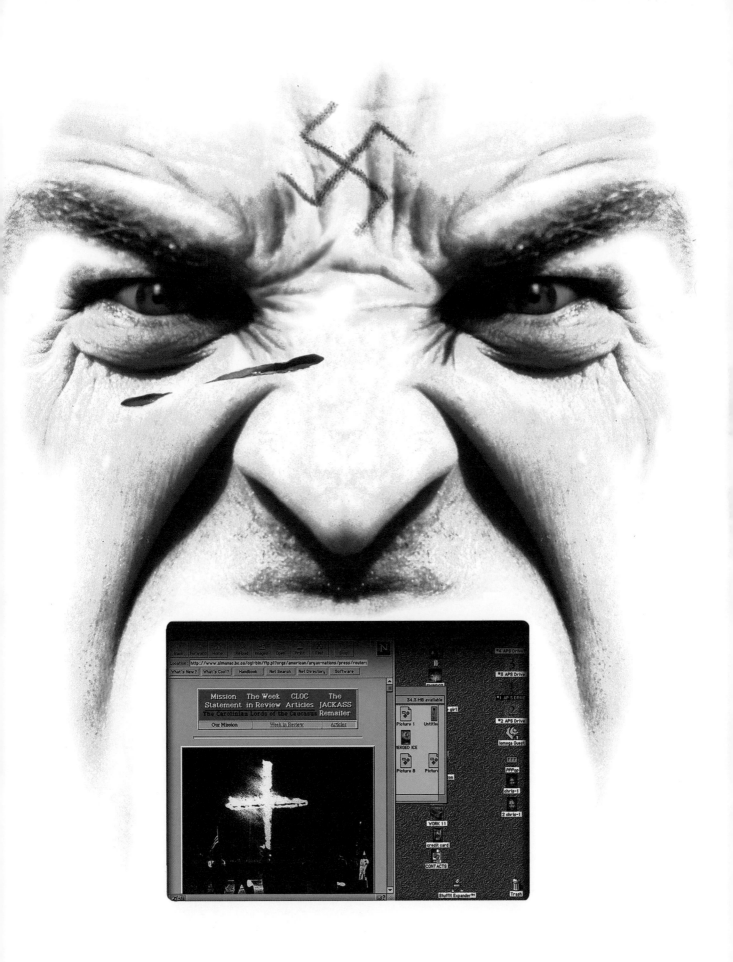

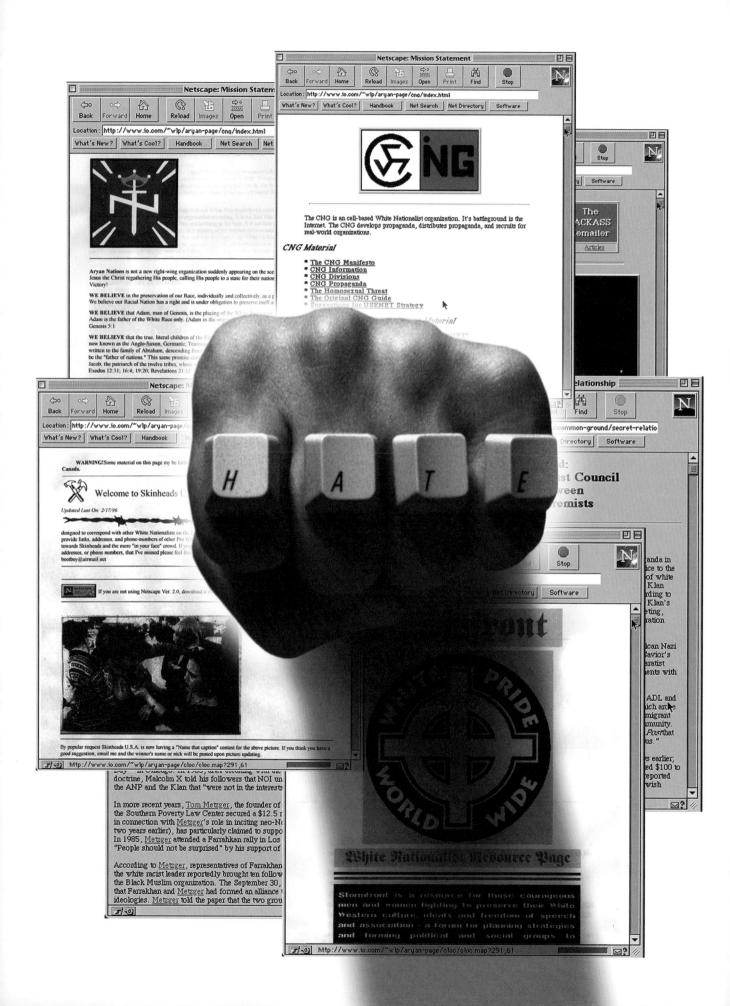

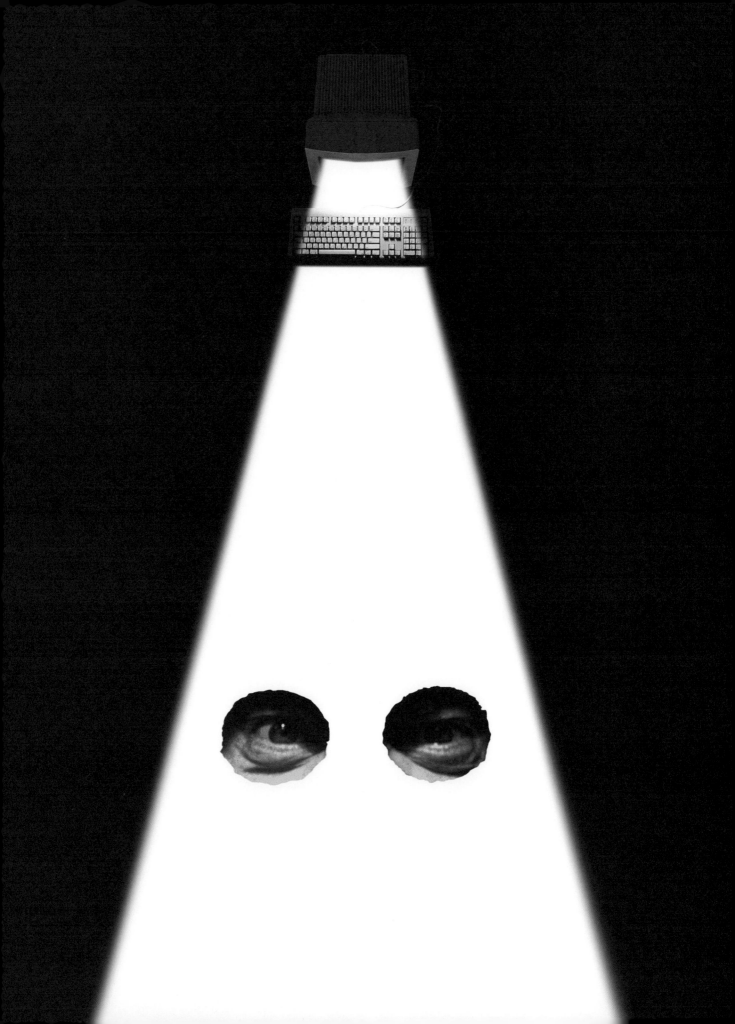

Mirko Ilić Corp.

1995 and beyond

AT THE END OF 1995 ILIĆ FOUNDED MIRKO ILIĆ CORP. and settled the office on the third floor of a small building in the heart of Manhattan, where a few other famous residents had their studios as well: Milton Glaser on the first floor, and above it, the studio of Walter Bernard. The entrance of the building was marked by Glaser's commonly known slogan, "Art is Work," which was also used for the title of his second monograph (Overlook, 2000.)

"When we first met, I did not accept the desk he offered me, but I came to him ten years later and asked him: How about the entire floor? PushPin Studio was located in this building since 1965, *New York* magazine was started in it, the I heart NY logo was conceived there, and thousands of other things."

A special relationship developed between Milton and Mirko during the years, not just occasional collaboration and exchanging the of roles of art director, illustrator, and designer, but the exchange of ideas, information, and opinions about design, life, and politics, with many walks taken in between floors. In the preface of the interview for *Graphis*, Laetitia Wolff wrote, "Some would say that Mirko was Milton's protégé, although Milton is not showing any signs of a patronizing attitude, which apprenticeship with a great master might include."

Though generations separate them, a true and deep connection was established between the two men. "Milton is a wonderful person; there is no difference between him as an artist and his work. In fact, one can say that he is a better man than designer, and he is a great designer. Unfortunately, this cannot be said for some other artists. From the first moment I felt that the two of us were much closer than you would think possible given our ages, as he is eighty-two now. When I go for a lunch with my associates from the studio, which is typically two times a week, I invite him, too. We talk about politics, women, ordinary things."

Commenting on their relationship, Mirko once said, "Milton adopted me as a son, and I adopted him as a father." Given the turbulent relationship between Mirko and his father, this is of course a very interesting observation, which Ilić made in a conversation with Milton for *Graphis*. "For example, you are a new father figure for me and I'm jealous that you can do all these wonderful things, partly because I cannot, and partly because I need the resistance. I have a feeling that people like you work for themselves. I always work against someone. I need to get a job where I will be told the precise fee, and given the deadline. Otherwise I would probably go to the movies."

Together they did a series of jobs, from magazine covers to corporate annual reports, but probably the most famous joint work is the credits for the Nora Ephron movie *You've Got Mail,* with Tom Hanks and Meg Ryan.

"I worked for Milton when he was the art director at *U.S. News.* After that, as my revenge, I called him to work for me a few times. I constantly claim, even though it sounds stupid, that the amount of freedom that I take is equal to the amount of freedom that I give. For someone to illustrate my design ideas, one would have to do exactly what I tell him to do. So I'm in this stupid position of dictating to someone: No, this must be straight, I want a tree here… This is why it is much easier for me to do it by myself. Milton would engage me if he knew that he could not draw it in that way. So you go out when you are looking for something that you definitely cannot do by yourself."

"By American standards I make terrible mistakes when it comes to mon-

Cover of *Graphis* #350, 2004

PHOTO: Antonin Kratochvil

ey. I design web sites, books, credits for movies, I do illustrations, edit books. Each of these jobs could be a separate profession. If I split them up and specialized in just a few of them, I would do much better financially. But doing them all at once, keeps me from getting bored. The most important thing for me is the freedom I get when I am working on something. It's great when I can tell my coworkers that we will stop to do illustrations for a month and then work on a web site or movie credits.

I do not advertise myself at all so I don't get invited to a bunch of events that I don't want to go to anyway. I always insist on some degree of equality and thus I do not hang out with clients and I don't have business dinners. I come to the studio at nine-thirty and go home at six, except on Mondays and Wednesdays, when I leave at five-thirty because I go to the gym. If I screw something up in work, I may stay fifteen minutes or half an hour longer, but that's rare. I do not work on Saturdays and Sundays. I rarely go to business lunches; I am very picky about with whom I dine. I prefer to take my entire team out to lunch, and that's uncommon in America. It relaxes me because then we can talk about things that have absolutely nothing to do with work. I want my colleagues to love to work together, not to be there because I pay them. I want them to see everything as ours in common, and not just mine."

Ilić is a frequent guest at American universities and is also a lecturer in postgraduate studies at the School of Visual Arts and Cooper Union.

In a 1999 interview with Igor Masnjak for the magazine *Oris,* answering the question of what his message is for people at the beginning of their studies, he said: "I try to persuade them to change their occupation. This is pretty much a desperate profession, because you sell your soul, and in fact more or less always come across disappointments. If you are not ready for disappointments, don't do this. Most designers are emotional people, and therefore it is hard for them to bear disappointments; they get hurt easily."

He points out that during his lectures he especially addresses young people and women because they are rarer in the profession and because their position is underestimated.

"I love teaching children. I like to work with young people; it's nice to help them understand the power of design. I think that successful people are mostly good people. Those that are halfway to success and think that they have been taken advantage of, those are the people that never have time and are constantly in a hurry. And yet, America has given a lot to me and I have a moral obligation to give that back. Why should young kids have to go through the things that I went through? I am grateful that I first went to school in Yugoslavia, and then came to America to work, rather than the other way around and I see no reason whatsoever not to convey some of my experiences to young Americans."

The title of one of his lectures includes the question how to sell the body of your work without selling your soul. It is the question that he is obviously constantly facing, and the topic that he returns to in a series of his interviews: "I came to America because I wanted to have artistic freedom, and not squander it for commercial reasons. I did not come to get rich, but to test my possibili-

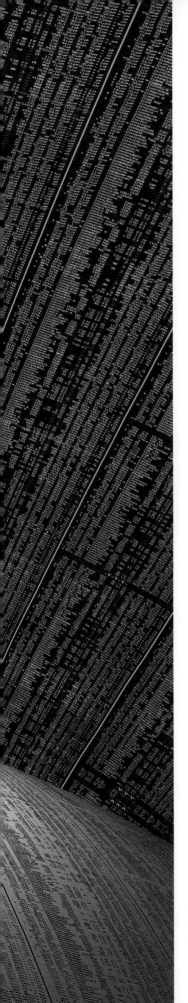

ties and see what I could really do and know how stacked up in comparison to the 'big boys' at the top. I came to America not to change, but to stay my true self. I was afraid that America would change me, that I'd turn into something that I did not like, and that I would not even notice it. That I would sell some part of myself that I care about. I have nothing against money in life, but I do not want it at all costs. That's why my studio has only three employees. I am not interested in mass production and exploitation of people; I do not want to run around, sit in stupid meetings, while some other people work hard for me and play with my toys. I walked into this business because I did not want to be like my parents and many other parents or the guy wearing the tie. Being an artist for me meant pushing boundaries, having fun, attacking institutions. I would betray myself if I institutionalized myself after all." ▶

The One Investment Guide You really Need Now,

Smart Money, 1998

AD: Amy Rosenfeld, D: Julie Lazarus

Wall Street Versus America,

Portfolio – Penguin 2006, AD: Joseph Perez

Enron, *The New York Times*, 2002.

Bad Medicine,

Smart Money, 1998

AD: Amy Rosenfeld

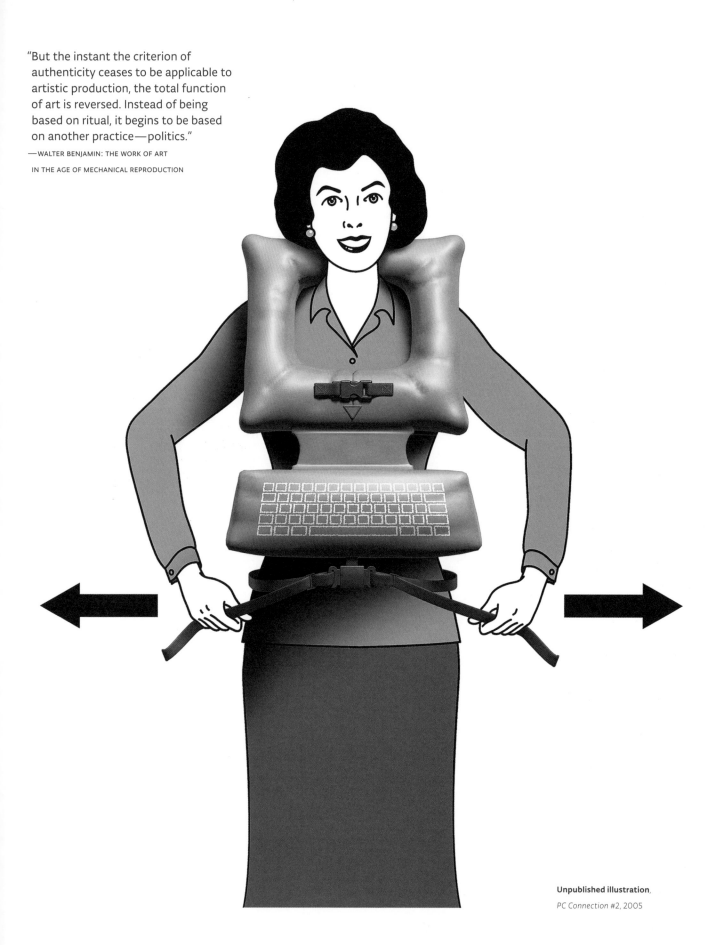

"But the instant the criterion of authenticity ceases to be applicable to artistic production, the total function of art is reversed. Instead of being based on ritual, it begins to be based on another practice—politics."
—WALTER BENJAMIN: THE WORK OF ART
IN THE AGE OF MECHANICAL REPRODUCTION

Unpublished illustration,
PC Connection #2, 2005

In the Realm of Digital Rendering

Would you recognize a digital paradise?

IT WAS BERTOLT BRECHT WHO SAID that nowadays, "less than at any time does a simple reproduction of reality tell us anything about reality." What is the role of an illustration in time of highly commercialized, digital and digitized images? The very word *illustration* puts us on the wrong track, because a good illustration today does not *illustrate* in the usual sense of the word; it does not represent a literal view of something from reality, but instead indicates the traumatic *real*, what is usually excluded from the field of representation (as in our world, a world of spectacle, there are actual political relations, relations of power). Thus, some of Ilić's surreal illustrations say more about the realities of today than even a photograph.

Many have wondered and complained about Ilić's transition to creating digitally rendered illustrations, but there is some logic in the move. Drawing is a complex, but not necessarily complicated, activity—everyone can draw somehow. But even the best authors cannot fully control their strokes, everything that takes place in the area of transfer between the head and paper, which is unconscious and mechanical. Although he was praised for the accuracy of his drawings at the beginning of his career, Ilić never fetishized his drawings, perhaps because at the School for Applied Arts and Novi kvadrat there were at least two or three better drawers. It is an open question which one was more talented and who of them managed to transfer their natural talents into more interesting works, but certainly Igor Kordej, Krešimir Zimonić, and Radovan Devlić worked much more easily. They were guided by the hand, that specific *mano*, and their oeuvre is surely more coherent in terms of drawing.

Contrary to this, Ilić has always been a toiler. He used to work hard on his drawings, and as he often has said in interviews, he was never satisfied.

"I am a perfectionist. I spent many hours drawing comics, but the next day they would seem awful to me. I would see all of my mistakes, everything that I did not do well, and when you are doing work for international magazines, the dynamic differs from the one at *Polet,* where we did not have time to think about errors because of the time crunch. I would throw one version in the basket, and the next one would be published. However, this way I work on the comic for two months, send it in, and then I wait a year before it gets published. And then, after a year I see the comic and I hate every line, 'Ah, I missed this and I didn't do that'. That was almost unbearably humiliating."

He worked in a variety of styles, and tested various techniques and options. "I tried all kinds of things, whatever came to my mind," he said. Brush, pen, rapidograph pen, sprinkling India ink with a toothbrush or a blower brush, scratchboard, airbrush. For photo-illustrations in *Danas* he made collages and photomontages, created models, made cutout paper characters, and modeled figures out of Play-Doh. The frequent use of Letraset raster tones in comics and illustrations clearly testifies to the aspirations for the "mechanization" of drawings, the idea of the invisible hand. Scratchboard is also an attempt at 'objectification' of drawings, to minimize as much as possible the role of chance, the uncontrolled expression of the hand.

Though he was often criticized for it, the coldness of his drawings, the geometry of form, can be understood as an attempt to move news illustration as far away as possible from its close relative—the caricature. Through his distinctive style, the caricaturist is expressing his personal opinion, his criticism of the indecency of the world. Ilić is avoiding the position of a satirist

Sketch and final version as it appeared on the cover.
A Long Slog to Someplace,
The New York Times Book Review,
April 04, 2004,
AD: Steven Heller

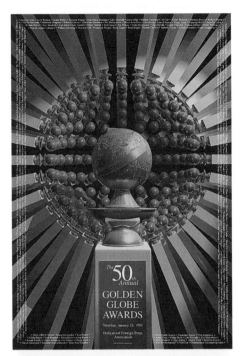

The 50th Golden Globe Awards, 1993
The 51st Golden Globe Awards, 1994
BOTH DESIGN & ILLUSTRATION: Oko & Mano /
Alejandro Arce & Mirko Ilić

OPPOSITE PAGE:

Great Tape Hits of the '60s,
The New York Times Book Review,
October 19, 1997, AD: Steven Heller

and any moralizing associated with it. He is forcing us to read the meaning of his metaphorical constructions and to take our own active stance.

The mechanical aspect of Ilić's drawings provide just the necessary dose of abstract universality with which we can all communicate—his illustration is most obviously not about any particular person, but about the "man as such," devoid of all unnecessary character details, in the reduced, often totally abstract space. If there are more characters, they are the same, as multiplied figures, stripped of any unnecessary psychologizing, dolls, toys in the hands of social, political, and economic forces that they cannot control, but which, at least occasionally, they resist. There is nothing superfluous in his drawing, so that the basic idea, the message could more easily find its way to readers.

A frequent objection about the "coldness" of his drawings has its explanation in the medium. According to Marshall McLuhan, "cold" are the media of "low resolution," those that force us to fill in the gaps by ourselves. The high contrast of newspaper graphics drives us to this activity, the work of completing and connecting.

Digital illustration at high-resolution in color works with a different logic, but in a similar manner. The media quality of 3-D illustrations lays precisely in its "unreality." We know that it is easy to manipulate photographs—selection, contextualization, framing, retouching, and photomontage often challenge our confidence in the fidelity and validity of a photograph. Despite the fact that we are aware of that, we often accept a photograph as valid with ease. That's why today photography plays a much bigger role in newspapers and magazines than illustration.

Rendered illustrations may confuse us for a moment, but an inexperienced eye is soon aware that this is an illusion, a construction, and not a direct view of reality. Three-dimensional rendered characters look like people but they are not people, regardless of the skill and technique, the quality and price of software and hardware; they are a bit plastic. This artistic choice should not be seen as a flaw or an imperfection of technology, but rather as a "hidden agenda," that provides the necessary element of abstraction. This approach introduces a sense of detachment that allows and requires consideration and calls for reflection.

The choice of digital simulation also has its political applications. In today's post industrial society, a society of spectacle, the world of digital communications and mediatized pictures, which discusses the possibilities and dangers of virtual reality, genetic manipulation, hand-drawn illustrations critically intoned would mean, at least implicitly, if not overtly, to take a unique romantic, somewhat nostalgic, conservative or even retrograde attitude. The attitude that warns from a humanist position about the strains of modern society and the dangers of technology that dehumanizes, alienates, and enslaves us. But Ilić is very far from that attitude. He embraced these modern means and he is using them to effectively present critical messages about today following that Wagnerian advice that "The wound can only be healed by the spear that made it."

This attitude is in a way analogous to his attitude towards the new country, the United States: he embraced all the positive aspects of American society and right in its foundation—the spirit of the Constitution which guarantees freedom of speech—he has remained critical of politics, politicians, and the corporate attitude that rules America and the world.

His style is his way of thinking and that is why—as we can see in this review of his work—he could go through such a range of techniques and styles "unpunished." Of course, there is always a question of that "surplus," something extra, that the artist's "handicraft" brings to the work, some specifics of handwriting, stylish, compositional, and coloristic idiosyncrasies that are

emerging from the unconscious without control during the working process? So, have Mirko's illustrations lost something in the moment when, from the domain of handmade work of art in the age of mechanical reproduction, they break into the sphere of digital simulation? Despite his loyalty to the initial sketch that precedes rendered illustration, the standard, probably conservative, answer would most likely be: Yes, they lost the personal touch, some "pathological" moments that are inevitably automatically and unconsciously shown by the handwriting—no matter how controlled by skill, or pressured by technique, method of work.

In his defense, is such "heroism of alienation" just a fidelity to the truth? Should not the "sacrifice" be more appreciated since it came from the master of the craft who dared to continually experiment, to leave the safe limits of his own conquered skill? ▶

"A murder in New York becomes the news of the day, while in Western Europe five people need to die for that to happen. In Eastern Europe it needs to be more than twenty. In Africa more than a hundred, and in Asia more than five hundred people, so that news appears on the front page of local American newspapers."

—MIRKO ILIĆ, "THE DREAM COVER," MAG, LJUBLJANA, MAY 17, 2000

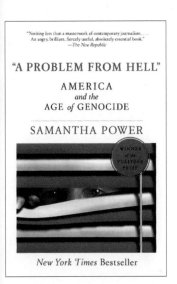

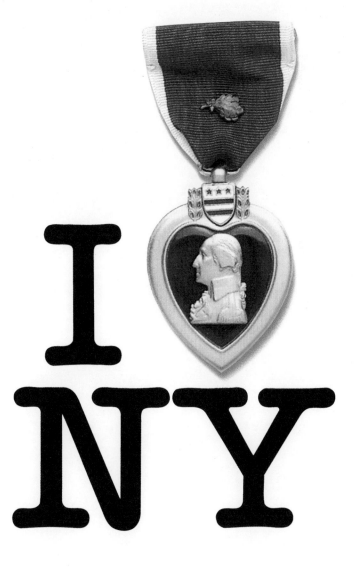

Samantha Power: A Problem from Hell – America and the Age of Genocide
Paperback, Harper Perennial, 2007
ILLUSTRATION: Mirko ilić

The New World Order
The New York Times Book Review,
October 14, 2001
AD: Steven Heller

September 11, 2001, *Rolling Stone* # 880, September 25, 2001, AD: Fred Woodward
The illustration is a reference to the famous I♥NY logo designed by Milton Glaser.

Ilić communicates through pictures. It is an undeniable fact. He convinced Americans immediately upon his arrival to the Promised Land. He did not need words because his presentation of the real and the imaginary world that we live in was assuring enough. He was the same when he lived in the former Yugoslav part of the Europe that he came from, but even then, he was reaching beyond those borders with the quality of his independent and engaged graphic design.

Ilić is above all an excellent illustrator and a designer: lucid, innovative, high-tech, creates a new, recognizable Ilić's phantasmagorical world without all [or together with them] co-signed art directors.

—STANE BERNIK, "TO WHAT EXTENT IS SLOVENIAN DESIGN REALLY BORING?", *DELO*, JUNE 20, 2000

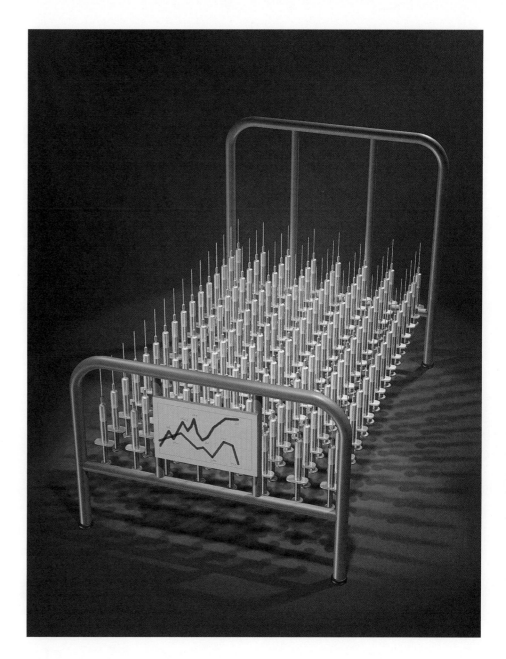

Needle Exchange, *Readers Digest*, 2000, AD: Hannu Laakso

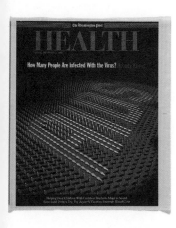

How Many People are Infected with the Virus? Nobody Knows,
Washington Post Health, September 1997
AD: Sandra Schneider

"Since 1995, I have not drawn any work by hand, it's all done on the computer. Sometimes I'll make a rough hand sketch of a design or picture, but only for the basic idea; the rest is computer generated. In fact, almost none of my work in recent years has been on paper."

—MIRKO ILIĆ, "SEX, LIES... AND A CIGARETTE AT THE END," APRIL 16, 2002

ABOVE AND LEFT BELOW:
Sketch and illustration, *Danas*, 1984.

BELOW RIGHT:

The Third Annual Village
Voice Film Critics' Poll,
The Village Voice, 2002,
AD: Minh Uong

GLASER: Let me ask you another question about the evolution of your work. Most people in the field who now do computer illustration are people whose knowledge of drawing is very limited, or they haven't had enough experience in a traditional sense. So, you see a kind of work that is characterized by great technical skills, but there's something unconvincing about the work. Like computer-generated figures and animation, you get the sense there's no spine and no bones underneath the skin. But underneath your computer image, one can read your experience, in conventional terms, as a draftsman, having learned to draw from observation. And I think that separates your work from everybody else around who basically works on the computer. My sense is that the computer is a choice that comes out of a pre-existing knowledge as opposed to a way of avoiding a certain understanding. It's like the difference between somebody who draws things in a distorted way, because they can't draw, and someone who can draw, who chooses the distortion in order to produce an expressive idea. How do you think your previous work—when you were observing, drawing, and usin, what you might call, traditional tools—informed the way you use a computer?

ILIĆ: When I started to illustrate, and doing things for youth magazines, the print quality was extremely bad. The first few times, I tried to match the quality of my drawing to the print, but the print quality was so bad that whatever I did, it would print badly. Then, I decided to take control. I started to produce illustrations that technically looked perfect. I was trying to avoid

mistakes and not use the white correction paint because the white paint is always a different shade of white than the paper. I wanted the surface to be perfectly smooth. Then I started to do pen and ink and crossetching. I even tried to deny my hand stroke (thick and thin lines) to make the lines look even and mechanical, as if no human hand was involved. I wanted it to look as perfect as a Dürer etching print. Dürer and Doré's etchings appear perfect from top left corner to the bottom right corner. I didn't want to surrender just because of bad printing quality. Because of that I never developed a certain style or a certain look. That's why I was able to switch styles. When I arrived in the United States, from all my different styles, the first two art directors I worked with asked me to do scratch board work. Suddenly I got this label "Eastern European artist specializing in politics, doing scratchboard." And if I didn't do a scratchboard, they would say, "Oh, you didn't have time to do a scratchboard. Oh, we didn't pay you enough to do a scratchboard." [*Laughter*] I was doing it with an X-acto knife; there were approximately a couple million lines in my drawing—once I even counted. Toward the end, I would even catch myself almost asleep with my hand drawing and filling in those spaces. I was stuck, I was typecast and they all expected the same kind of work from me, even *The New York Times,* which at that time didn't have the best printing technique either. I was thinking of this idea about the fastest communication between your head and your hand being either a pencil or a stick drawing in the sand. The less you have in between, the more immediate the idea, the less work. My stick in the sand became the computer. Why was it necessary to do it by hand when the computer arrived—the Mac IIfx was the first computer that was capable of doing this—I bought it immediately. I started to play with it, and I went back and forth between different styles, in Photoshop, Illustrator, and later 3-D, etc. I was finally getting results that looked printed. Smooth and nice. I was doing my little thing, it was looking great. Probably because of that little, stupid, fixed idea from my past—I just went into photo illustration without thinking about it. I still do roughs first and then go to the computer, never vice versa. When I'm doing a rough, I have on my mind all the possibilities of technology, which kind of light I can get (in 3-D computer programs), which kind of mood, texture, and all the possibilities of computer effects. When I finish my rough, which I usually do with marker directly on paper, I the decide which technique is appropriate for a particular idea, photomontage, 3-D, etc. Then I try to be as truthful to that rough as I can. I keep the same lighting, same shadow, from the same direction, the same cropping, and I force the computer to follow that exact idea I had originally drawn. I think one of the biggest problems with using computers is to sit in front of it and let it guide you. Then hundreds of people end up in the exact same place, again and again, because programs have their limitations. It's like water that flows downhill and you're avoiding stones, pure gravity. In the end, you all end up in the same ocean. That's the problem. I think that's why if you see it, and I'm grateful you do—can see under the computer rendering and still feel that rough. And I think that may be the difference.

"MIRKO ILIĆ & MILTON GLASER: THE KING AND THE JESTER,"

GRAPHIS ISSUE #350, MARCH/APRIL 2004, INTERVIEW EDITED BY LAETITIA WOLFF

The ugly side of the world

Danas no. 140, October 23, 1984

Coming Home

Los Angeles Times Book Review,
October 6, 2002, AD: Carol Kaufman,
front cover and article illustration

"It became boring to draw illustrations by hand. It got to the point that after drawing for ten hours my arm drew lines by itself automatically while I was snoozing, and my head was falling from boredom and exhaustion. That's when you realize you do something just to do it. When you do that with something you love, it's a bit sad."

—MIRKO ILIĆ,

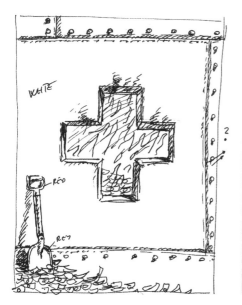

Sketch and unpublished illustration for *The Village Voice* from 2002, about how the Red Cross used to spend money collected through donations after September 11th.

"Anyone who remembers Ilić from the illustrations published in *Danas* and *Start* will immediately be tempted to compare his present work—when his visual ideas are fully mediated with computer techniques—with the time when the author's own hand shaped the forms on the paper. Ilić's forms were always crystal clear, precise, deindividualized, or deprived of their author's 'touch'. Also, Ilić always had a coldness and staticness in his composition, and a kind of mechanicalness, which was characterized by the stressed themes of machinery and technical equipment, or in reducing people to mechanical units that were impersonally and properly moving into some kind of order or were uniformly cloned in a geometrically arranged crowd.

Ilić's earlier graphics had a charm of cold aesthetic, and one would know that they were hand-drawn and that he tried to hide that, i.e., to make them impersonally correct. This aesthetic echoes that of the historical avant-garde and pop art movements. Ilić's deindividualized poetics fit into the cultural context of fine art, in which he had artistic legitimacy, and it was highly functional as irony, a powerful weapon in illustrating articles that have commented on the political reality of a meaningless bureaucratic system."

—SANDI VIDULIĆ, "WORLD CURRENT TOPICS," *SLOBODNA DALMACIJA*, SPLIT, JUNE 1, 1999

"With his new work the context was radically different. Ilić's illustrations for U.S. magazines show that the characters were less flat now, the volume, i.e., the 3-D illusion, was more pronounced, colors were more aggressive and glamorous. Ilić's slightly dark irony here was differently intoned, 'tingling' of the social system shows a pronounced symbolic aggression. Contrary to his European poetry (which he kept during his work at *Time*), Ilić became more explicit with the transition to computer graphics, more Hollywood like luxuriousness and visual aggression. A part of Ilić's fine-art subtleties in this cyber-Hollywood mannerism is surely lost. His humor is less intellectual in the European way, which may seem a bit hermetic and gloomy to Americans in its Kafka-like absurdity and unhumanity. The computer age of his career was a sort of drift into the new, where he was partly sucked in by the local machinery, but ends up surfing skillfully and lucidly on the foam of its waves. Maybe we are Eurocentrically limited when we reproach him for the loss of subtlety; perhaps the new visual paradigm is on his side? Maybe we are reaching the point where the taste begins to decide?"

—SANDI VIDULIĆ, "WORLD CURRENT TOPICS," *SLOBODNA DALMACIJA*, SPLIT, JUNE 1, 1999

Sketch and illustration

Caged Cargo,

Emerge, 1997

AD: Wayne Fitzpatric

Sketch and published illustration

Plug-and-Play Storage, *PC Connection*, vol 2, #4,

AD: Jenn Ste. Marie, D: Don Morris Design

Surveillance City,

The Village Voice, October 6, 1998

AD: Ming Uong

LGBT Marriage and Family Legal resources and

So, are you two gonna get married?

Brochures

The Massachusetts Lesbian and Gay

Association Family Law Section, 2004

AD: Nicky Lindeman, D: Nicky Lindeman & Mirko Ilić

LEFT:

I'd Leave the Country,

But My Wife Won't Let Me,

The Village Voice, 2004

AD: Ming Uong

Unpublished illustration

Liberty Cross (above)

and approved version:

Will Liberty Survive?

National Council of Jewish

Women Journal, #2, 2005

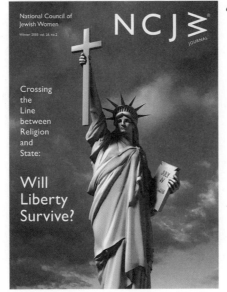

"We do a lot of pro bono work for some institutions, organizations whose causes I personally believe in. We have worked for several years for Gay Pride, the Auschwitz Jewish Center, and associations fighting against the mistreatment of animals; projects that make me happy and that are important to me. I also should note that I am neither a homosexual nor Jewish, but I like to support things that I think are correct."

—MIRKO ILIĆ, "IMMATURE AND INSECURE ARTISTS LOVE TO SNUGGLE NEXT TO THE GOVERNMENT," MEDITERAN, *NOVI LIST*, RIJEKA, JULY 13, 2003

Justice Turns on the Cams

The New York Times Book Review,
February 22, 2004, AD: Steven Heller

"As an art director I have given many illustrators difficult themes that I personally find impossible to visually interpret. I rely on the illustrator to conceive ideas and am beholden to their sleight of hand, which is an imprecise way of saying the neurological hardwiring that enable these conceptualists to discover ideas that are inaccessible to other mortals. By way of example, one such image that I used as a cover illustration for *The New York Times Book Review* is by Mirko Ilić. It represents the dangers involved in temporarily abrogating certain civil liberties by legalizing such intrusions as surveillance. Rendering the American symbol for justice in such a realistic, Oscar-like manner invested power into the image (a pen sketch would not have been as startling). By adding the cameras to Justice's head Ilić transformed the symbol into a memorable icon that telegraphs danger more effectively than most words.

—STEVEN HELLER, "ODE TO ILLUSTRATION,"
AIGA JOURNAL OF DESIGN AND ILLUSTRATION
MARCH 18, 2004

Unpublished illustration

for *Rolling Stone* magazine,
2003

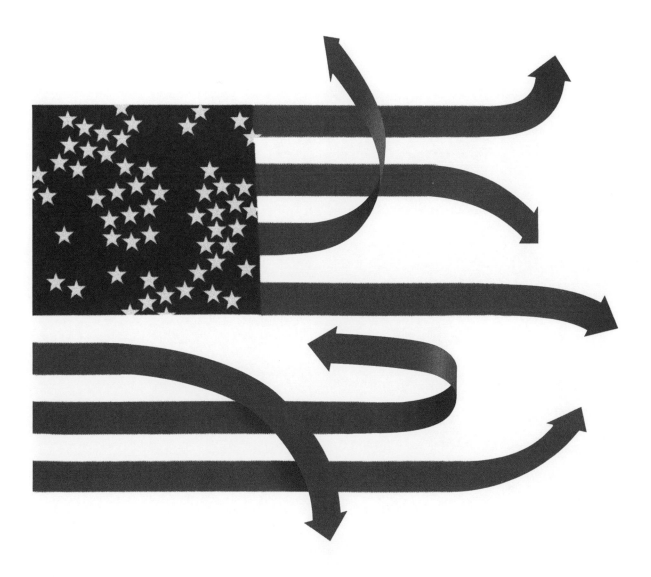

Where Do We Go from Here?,

The Nation, December 2, 1996

ADS: Milton Glaser & Walter Bernard

"I think that there are about fifty thousand designers in Manhattan alone. Probably more than in the former Yugoslavia combined with Italy, Austria, and a couple of other countries. Manhattan is only slightly larger than downtown Zagreb. It is a great concentration of information, that produces both good and bad work. I think the ratio of good to bad work is similar in every environment and since there are so many people here, there is a lot more of both."

—MIRKO ILIĆ, "GIVE ME A DEADLINE AND MONEY," *ORIS* # 02, ZAGREB, 1999

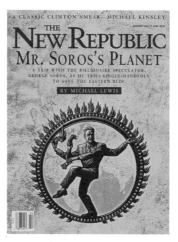

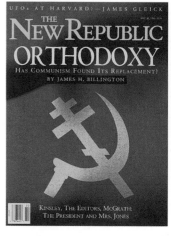

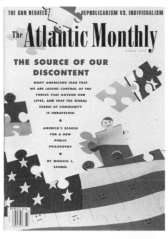

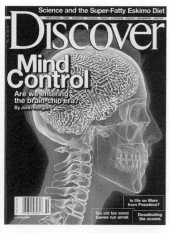

LEFT:

Would you want to know…, *Discover*, June 1987, AD: Eric Seidman

Quest for beauty, *Psychology Today*, May 1988, AD: Wayne Fitzpatrick

Mr. Soros's Planet / Orthodoxy, *The New Republic*, January 10 / May 30, 1994

The Source of Our Discontent, *The Atlantic Monthly*, March 1996

Politics of Travel, *The Nation*, October 06, 1997, AD: Walter Bernard & Milton Glaser

The Drug War's Phony Fix, *The Nation*, April 28, 1997, AD: Milton Glaser & Walter Bernard

Real Estate Mania, *New York*, April 12, 1999, AD: Michael Picon

European Design Annual, *Print*, April 1998, AD: Andrew P. Kner

Cybercash, *Worth*, September 1993, AD: Ina Saltz

Power Surge, *Mother Jones*, August 2002, AD: Jane Palecek

Double Agent, *UpFront*, August 2001, AD: Ron Gabriel

Identity Theft, *Newsweek*, July 4, 2005, AD: Bruce Ramsay

THIS PAGE:

Mind Control,
Discover #10, October 2004
AD: Michael Mrak

Tempted by Apple
PC Connect, 2005
AD: Jennifer Ste. Marie

**What's Wong With Energy
Independence?** *Stanford*,
November 2006
AD: Amy Shroads

Deep Trouble,
Business Week, 2009

AD: Ronald Plyman

Kosovo: A Country Reborn,
Diplomat, September 2010
AD: Jeannine Saba

Grave New World,
Chicago, June 2006
AD: Mary Ruth Yoe

Shades of Green,
Chicago, July–August 2010
AD: Lydialyle Gibson

Modern Times,
Der Spiegel, March 22, 2010

AD: Stefan Kifer

Cold War on the Internet,
Der Spiegel, March 29, 2010
AD: Stefan Kifer

The Power Issue,
Print, February, 2011
AD: Ben King

99%,
Crisis, Fall 2011
AD: Wayne Fitzpatrick

Der China-Böller
Warum Künstler Olympia so lieben

**The Chinese Fireworks – Why the Artists
Love the Olympics So Much**,
Der Spiegel, 2008
AD: Stefan Kiefer
ILLUSTRATION: Mirko Ilić

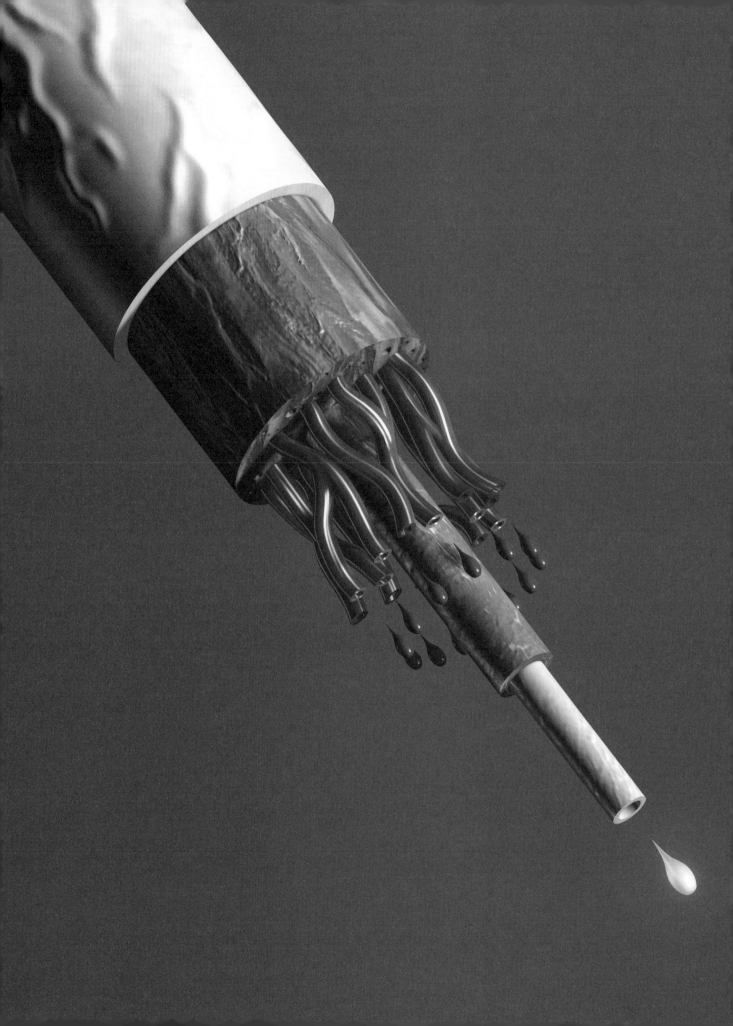

Sex and Lies

by **Steven HELLER**

WHEN I WAS A LITTLE BOY I CALLED THEM *peanut* and *pajama*. When I eventually realized that's not what they were really called I nevertheless continued to say *peanut* for penis and *pajama* for vagina. And I still refer to them this way.

It's certainly a sweeter way of talking about our respective body parts with family and friends.

For my formative years the word *sex* could not be mentioned in polite company—or in church, elevators, or on TV. Forget about saying penis or vagina even though these are, in fact, the polite (and anatomically correct) terms—they were taboo.

Now, you can say *sex* all you want. And penis, vagina, even breasts are vernacular in all manner of mass media. Yet S–E–X are the three most charged letters in the English language. I have no idea how sex is spelled in Croatian, though I presume it is equally provocative.

The word embarrasses and arouses in much the same way that Mirko Ilić's huge penile and vaginal visualizations do.

That Ilić has used his incredible conceptual and technical skills to make us uncomfortable is no surprise, but the magnitude of these images is a shock to senses I never even knew I had.

While I defy anyone to see a real penis or vagina or, for that matter, a breast in these overtly sensual visual puns, the effect is the same. For me this is the most hardcore eroticism I've seen. But what the hell do we see? Are these parts or parcels? They may be graphic, but are they pornographic? They may seem real, but they are really abstractions in a most preternatural way. Ilić proves that sexuality and sensuality are in the mind. Freud was right, "sometimes a cigar is just a cigar," but sometimes a penis is a penis. And while these may not really be what they seem, they are more disturbing than any vivid depiction of real sexography, and also funnier than *peanut* and *pajama*. ✖

TEXT FROM THE CATALOGUE OF *SEX & LIES* EXHIBITION, STUDIO JOSIP RAČIĆ, MODERNA GALERIJA, ZAGREB, APRIL 16 – MAY 14, 2002

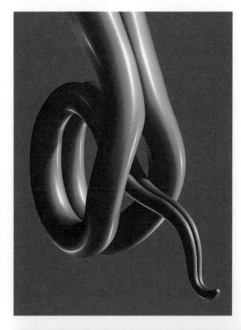

Topsy-Turvy, 2002

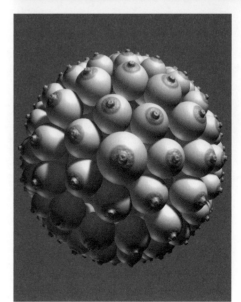

ABOVE: **Mr Moebius**, 2002

LEFT: **Pollenation**, 2002

PREVIOUS PAGE: **Cable**, 2002

ALL WORKS, 3D: Lauren DeNapoli & Mirko Ilić

"If the president of United States was willing to risk his career because of a sexual act, the question is: what is more important—the sex or to be the president of America? I think that the sex is the most important thing. Otherwise, if to all those priests who have been convicted of sexually assaulting kids the sex was more important than going to heaven, it is clear that there is a powerful force that they either cannot or do not want to control."

—MIRKO ILIĆ, "SEX AND LIES ARE PRESENT IN ZAGREB ALL THE TIME," *VEČERNJI LIST*, ZAGREB, APRIL 18, 2002

Suspense, 2002

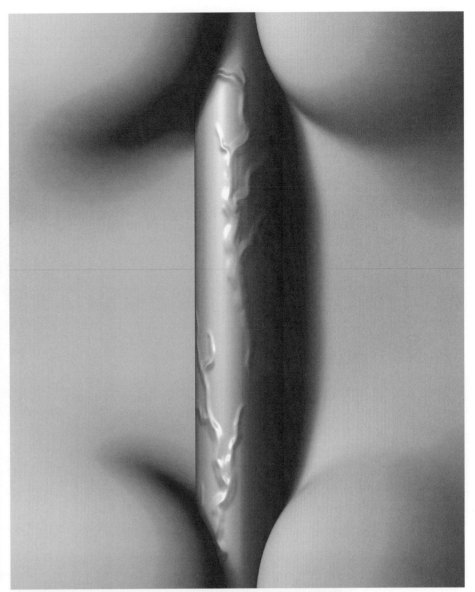

Balance, 2002

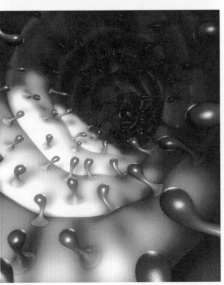

"Sex and lies are
the two things
that often go
together…"

—MIRKO ILIĆ, "GLAMOUR
CAFE," HTV APRIL 19, 2002

Race, 2002 • **Dew**, 2002 • **Insider**, 2002   **Nation**, 2002, ALL WORKS, 3D: Lauren DeNapoli & Mirko Ilić

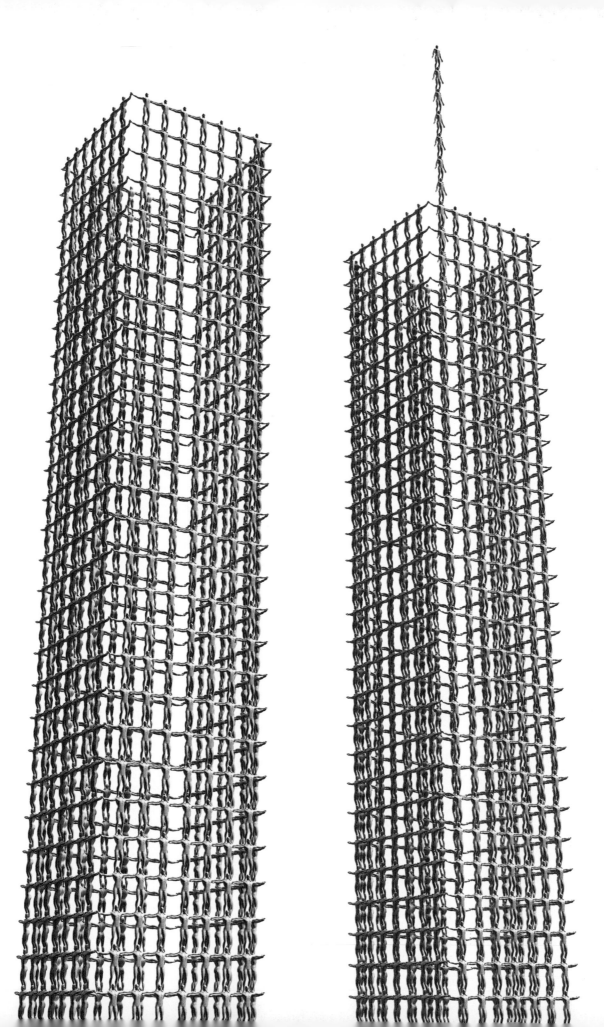

The Policies and Politics of Design

SPEAKING ABOUT THE DIFFERENCES between the contexts in which two periods of his career occurred, Ilić said, "In Yugoslavia, art was like ice hockey. In the United States, it was more like figure skating." But even within this much smoother situation, corporate America certainly provides Ilić with friction that he finds absolutely necessary. Everywhere else, he would already be big enough so no one would dare complain about anything, and his work would be commissioned only by those who were prepared to accept, and even expect, the "excess value" that he puts into an illustration or a design.

"Actually, what I do in America is identical to what I was doing in Yugoslavia. And when I do the official newspaper, I have my own attitude. I still criticize the system, and I do a lot of work for alternative groups, animal rights, and minority groups. I work for the black newspapers, feminist themes. But despite the fact that I'm on 'the other side', I get commissions for illustrations from the most conservative of American newspapers, such as *Spectrum,* which I reject out of my own convictions."

Luka Mjeda has precisely summed up Ilić's position: "From the beginning, he worked for major magazines with the proviso that he never forgot to work for the small ones."

His *Start* magazine illustrations had usually offered a different view and showed an aspect of a topic that even the editors did not consider. When asked how much of his commentary, ribbing, or even subversion his illustrations could take these days, he replied, "A lot less since 9/11. They are all scared shitless, literally afraid of everything. Everyone is extremely careful. With *Start,* I never had to do sketches and show them to the editor. In this sense, the situation has worsened. But expressing the attitude, I don't see it as subversive. You can always slip something under, but that's not the point. I do not want to push stuff under the table. I think it and say it. Subversive is not saying what you think publicly. In *The New York Times,* there were two editors in charge of the weekly Week in Review supplement. One did not like Reagan, and the other one did, so I always knew when to bring my Reagan. Here and there there's room for petty fraud, a stunt that is not immediately obvious, for my own satisfaction, but it is not a stunt that will change the meaning of an illustration. Lately, I've had many illustrations killed and they say: *It's too creepy, it's too scary.* In the studio, we had an image of a dandelion, so we joked—let's fax it and ask if that's OK? It means nothing, but it's not *scary*! One of the reasons why my illustrations are not successful in a business sense is that I can't change my mind; I stick to my opinion. Because at the end, this is what I'm recognized for. And, whether it's with scratchboard or Photoshop is not that important. The only things that I have are ideas and a way of thinking. And that is the biggest problem in selling an illustration. The relationship between a customer and an illustrator is getting worse and worse."

In response to Glaser's explanation that an illustrator is not hired because of ideological beliefs, but because of his drawing style, Ilić replied, "I consider it a bonus: you pay for one thing and get the other one free. You can always fire me."

He does not express his political convictions merely by working for minority groups or charitable projects—such as putting on workshops with talented high school children from economically disadvantaged New York neighborhoods—but also (like other New York peers Glaser, Kalman, and Sagmeister) by flatly refusing to work for some clients whose political or

Still Standing, 2004 a poster in memory of victims of September 11ᵗʰ attack. Number of figures corresponds to the number of people killed at the WTC. Poster is now in collection of the 9/11 Memorial Museum, NYC.

social standing he disagrees with. And that includes not only publications of openly right-wing views, but also a good deal of advertising.

"I could perhaps do some interesting work and make tons of money promoting vodka and cigarettes, but that does not interest me," he said. "I do not want to lie to people to buy products they don't need. Maybe I'll do advertising for those things that I think are important and good, where I can find an interesting angle."

His attitude is perhaps best demonstrated by the answer to the question of who the real client is to a designer—"Not those who pay us, but those we work for! In other words, people, the audience." He formulated his design policy in brief: "I try to find another angle, to earn some money along the way, and to give, at the client's expense, a little more to the final consumer." ▶

Opening Soon: New York's Toughest Prison, *The Village Voice*, May 25, 1999
AD: Minh Uong

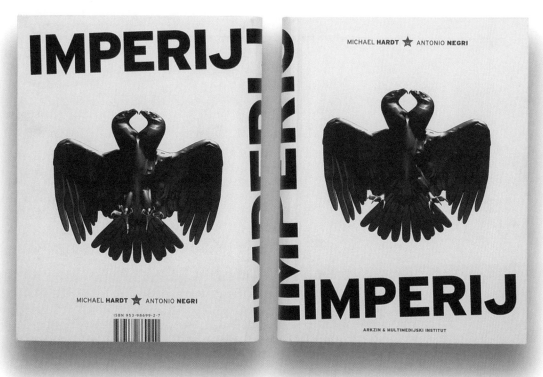

Michael Hardt / Antonio Negri: *Empire*, Arkzin & mi2, Zagreb, 2003
AD: Dejan Kršić,
ILLUSTRATION: Mirko Ilić

Final Solutions, *The Village Voice*, 2003, AD: Minh Uong

"For me, social critique is the 'secret mission' of design. For me, 'pretty' is shown in the truth. If I'm to illustrate an article on abortion and I disagree with the author's opinion, I search for a solution that projects my belief but still works with the article. Subtle, but present."
—MIRKO ILIĆ, "COMICS DIED IN THREE EPISODES," *GLAS JAVNOSTI*, BELGRADE, JANUARY 23, 2001

GRAPHIC ACTIVISM
IN
MEAN TIMES

GLASER: The truth is there's an inherent conflict between business and *art*, whatever that word means. So objectively this is not a good business. It's not something that people get rich at, generally speaking, because you never get rich based on your own efforts. You get rich by engaging other people who are helping you get rich. But the fact of the matter is, that anybody who is good in this field—what does *good* mean?—whose work represents something that goes beyond business or professionalism, are good precisely because of the idea of making something beautiful that represents their skills well. It is much more important to them than being paid appropriately for the job. If you're only working for money, eventually, you will give the least possible effort to every project, because you evaluate the reward in relationship to the work that you're doing. In our field, that does not work. Eventually, the energy just disappears from the work and people become hacks. They get used up. And incidentally, you see that happen to people, who go into the field with enormous talent, and then are robbed of their energy, because they decided they have to make a living and want to look at it as a profession or a job. And ultimately the best people in this field—everybody that you and I could name on our fingers—are people who do not have that objective, who would work for nothing because the meaning of the work goes beyond the payment for the work. So I think that you could almost identify the best designers in our terms by that characteristic.

ILIĆ: In the meantime, it's extremely sad for our profession. People who would work for free! That kind of value does not bring you any respect from corporate America.

GLASER: Corporate America can't have any other value. Corporate America can't value art. Why should they value art? Or value dedication that goes beyond making money. Corporate America is only about the ability to make money. So there's no way they could ever acknowledge that there was anything else in life, except making money.

ILIĆ: Exactly. And that's who we work for. And then, fight the power.

"THE KING AND THE JESTER," GRAPHIS NO. 350, MARCH/APRIL 2004

Graphic Activism in Mean Times,
AIGA NY—Fresh Dialogue, 1995
flyer/poster, double-sided print

Take Back the Net,
The Village Voice, May 16, 2000
AD: Minh Uong

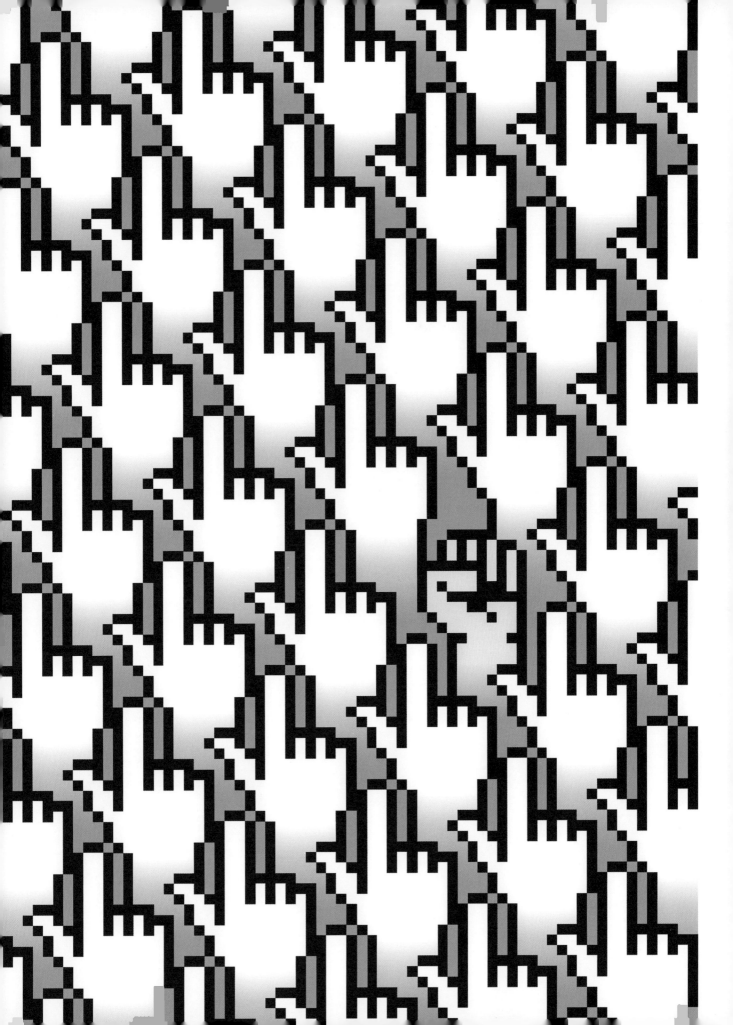

One of Ilić's most controversial illustrations appeared in a 2000 issue of the *Village Voice*. The theme of the issue "You've Got Porn," talked about how America OnLine presents itself as family friendly, but profits from pornography. Ilić had the AOL logo shaped like women's "intimate haircut." But instead of that solution, they published a picture of a cardboard penis that jumps out of a box whose one side represents a computer screen with the AOL logo. As Jesse Sunenblick says in the text *Little Murders*, when you compare the two illustrations, you can't help but feel cheated.

The illustration was not completely rejected. It was shown over an entire page with text, but in an illustrator's world this is a hard blow as well.

Realistically rendered illustrations perhaps could have been published if Ilić, as he admits himself, hadn't made an error and submitted the illustration before the deadline, on Friday, because he traveled out of town for the weekend. "So, they had time to think." There are various competing claims about what really happened. Ilić says that the female editors objected to the exploitation of female body, while the PR office claimed that the magazine's editor-in-chief Don Forst, chose another front page because this one looked "too physical, sexual."

However, the back pages of the *Village Voice* are full of tempting images and ads for sexual services, and the money earned from them enables it to survive as the largest free newspaper in America.

Ilić called the art director. "I told him: You are the biggest because of pimps and whores, escort agencies, and sex phone lines, which are a direct exploitation of women. And it's okay to post these ads, and this is not? So, the editor felt that the illustrations were offensive to women, and her wages are paid directly by pimps. Isn't that controversial? When I put it that way they said: 'Aha, well, yes...' But it was too late."

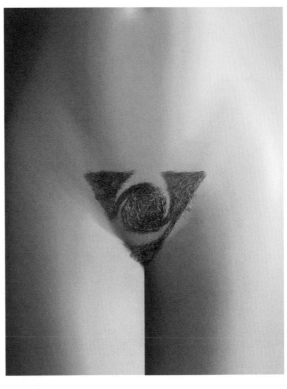

You've Got Porn,
The Village Voice, October 24, 2000

Suddenly Not Susan,
The Village Voice, November 23, 1999

The Burden of Being a Woman,
The Village Voice, December 22, 2004

ALL: AD: Ming Uong

"An illustration I did for the *Village Voice* caused demonstrations. It accompanied an interview with a woman who had undergone many sexual reassignment surgeries to become a man. My illustration showed Barbie with parts of Ken. A group of transgender people thought that I wanted to portray them as monsters and so they organized a large demonstration in front of the *Village Voice*. They did not attack me personally, but when I later did an illustration for *The New York Times* on the conflict between Serbs and Croats, both sides started to call me at home and threatened to slaughter me. The fact that it got the same reaction from both groups was confirmation that my illustration reflected reality."

—MIRKO ILIĆ, "BECAUSE OF MY ILLUSTRATION TRANSVESTITES ORGANIZED DEMONSTRATIONS IN NEW YORK," PLUS 7, *NOVI LIST*, RIJEKA, JULY 10, 2000

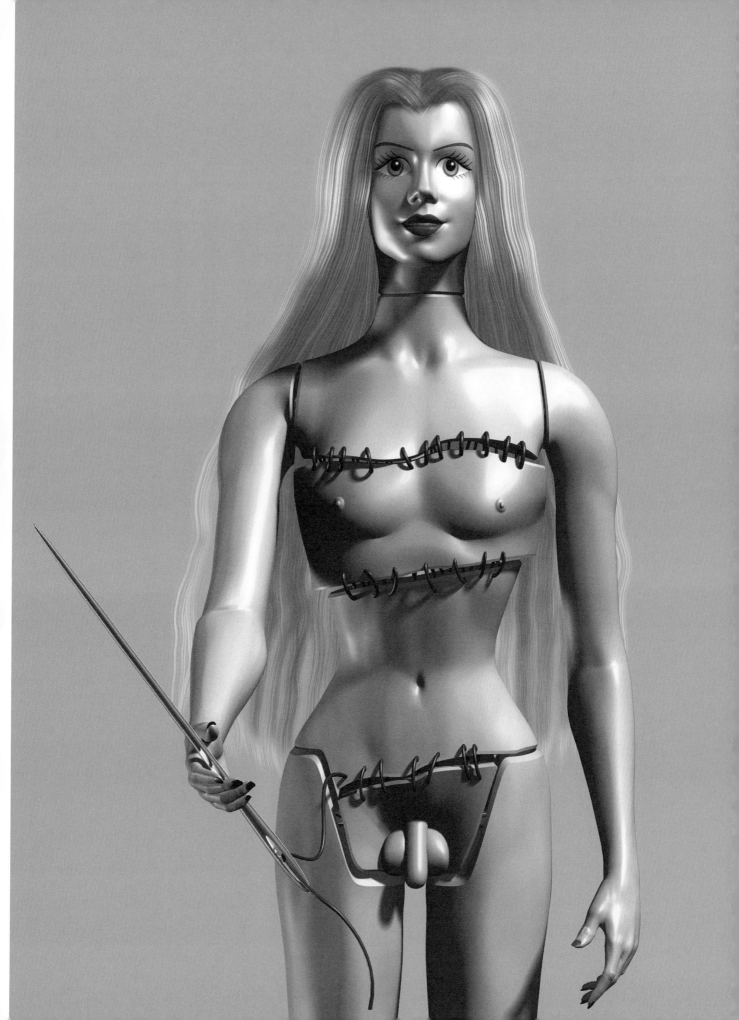

Ewe Two, *The New York Times Book Review*, December 1997, AD: Steven Heller

"The praise that Mirko Ilić received as a graphic designer in the U.S., as well as his successful experiments with computer animation, confirmed the incitement of Novi kvadrat ideas within the virtual reality of new electronic technologies."

—DARKO GLAVAN, "NOVI KVADRAT OF MIRKO ILIĆ: CULTURAL FORGERY OR THE REVOLUTION OF CROATIAN COMICS," *GLOBUS*, DECEMBER 3, 1999

Fat Free, *University of Chicago Magazine* #4, vol. 97, April, 2005, AD: Allen Carroll

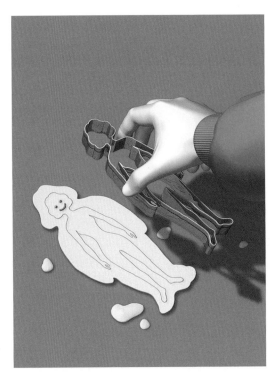

The hard facts, (The sexual male, part five), *Playboy*, 2008 AD: Rob Wilson

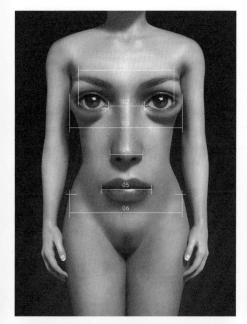

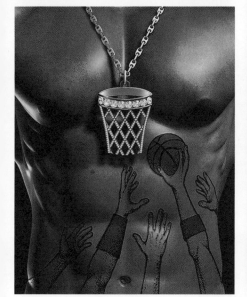

The look of love, (The sexual male, part four), *Playboy*, 2008
AD: Rob Wilson

Love Hurts,
Vibe Magazine, March, 2005
AD: Florian Bachleda

36 Tattoos,
The Village Voice, October 16, 2002
AD: Minh Uong

No Masses, No Movement,
The Village Voice, May 28, 2002
AD: Minh Uong

"I don't care if the country is led by a Republican, a Democrat, an Independent, a black, or a woman I will be equally critical of every president if I think it is necessary."

—MIRKO ILIĆ, "THE KING AND THE JESTER," *GRAPHIS* NO. 350, MARCH/APRIL 2004

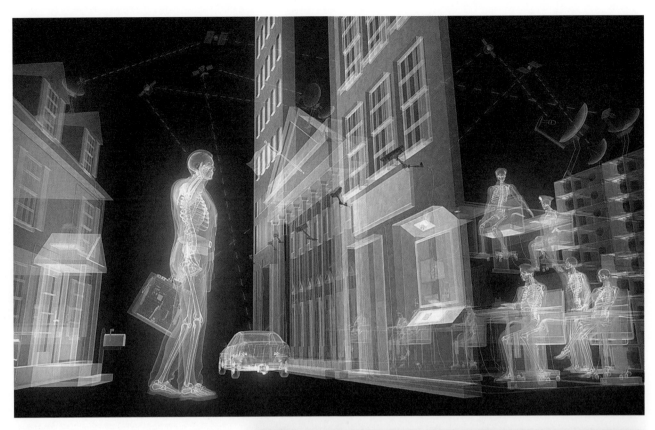

Data Trail

National Geographic, 2003

AD: Jeffrey Osborne

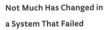

Not Much Has Changed in a System That Failed

The New York Times,
September 8, 2002,
AD: Tom Bodkin

C.I.A, *Emerge*, 1997
AD: Wayne Fitzpatric

When the magazine *Emerge*
ordered the cover for the
January 1997 issue about
the alleged involvement
of the CIA in a planned
distribution of narcotics in
black neighborhoods of Los
Angeles, Ilić acquired seven
crack-pipes in the search for
the one that would perfectly
suit his idea.

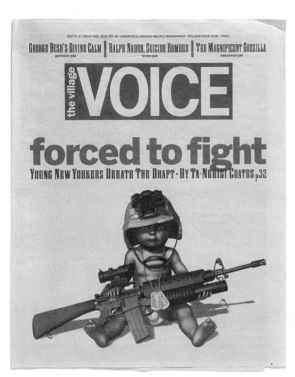

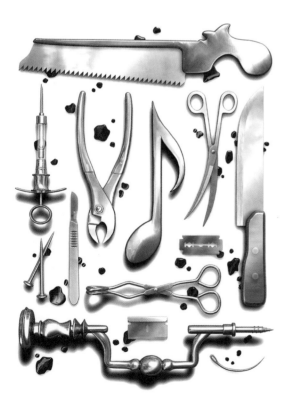

The Scent of War

The Village Voice,
November 13, 2002
AD: Minh Uong

Audio Torture

Best Life, March 2005
AD: Brandon Kavulla

Forced to Fight

The Village Voice,
May 5, 2004
AD: Minh Uong

"In the field of design, Mirko is a rare species. His powers of imagination, invention, and visualization are so extraordinary and so fast it seems unbelievable. And he does everything with a great knowledge of design history and classic design principles. On top of everything, he has a strong social conscience and uncompromised political honesty. Because opposites attract, I go upstairs from my studio every day to visit Mirko and steal whatever I can. Whenever Mirko helps me, it makes my crude ideas presentable. We work well together because we don't give a shit about credit. We just want the work to do its job of making the world better. The vast majority of design is professional pimping for corporations. A small and precious minority is primarily concerned with humanistic values, with freedom, with tolerance, and with goodness. I hope to be counted with him in this group.

—DANIEL YOUNG

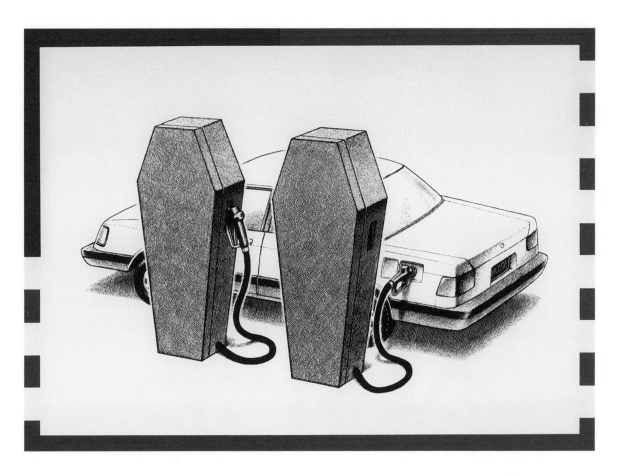

Fuel, 2002
silkscreen poster

Black and white illustration
(**Make Fuel Efficiency Our
Gulf Strategy,** *The New York
Times*, 1990, AD: Michael
Valenti) was redesigned as
a protest poster against
intervention in Iraq.

Bushit, "flyers", Produced for anti-Bush campaigns during the presidential elections in 2004
cw: Daniel Young,
d: Mirko Ilić

Radioactive waste from nuclear power plants stays radioactive and deadly for hundreds of thousands of years.

We can generate electricity in safer ways.

Radioactive waste from nuclear power plants stays radioactive and deadly for hundreds of thousands of years.

We can generate electricity in safer ways.

Radioactive Waste (glow in the dark poster), 2010,
AD & D: Mirko Ilić, Daniel Young, CLIENT: Paradoxy Products

All these works were conceived, created, and funded by Daniel Young and Mirko Ilić.

Fix the Mistake!, 2004
Project realized for the
2004 Presidential elections.
A signage flown daily for
about 10 days, in Florida
from South Beach to Fort
Lauderdale. The project was
financed by Daniel Young,
Stefan Sagmeister, Louise
Fili, and Mirko Ilić.

Tolerance is Holy, 2005,
D: Daniel Young & Mirko Ilić
Poster was made for
Jerusalem Gay Pride,
when leaders of all
opposed religious groups
were equally engaged in
opposition to Gay Pride
parade in "Holly City".

Greed, Occupy Wall St.
T-shirt design
PHOTO: Jacquie Osman, 2011.

Occupy Wall Street,
d: Dallas Graham and
Mirko Ilić, 2012
Piece is created out of bits
of logos from different
banks and financial
institutions.

Dachau — Nazi concentration camp in G

Auschwitz — Nazi concentration

Radogosz — Nazi concentration c

Flossenbürg — Nazi conc

Ulven — Nazi concentration camp in Norway

Ravensbrück — Nazi con

To help, contact: www.ajws.org   www.genocideinterventi

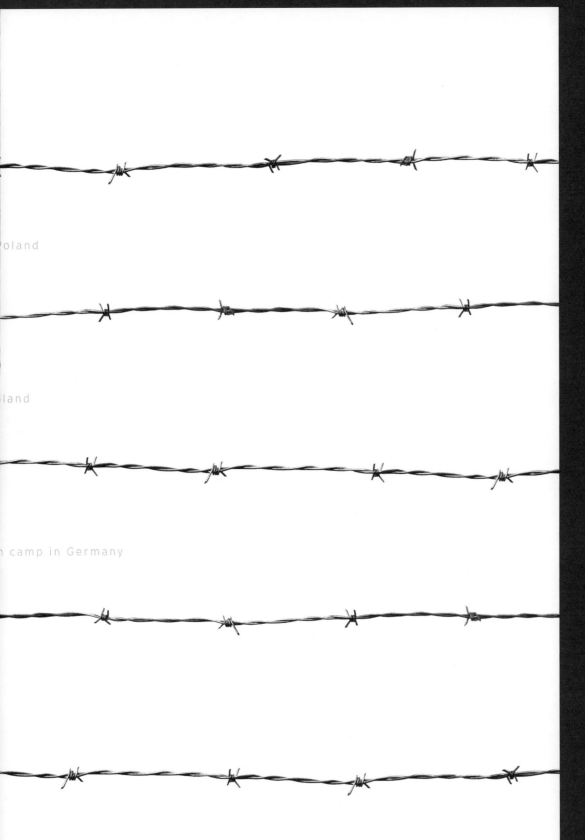

Poland

land

camp in Germany

on camp in Germany

www.savedarfur.org   www.theirc.org   www.unicefusa.org   www.worldvision.org

Darfur poster, 2006
D: Mirko Ilić & Daniel Young
The poster has caused
much discussion on the use
of Holocaust motifs outside
the context of suffering
Jews from Nazi and other
pro-fascist governments.
Conceived, created, and
funded by Daniel Young and
Mirko Ilić.

222

> "There are a thousand reasons not to give something to someone, and there is only one reason to do so. There are a thousand reasons why homosexuals are not allowed on Croatian television, and only one why they should be: we want to hear what they have to say."
>
> —MIRKO ILIĆ, "SEX AND LIES OF MIRKO ILIĆ," FORUM, SLOBODNA DALMACIJA, SPLIT, APRIL 17, 2002

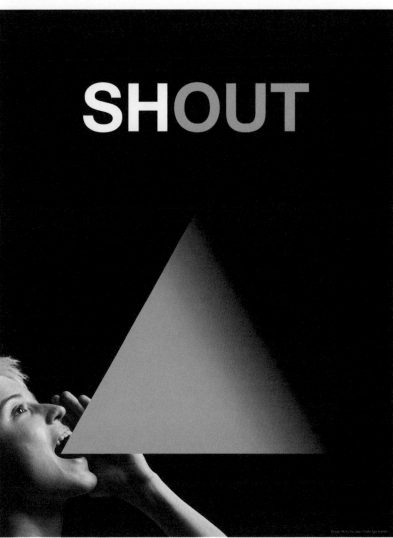

SHOUT—Gay Pride Parade, 2011
Poster design for New York's Gay Pride
Parade 2011 is a combination of Alexander
Rodchenko's poster, "Lengiz-Books" (1925)
and the famous "Silence = Death" (1986)
poster about AIDS.
PHOTO: Igor Mandić

Calderone / Provocateur poster and program booklet
for a party during Gay Pride Weekend 2002
D: Heath Hinegardner, Mirko Ilić
3D ILLUSTRATION: Lauren DeNapoli, Mirko Ilić

ABSOLUT TIMES.

"A problem arises with clients that do not see that they could earn money from a good design, but at the same time they run to buy a new car because it looks nice! They buy it because of the design, and here they do not believe that design equals money. Fashion design and advertising in fashion magazines dictates what you wear. If design can dictate how you are going to look, it obviously can propose and suggest some other things as well. With that kind of design you never know whether you succeeded or not. It is always a crapshoot. With shoes you always know how much you sold."

—MIRKO ILIĆ, "THERE IS A LOT OF BAD DESIGN IN POLITICS, BECAUSE EVERYONE WANTS TO CARRY FAVOR WITH THE MASSES," *VJESNIK*, ZAGREB, MAY 14–15, 2005

Illustration, the Method

WRITING ABOUT ILLUSTRATION IN AMERICA, Steven Heller points out that the artists who came from the former Eastern Europe have strongly influenced the trends of American illustration with their metaphorical visual vocabulary.

"Criticism, cynicism, and a great deal of sensitivity to social and political issues have made Mirko Ilić a leading graphic commentator on current events, for which in some situations it is just incredible that he identifies them, not being a native to the American culture..." [01]

Ilić's mastery of political illustration is reflected in the way that he involves the viewer in the game. His illustrations often seem like a frame from the comic in which we never see the following one, we have to imagine it, to construct a picture in our mind and complete a story. The fact that we must engage in solving a kind of rebus, means that we must stay a few seconds longer on the illustration because it draws out our attention, and in an ideal sense, forced us as readers to think of the political problem it represents and ultimately to take a stand about it. Ilić himself says that many of his illustrations are based on the manipulation of two quite ordinary, everyday objects linked in an unusual way. We could say that the key characteristic of his illustration work is the use of metaphors, which he often manages to extract from the most ordinary things, topics dangerously threatened by banality.

Illustration on the topic *digital city* would lure many illustrators to some sci-fi vision of the city of the future, variations on the Orwellian, or virtual reality. Ilić however is moving in the reverse direction. Instead of the futuristic vision of the city wired with digital communications systems, he sees the city and structure of streets, and turns it into a picture of a typical American city, with a bank and a hospital, park, and monuments. Simple? Yes, why have we not thought of that before! Banal? No, and exactly because we did not think of it before. But after that illustration—whether we see a chip or hear something about the "digital city," we shall never be able to avoid that association.

He has achieved a similar effect with the work that he considers as one of his greatest successes, the cover of the *Time* magazine picturing the conflict between the Francophone and Anglophone populations in Canada, bearing no text. When he drew two faces in simple strokes around the recognizable symbol of maple leaf of the Canadian flag, perception of that symbol was forever changed for many.

"After that, Canadians called me and told me that I have changed their flag forever. I made it so that people can no longer see the Canadian flag without seeing two profiles in it. Such things make me happier than any award. It's when you point to someone something that existed before, but people did not see it that way."

Such an approach is precisely in the spirit of the idea that we just need to learn to observe. As the designer Bob Gill has said, "Each of my works is based on things that people could have perceived by themselves if they only tried a little harder."

"That is correct. It's all there," Ilić confirms but adds: "If I take someone's idea and draw it in my own way, in most cases, my work would eventually be stronger, because ideas are often not supported by technique. Everything is already around us, but the road from the head to the paper is different, and art is happening on that road. I am not fascinated by intellect anymore. All intellect has two or three systems of functioning. I am totally fascinated by stupidity. You'd say, how in the world did he think of that! Stupidity is much more fascinating. ▶

01 | Heller quoted in catalogue of the exhibition *Mirko Ilić: Graphic design, illustrations*, Art Pavilion, Zagreb 1992

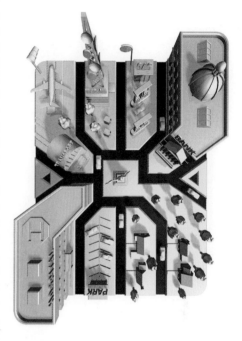

Digital City, Schlumberger
Annual Report, 1996
AD: Milton Glaser & Walter
Bernard

PREVIOUS PAGE:
Absolut Times,
Times Talk, newsletter of
The New York Times Company, 2001
AD: Richard Press

**Bidu Sayāo: Opera Arias
and Brazilian Folk Songs**

CD digipak, Sony 1996

D: Nicky Lindeman & Mirko Ilić

From Gershwin's Time

CD digipak, Sony 1998

Lily Pons: Coloratura Assoluta

CD digipak, Sony 1998.

Gregor Piatigorsky:

Great Cello Concerts

CD digipak, Sony 1997

George Szell &

Cleveland Orchestra:

Prokofiev / Bartók,

CD digipak, Sony 1999

Lotte Lenya Sings Kurt Weill,

The American Theatre Songs

CD digipak, 1999

ILLUSTRATION: Karl Ericson

ALL COVERS

Sony Classical • Masterworks Heritage

AD: Allen Weinberg

D: Mirko Ilić

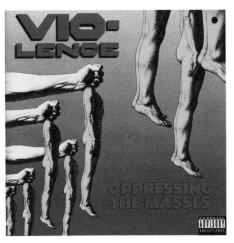

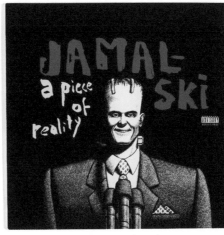

C+C Music Factory,
Logo, Sony Music, 1990
D: Nicky Lindeman & Mirko Ilić

Violence: Oppressing The Masses,
Atlantic Records Corporation, 1990
AD: Bob Defrin, ILLUSTRATION: Mirko Ilić

Jamalski: A Piece of Reality,
Sony BMG, 1992

Rage Against the Machine:
Bulls on Parade
CD single, Sony/Epic, 1996

Rage Against the Machine:
Evil Empire
CD single, Sony/Epic, 1996

RIGHT: **RATM t-shirt**

Buldožer: Night
Helidon 1995, 6751750

"It's good that trends don't typically happen all over America at once. A few years back a big trend in Seattle was the grunge movement. At the same time in Los Angeles there was overlapping type designed on a computer. In New York, Stefan Sagmeister was doing something completely different from everything that was happening in the West or in the rest of the U.S."

— MIRKO ILIĆ

Urban & 4: Hello!
Croatia Records 2009, CD 5832478
PHOTO: Milica Czerny Urban

Primož Grašič: My Wish
(Nika 2000, NR-CD-Y-0040)

**SVA To Help See
Possibilities**

The School of Visual Arts
poster, 2008
CD: Anthony Rhodes
AD: Michael Walsh
D: Mirko Ilić
ILLUSTRATION:
Mirko Ilić Corp.

Designer as Author

How we survived deconstructivism and even laughed

AS AN EXPRESSION OF THE MODERNIST IDEOLOGY (developed by the Bauhaus and its followers), the position that design should be "anonymous," that good design is not an individual author's expression, but a result of specific needs and a rational response to existing problems, was dominant until recently. As Rick Poynor pointed out, there were always a handful of famous designers who, like Raymond Loewy and Charles Eames, became famous, but for most designers—especially graphic designers—anonymity was their professional destiny. In the last twenty years, though, that has changed.

"A class of design stars has emerged and for anyone going into design now, it must be clear that fame is an achievable goal. There are various reasons for this. In broader terms, it corresponds to deep changes within the culture..."[01]

But still, to most people, the term "designer" unfortunately does not suggest someone who is solving problems—as Tomás Maldonado defined it—instead, they often think of a fashion designer or even a hairdresser. Magazines with the word "design" in their name are mainly focused on interior decoration. We have not only designer furniture and designer jeans but also designer beer and water, even designer drugs.

At the same time, inside the design profession itself, many designers and writers argue that contemporary design has reduced its role to being the handmaid of marketing and advertising. Critics point out that there are many more important issues and communication problems that really deserve designers attention. The *First Things First 2000* manifesto was one such attempt at addressing the problems of contemporary design and its shifting role by the profession as a whole. If conservatives limit the role of design to the service of commerce, radical critics point out that in the development of design as profession many theoreticians and practitioners—from Bauhaus to Victor Papanek and the Antidesign movement of the late sixties—have been emphasizing social aspects and meanings of design. Design was regarded as a device for social progress, not just a tool to raise productivity and sales.

"When did you last see an advertisement for bread?" Ilić asked. "Bread is not advertised because everyone eats it, but why are there so many commercials for bottled water? Because we have tap water and in fact we do not need to buy it! So, advertising and design are just pushing stuff that we don't need. What we really need, we buy anyway. The entire marketing, advertising, and the design, create in us the need to buy something that we probably do not need at all. Of course, design can deal with other, more important social issues, but this is done by a smaller number of people who get less media exposure and earn far less than the design stars whose names everybody knows.

"It has been extremely common in the last ten or fifteen years for young designers to start their own studios and collectives soon after graduating," Poynor said. "There is great pressure on those who want rapid success to devlop a distinctive style while still a student. By comparison, twenty or so years ago, young designers usually worked for established design companies for a number of years, learning all aspects of the craft and business, before setting up their own companies (if they did this at all)."[02]

"Ten years ago, only the most stellar and durable design figures would find themselves lauded in career monographs, which design book publishers regarded as commercially risky ventures. Today, publishers compete with each other to sign deals and publish lavish, celebratory tomes. None of this would be happening if there wasn't a huge appetite within the design profession, particularly among younger designers, to admire, learn about, and learn from its inspirational figures. At the same time, there is a growing interest outside the design world in the people who shape our visual reality. Three-dimension designers are the usual beneficiaries of this attention, but occasionally a graphic designer—Neville Brody, Tibor Kalman, David Carson...

—RICK POYNOR, "BARING IT ALL—STEFAN SAGMEISTER & THE RETURN OF IDEA-BASED DESIGN," *HANDARBEIT*, MAK, VIENNA 2002

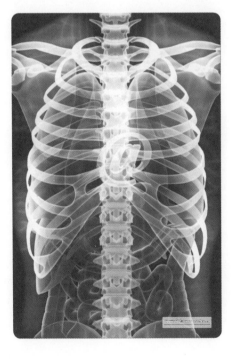

Punct'd, limited edition poster on the subject of typographic sign, Neenah Paper, 2004

01 I Rick Poynor: Baring it all – Stefan Sagmeister and the return of idea-based design, in Handarbeit, MAK, Vienna 2002, pgs. 54–55

02 I Ibid, pg. 55

In that aspect Ilić's professional development was quite unique as well. In the early days, he first received attention for his comics and then he expanded his scope of action to almost everything that a graphic designer in socialist Yugoslavia could do at that time. When he came to the United States, a new professional environment with quite different corporate rules, he again established his position as an illustrator first and then used it to expand his activities to other areas of graphic and visual communications.

His work in socialist Yugoslavia was often criticized for lacking a unique and distinctive style. But that aspect of his work can be seen as a certain post-modern "death of the author" form. Rejection of classical narrative comics also represented an equivalent to the disappearance of the omniscient narrator. In the same way that the short story was an ideal medium of postmodern literature, short experimental forms in just one or two tabs were the same for new comics. Those Ilić defined as "comics without obligation," without the burden of permanent characters, a recognizable but repetitive style, or even the continuity of publication. For his eclecticism Ilić is undoubtedly a postmodernist, but this kind of postmodernism has nothing to do with a parasitic strip-mining of the past or uncritical acceptance of the consumer culture. On the contrary, he always strived towards provocation and innovation. In what seems established and well known he works to discover something new.

His approach is self-reflexive. It includes his own position which cannot remain intact and unchanged. It is an active position, by which the author includes himself in the whole picture. A kind of a metaphor for this is his frequent introduction of himself or a look-alike as a character in his comics and illustrations. *Otvoreni strip* (Open comic) was entirely about the process of drawing comics, and comments on the context of its own publication in newspapers.

This is what literary theory calls metafiction. Many comics emphasized their own media nature as well and self-reflexively pointed out to the reader the means of their production and in so doing increased awareness of their own artificiality. This is an educational process of Brechtian type; it is a type of art, comic, or illustration that does not allow us to stare at it romantically, but instead wants to snap us out of our dogmatic slumber.

His faith in development, overcoming limits, and rejecting the conventional limitations in thinking, makes Ilić a follower of the radical spirit of modernism, and not an empty formal shell of late-modernist design (exemplified, for instance, in the formal use of Helvetica and the grid that through the decades have become signifiers of the international corporate style). Thus, it is easy to see that the authors he deeply admires, such as Milton Glaser and Robert Massin, are in a way similar. In terms of form, they were postmodern when postmodernism did not yet have a name, and today they still defend the basic progressive cultural values of modernism.

Proposed design for the passport and paper bills of the Independent Republic of New York. Illustrations for the text **The independent Republic of New York**, *New York Magazine*, August 2004, AD: Chris Dixon, IL: Mirko Ilić

The expansion of Apple's Macintosh computers as a design tool opened up great opportunities for experimentation with typography, which served the development of so-called deconstructivist approach well. Under the influence of Wolfgang Weingart, deconstructivism spread in the United States in the late eighties from institutions such as the Cranbrook Academy of Art, Cal Arts, and *Emigre* magazine. Radical, eccentric layouts, strange new typefaces and the typographical complexity of the West Coast in the late eighties and nineties did not affect Ilić much. Undoubtedly, this was partly the result of the internal U.S. division into East and West Coast scenes. Already, he was a New Yorker. In terms of typography, he has favored the work of Jonathan Hoefler and Tobias Frere-Jones, who rely on American typographic tradition. Taking over the ideas and achievements of the past—past artists, periods and styles—is a legitimate part of design practice. In a way, graphic designers have always been postmodernists (relying on the work of other authors, from other contexts and times, when creating their own narratives).

Designing the op-ed pages of *The New York Times* was one such example where an almost forgotten idea from typographic history was creatively transformed for new purposes in a new medium. Just at the moment when the expansion of the Internet, e-mail, and the Web, turned the old print magazines and newspapers into a new art form—which was particularly evident in magazines such as *Emigre* and *Ray Gun*—Ilić made a similar creative breakthrough, not in the field of alternative publishing intended for young and radical readers, but in the heart of the American corporate media-culture—*Time* magazine and *The New York Times*. The counterargument to the thesis that old media dinosaurs simply reacted to the appearance of new visual and cultural tendencies, wanting to modernize the look and thus make themselves more appealing to a new audience, can easily be found in the more conventional design of these newspapers after the termination of Ilić's cooperation with them. Obviously it was all about individual creative breakthrough as well as about personal strength and ability to convince editors of the value of his solutions.

At that time when the design world was strongly marked with new digital typography, Ilić and his associates created an entire calendar using a hand-drawn mixture of Cyrillic and Latin letters in the 2001 project Antiewall. He also anticipated the interest expressed in the book coauthored with Steven Heller, *Handwritten: Expressive Lettering In The Digital Age* (Thames & Hudson, 2004)—a kind of backlash at the moment of saturation with digital innovations. Examples gathered in the book show that strange things were done with typography even before computers and that they could be done without it too, i.e., they point out that typographic experiment is by no means related to modern digital technology only.

The revolution in graphic design is usually associated with the emergence of personal computers, which enabled designers to fully perform complex and demanding professional jobs, which, in the technical sense of designing, composing, and creating layouts, scanning, and prepress, until recently was done by a whole team of professionals. This is certainly important, but there is another side to it. The democratization of digital media has enabled a large number of people who are not, narrowly speaking, graphic designers, to realize their own needs in that area, and it gave them some of the special technical tools of professional designers. What, then, makes one designer different from another, or from everyone else who is able to work in desktop publishing software? It can only be in his way of thinking. Contemporary graphic designer can no longer be limited to knowing the "rules of the profession"—although the extent to which new generations of digital designers often neglect finer points in typography can be painful. Designers now have to devote more attention to what a computer is not able to do. They need to think creatively, to be politically and socially responsible. There is nothing new for Ilić in this situation. The computer releases him from hard manual work, giving him greater control over the whole product, but the most important thing remains the same—the notion that the idea is paramount. ▶

"If you work on someting that's a fad one minute, it will be out of fashion the next. In this way design is similar to the music industry: there are musicians who constantly sell albums, and there are those who make a trendy one hit wonder and then disappear. The question is who would you rather be, David Bowie or the Spice Girls?"

—MIRKO ILIĆ, "GIVE ME A DEADLINE AND MONEY," *ORIS* NO. 2, ZAGREB, 1999

The Bells Are Ringing • Where's Charley? • Lost in the Stars, Theatre posters illustrations, Spot Co, 2010, AD & D: Nicky Lindeman, ILLUSTRATION: Mirko Ilić

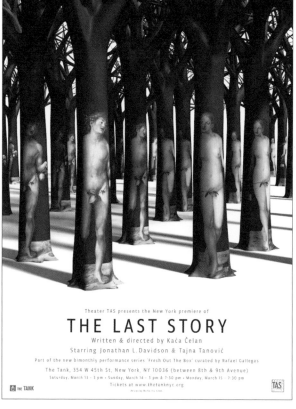

The Weeping Game,

poster, The Local Museum / KinoKamera, 2011

AD & D: Mirko Ilić

The Last Story,

poster, Theater TAS, 2010

AD: Mirko Ilić, Jee-eun Lee

ILLUSTRATION: Mirko Ilić Corp.

OPPOSITE PAGE:

Recycling Art

poster, The Philbrook Museum of Art,

Art Directors Club of Tulsa, 2004

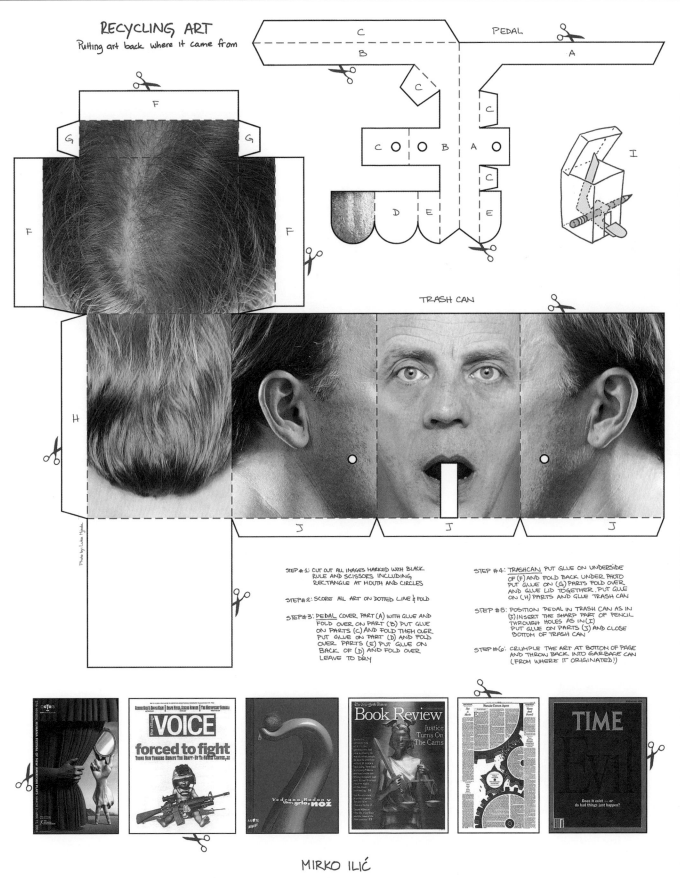

RECYCLING ART
Putting art back where it came from

PEDAL

C
B
A

C
C
C
C O O O B A O
D E E
F
G G
F F

I

TRASH CAN

H

J J J

Photo by Luka Hyodo

STEP #1: CUT OUT ALL IMAGES MARKED WITH BLACK RULE AND SCISSORS INCLUDING RECTANGLE AT MOUTH AND CIRCLES

STEP #2: SCORE ALL ART ON DOTTED LINE & FOLD

STEP #3: PEDAL COVER PART (A) WITH GLUE AND FOLD OVER ON PART (B) PUT GLUE ON PARTS (C) AND FOLD THEM OVER PUT GLUE ON PART (D) AND FOLD OVER PARTS (E) PUT GLUE ON BACK OF (D) AND FOLD OVER LEAVE TO DRY

STEP #4: TRASHCAN PUT GLUE ON UNDERSIDE OF (F) AND FOLD BACK UNDER PHOTO PUT GLUE ON (G) PARTS FOLD OVER AND GLUE LID TOGETHER. PUT GLUE ON (H) PARTS AND GLUE TRASH CAN

STEP #5: POSITION PEDAL IN TRASH CAN AS IN (I) INSERT THE SHARP PART OF PENCIL THROUGH HOLES AS IN (I) PUT GLUE ON PARTS (J) AND CLOSE BOTTOM OF TRASH CAN

STEP #6: CRUMPLE THE ART AT BOTTOM OF PAGE AND THROW BACK INTO GARBAGE CAN (FROM WHERE IT ORIGINATED!)

VOICE
forced to fight

Book Review
Justice Turns On The Cams

TIME

MIRKO ILIĆ

THE PHILBROOK MUSEUM OF ART   OCTOBER 21, 2004   ORGANIZED BY ART DIRECTORS CLUB OF TULSA

The poster reads:

AIGA DFW Presents Mirko Ilić

May 3rd, 2010 at Clampitt Creative Center

Reception at 6:30pm followed by presentat[ion]

AIGA Dallas Fort Worth
AIGA | the professional association for design
Design: Mirko Ilić Corp. Photo: Matthew Klein
Print

"I get bored very easily. It might sound pretentious, but if you look at my career you will see that I stopped making comics when I was on top of the game. When record design was my forte, I stopped designing records. When hand drawn illustration picked up, I stopped illustrating. It's simple, I get bored. I am not interested in what others expect of me; when I get bored, I see no reason whatsoever to keep doing it. Therefore, all of those different things that I do, make me happy because one should always challenge the brain with new puzzles rather than continue to solve old ones."

—MIRKO ILIĆ, "GIVE ME THE DEADLINE AND THE MONEY," *ORIS* NO.2, ZAGREB, 1999

Design, Money and...

poster, AIGA Dallas, 2010
AD & D: Mirko Ilić
The poster was designed with the help of Aleksandra Jakovljević and Eytan Schiowitz.
PHOTOGRAPHY: Matthew Klein

2010 – The Year in Culture,
The New York Times,
December 19, 2010
AD: Paul Jean
ILLUSTRATION: Mirko Ilić

RIGHT:

Jazz at Lincoln Center,
poster, AIC Foundation, 2009
AD: Mirko Ilić
D: Mirko Ilić, Jee-eun Lee

30th anniversary AIGA/NY,
AIGA/NY asked 30 NYC designers to
create commemorative posters for their
anniversary, 2012

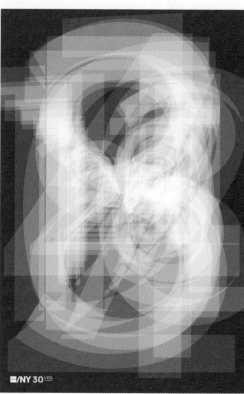

The Eye, Part II

by Laetitia WOLFF

MIRKO ILIĆ IS MY MENTOR.

Mirko is an eye, an image maker and an image matcher, who discovers treasure troves of inspiring imagery for both himself and others. The treasure trove he offered me, unsolicited, in the spring of 2000, was Massin. A single name that "I should have known," as Mirko put it, a name to which I could not as yet attach an image. Since then, Mirko has supported me in all my graphic endeavors: feeding me with exotic leads for the editorial direction of *Graphis* magazine, helping me curate the Young Guns 3 NYC show on whose board he sat, and designing the Massin exhibition poster. Under the benevolent eye of my mentor, I also learned a fair bit about design politics and I curated the Massin retrospective, when it was shown for the first time in America.

Mirko is the rare bird who gets as much excitement from creating images as he does from discovering them. He has brought an insatiable curiosity to the rich patrimony of culturally inherited images, safely stored in his head as much as in his file cabinets. This source material promises to yield even more compelling assemblages. Icons, books, and prints (new and old) are rarely gathered for their own sake, but rather so they can be transcended into a very personal picture alphabet. Without lapsing into the compulsive fixation of a collector, he draws sheer pleasure from cataloging these signs into specific interpretative contexts. Doctor Ilić curates them, translates them, "and prescribes" them via comprehensible, digestible groupings. Revealing connections is in fact one of his favourite games. While building bridges over ancient cultural discord he, by the same token, trains the eye to acknowledge similarities rather than differences.

Under the multifarious, enlightened identity of a designer-illustrator-cum-editor, Ilić has conceived many book projects in association with Steven Heller—an ubiquitous name in design criticism. Triggered from a pure and often personal visual statement, those projects reflect Mirko's desire not to forget the very origins of images, how they were generated and then used. *The Swastika: Symbol Beyond Redemption* is an incisive exploration of the meaning, mysteries, and misunderstanding of one of the most powerful symbols in the history of mankind. *Genius Moves* makes historical parallels to show how the best ideas perpetuate themselves over time. The *Hand Scrawl* is a record of hand-drawn lettering in the digital age. These projects have all been built from the ground up, with the secret intent of alerting our minds and senses to historical facts and truths (especially those that repeat), and ultimately, to elevating the viewer above the lowest common denominator of visual mediocrity. Ilić is like a corrosive solvent that reveals by exposing.

Hidden deep under Ilić's mania for imagery, I suspect there is a sense of ethical responsibility: i.e., the need to save nonvisual people from intellectual blindness. Or rather, to establish a visual history for the very industry that claims to be visual when too often short-term memory problems impedes its judgment.

The "mission impossible" of this dispenser of visual justice is by nature shared with others. By advocating for a better record of what's there to be seen and understood, he fights against oblivion and amnesia with the keepsake of all media: the book. And although he has taught regularly at various educational institutions, I am not quite sure the academic forum is necessarily the ideal arena for his exposés. The linear structure of the book seems more in tune with his design chronicles. Attached to his discoveries of unheard-of talents, incredible wacky typefaces, exquisite graphite drawings, and underground silk screens there is a delicious satisfaction in the act of finding, combined with the design "deed." With a mischievous pride taken in the discovery of overlooked visual artifacts, Mirko makes a book as a proof. The book, the magazine, and printed matter in general are definitely his preferred media. A book title or an author's name won't help much, but tell him the cover is black-and-white with lettering on a bathroom door, and he'll give you the exact page number where that striking image of a scarred body appears. The book brings organizational power to his rich visual memory and a sequence to his complex parallels.

To this day I keep asking him, "When are we starting our magazine together?"

Mirko Ilić is my mentor. ✖

NEW YORK, DECEMBER 2002

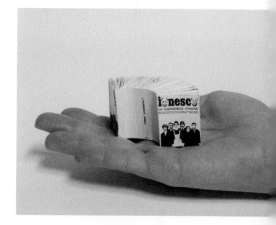

Poster for retrospetive exhibition
Massin in Continuo: A Dictionary, 2001
D: Heath Hinegardner, Mirko Ilić
DIAGRAMS: Heath Hinegardner
COMMISIONER: Futureflair

Poster could be folded into small book –
mini reproduction of Massin's famous
typographic interpretation of Ionesco's
La Cantatrice chauve, Gallimard, Paris 1964

The Books

1988 to today

NEW YORK IS A WORLD CENTER of the communication and information industies, and Milton Glaser believes that the diversity of his work was most certainly partly based on the location of his workplace. This also applies to Ilić. Paradoxically, what New York gave him as an added bonus was not an awareness of trends, knowledge of contemporary works and authors, or the availability of the latest technologies, but rather the opposite: the awareness of the past, of history. The access to new technologies is certainly faster and easier there, but his passion for old books and digging into the history of design rose to a new level.

"In America, I have achieved the two things I like most. One is that I love to travel, and another is that I like to collect books. I have a huge amount of old and new books, for example, the first editions of *El Lissitzky, Rodchenko*. I have Mayakovsky's *Poetry to be read aloud (For the Voice)*, which only three-thousand copies were released, out of which about a thousand have survived. Or a copy of the magazine *Nemoguće* (Impossible) that was published in Belgrade in 1932 and that probably no one in Belgrade has today. I have a huge collection of books and magazines from the period 1910–1950, and each of these pieces is extremely valuable. Not because they are expensive, but because their content is extremely valuable to me. I recently came across a book on architecture, *Visionary Cities: the Archaeology of Paolo Soleri*, which was published in America in 1971, and I was shocked to find out that the author, Donald Wall, was talking about things that some designers today, like David Carson, are quasi-inventing and using to make celebrities out of themselves. I sent the book to *Eye* magazine and they published four pages of it claiming that it was the most important typographic book in the world published in the seventies, and that almost no one today was aware of it because we, designers, read only books about design, while this is a book about architecture, it simply flew under the radar, and nobody noticed it. I bought the book for fifty dollars. I found three or four copies more and gave them to friends as presents. After the article in *Eye* and three other pieces in other magazines, everybody started to look for it, so it reached the price of fifteen-hundred dollars. These are my favorite successes.

I go to bookstores and I go through pages, I smell the paper, I look at the covers, and read the dedication. It's nice to hold a book that was once in the hands of Rodchenko, so I touch that page and it seems that I am touching him through history."

Said another lover of old books, Internet artist Vuk Ćosić: "Mirko and I have two themes: a sort of non-evil childish ego-match in which we praise each other about how brilliant we are, and collecting avant-garde printed things. We share a suicidal passion for design freaks from the twentieth century, mainly avant-gardists from between the two wars. These dialogues are interesting, because there are a few collectors of this material. So when we meet, we always harass each other by bragging about new pieces in our collections. And so, our macho dialogue continued for years—I show him Davičo's *Traces* from 1928 in five copies, and then he kills me with Mayakovsky. And so on. It's a horror."

Rewriting the Book,
Information Entertainment,
1996
AD: Milton Glaser &
Walter Bernard
ILLUSTRATION: Mirko Ilić

Herman Hesse: *Steppenwolf* and
The Glass Bead Game,
Henry Holt 1988, AD: Lee Wade,
D: Nicky Lindeman, ILLUSTRATION: Mirko Ilić

Elvis + Marilyn: 2×Immortal

Rizzoli, 1994

AD & D: Mirko Ilić

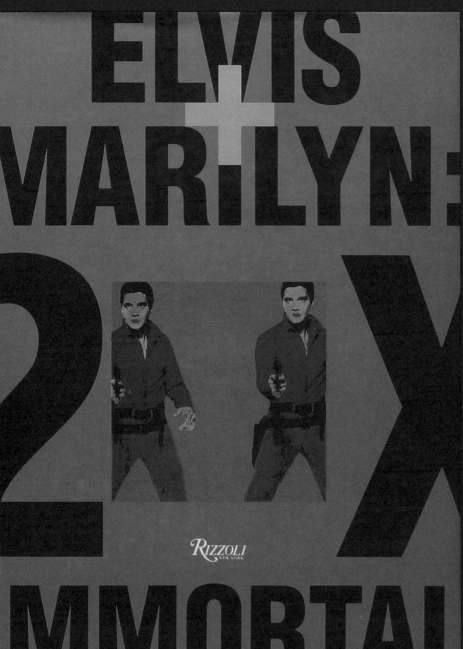

"Mirko Ilić looked to the Russian Constructivists ... blended typography reminiscent of Russian Constructivist El Lissitzky with images by pop artist Andy Warhol for the cover of a thoroughly modern book on Marilyn and Elvis.

Ilić obviously enjoys tweaking cranky editors. Take his design for the 1994 catalog that accompanied an exhibit at the Cleveland Museum of Art of images celebrating two American legends: Elvis Presley and Marilyn Monroe.

"Elvis and Marilyn were icons—they were worshipped by people. So my first draft was done to look like old Bibles, but with new typography. I used Beowulf, "says the designer." But the curators went bananas. They sent me a letter explaining exactly what I could and could not do. They said they wanted classical type. But they didn't say what shape the type should be in."

For the inside pages, Ilić again formed words into shapes. This time, though, his design was influenced by Russian Constructivism, not German poetry. "It's very bold, very minimalistic," he says.

The cover blends Constructivist type with pop art images by Andy Warhol. Ilić cites a book of poems to be read aloud designed by El Lissitzky in 1923: "All the illustrations were done from pieces Lissitzky found in the printing room. I'm trying to see what you can pull out with very minimal elements."

—BRYN M. MOOTH, "INSPIRING TYPE," *HOW MAGAZINE*, FEBRUARY 1996, PS. 95–96

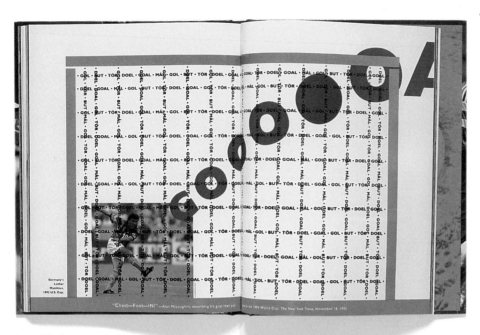

Soccer! The Game and the World Cup,
Rizzoli, 1994

Soccer! The Game and the World Cup,
Universe, 1998
AD: Mirko Ilić
D: So Takahashi & Mirko Ilić

"I learned about Bradbury Thompson from Steven Heller's books. Here and there I saw some of it, and as in the meantime I started to collect books, I gave myself the task of getting it, and now I have four complete books of Westvaco Inspirations. When I bought them, I was under such a strong impression that it can be really seen in the first book about soccer. There were some things that he did that I would accidentally touch on now and then. For example, Adi's LP that was assembled out of 4 CMYK inks after which the color would appear, I would occasionally touch something that he did, but at that time I did not know anything about it. He did everything that I thought about somewhere within myself, but I did not have a chance ... It is negative for me that I was under such influence, but it's always convenient for me to discover such people because it means that I do not have to do such things anymore and that I have to go a step further. What he would do if he was in my place and all that combined with several other people...

Although it has nothing to do with my work, I like Lustig a lot, because of that madness ... we are different as night and day, he is totally decorative, everything is nice, gentle, he has a beauty and freedom that I cannot afford, but I can enjoy it. I think I went farther backward, so Rodchenko's influence may be seen in my work, rather than the influence of someone appearing today. I was greatly influenced by the front page of *Fortune* magazine from 1932, because I was collecting those things. In some aspects of illustration I was influenced by Cassandre, for purity. From the fifties, sixties, a book here another book there: Massin, and on the other side you have this book on architecture by Soleri. I might be totally wrong, but I do not see any particular influence as I wander a lot. Naturally, I see a thing and say *whoo* and it immediately starts: so why not this, it could be that. And at the end, even if I am under the direct influence of something, the result turns out to be totally different. I am always trying to go one, two, three steps further."

—MIRKO ILIĆ

Soccer! How to Play the Game,

Universe 1999

AD: M. I, D: So Takahashi,

Ringo Takahashi, Mirko Ilić

3-D ILLUSTRATION:

Lauren DeNapoli

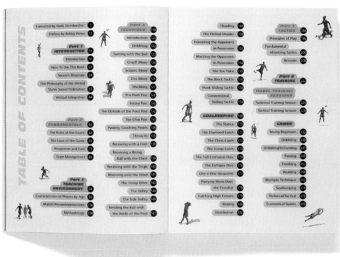

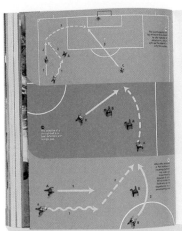

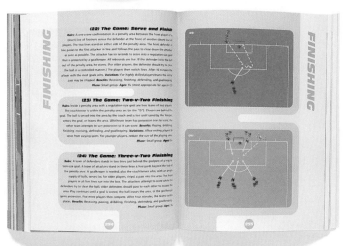

"I love books. Books make me very happy. When I lived in Zagreb, foreign books were quite rare. We all borrowed books from one another and made sure not to fold page corners, and not to tear them. A book as a book makes me happy and that's why I love to design them. I am not interested in things that cannot be fun."

—MIRKO ILIĆ

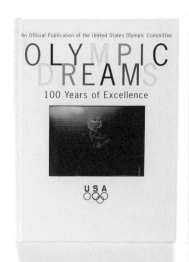

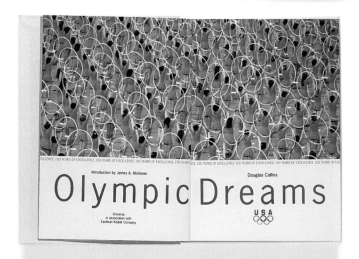

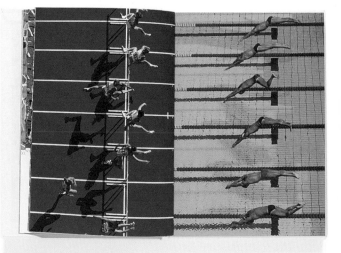

For the front page of the hardcover edition Kodamotion technology was used to achieve the illusion of motion in a two-dimensional picture. But, instead of 2 or 3 frames as usually used for example in the postcards, 16 frames were incorporated from the video footage of the winning performance of American gymnast Mary Lou Retton at the Olympics in Los Angeles.

Douglas Collins: Olympic Dreams,
Hardcover edition, Universe, 1996
in cooperation with Eastman Kodak

AD & D: Mirko Ilić, ILLUSTRATION: Nigel Holmes

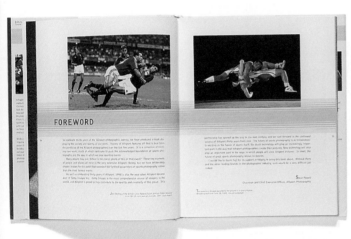

Visions of Allsport,

Universe, 1998.

AD: Mirko Ilić

D: So Takahashi & Mirko Ilić

Allsport is a photography agency specializing in sports photography. To mark the 30th anniversary of the work, they published a book which presents some of the best works of their photographers. The book was edited by Chris Beeson and Kate Donovan.

Newsletters Now: From Classic to New Wave

Steven Heller & Elinor Pettit

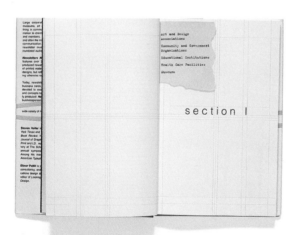

section I

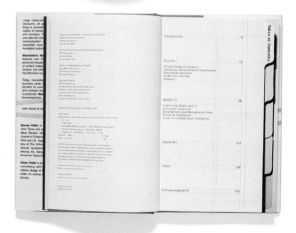

Introduction

Section I
Art and Design Associations
Community and Government Organizations
Educational Institutions
Health Care Facilities
Museums

Section II
Publishing, Music and TV
Consumer Industries
Development and Management Firms
Financial Companies
Utility & Transportation Companies

Appendix

Index

Acknowledgments

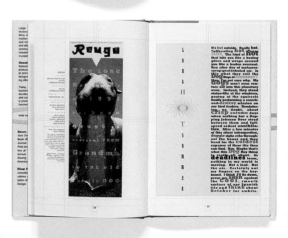

LEFT:

Steven Heller & Elinor Pettit: *Newsletters Now*,
PBG International, Inc., 1996
AD & D: Mirko Ilić

In the United States, corporate mail – the most frequent destination and the method of newsletter distribution – arrives in packages tied up with a rubber band. The design of the cover mimics that, to American reader, recognizable visual code.

Steven Heller:

The Swastika — Symbol Beyond Redemption?
Allworth Press, 2000
AD: Mirko Ilić
LAYOUT: Sharp Designs

In order to avoid the misuse of the book by neo-nazi groups, displaying of swastika on the front page was avoided by doubling its image.

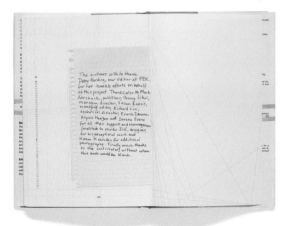

> "The quality of an illustration or design should be measured primarily in what social environment it was made and for whom it was intended. For the same work, an author can receive the top prize in one place, and end up in jail somewhere else. It's hard to say what the 'rules of the game' are. The illustrations or the designs will be successful if they satisfy the needs of their audience and not of editors and publishers. Unfortunately, editors and publishers often think that they are smarter than the audience."

—MIRKO ILIĆ, "WHEN THE GASTARBEITER BECOMES THE ART DIRECTOR OF *TIME*," VEČER, MARIBOR, JUNE 8, 2000

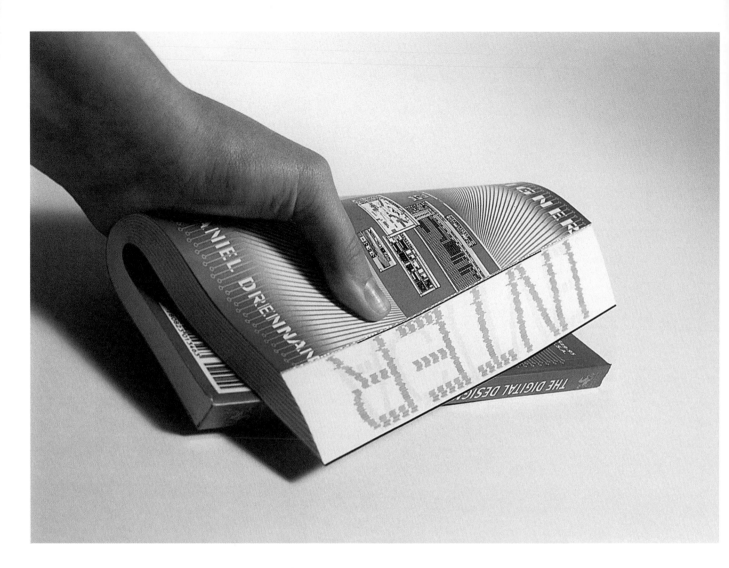

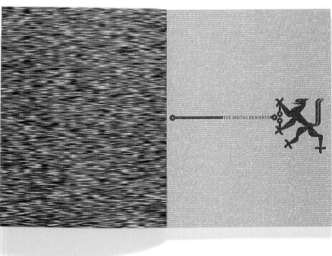

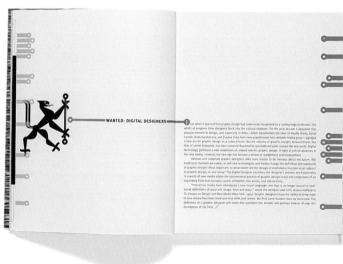

Steven Heller & Daniel Drennan:

The Digital Designer,

Watson Guptill, 1997

AD & D: Mirko Ilić

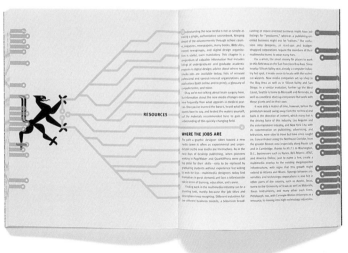

"Mirko is a fantastic designer who can draw and a marvelous painter who can design. While this accumulation of talent might have hurt him commercially, (the market prefers clean cut distinctions), it earned him the unending respect of all of us sadly singularly gifted people."

—STEFAN SAGMEISTER

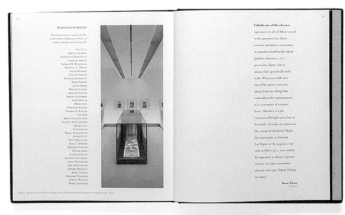

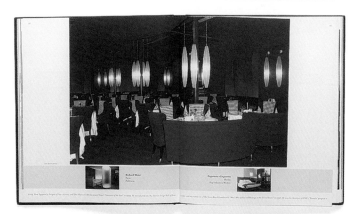

Adam D. Tihany & Marci Sutin Levin:
Tihany Style — Hospitality Design,
Mondadori Electa spa, 2004
AD: Mirko Ilić, D: Dario Tagliabue, Mirko Ilić

The book was printed in three versions of
fluorescent color on the inside cover: green,
orange and red.

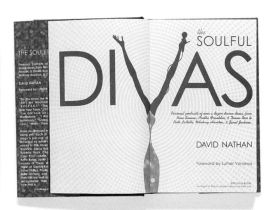

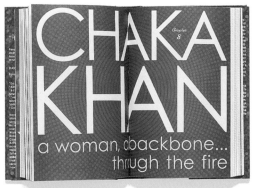

David Nathan: *The Soulful Divas*,
Billboard Books 1999,
AD: M. I.
D: Nicky Lindeman

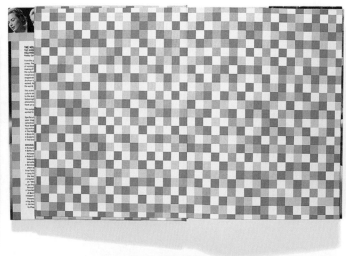

**Paddy Calistro &
Fred E. Basten:**
The Hollywood Archive,
Universe, 2000
AD & D: Mirko Ilić

The Beatles Now & Then /

Photographs by Harry Benson, Universe
Publishing 1998.
AD: M. I.
D: So Takahashi, M. I.
Photographer Harry Benson has went across
the ocean in order to follow The Beatles on
their first large american tour in 1964, and
stayed there for good. He has worked for
Life, Vanity Fair, GQ, Esquire, Paris Match.

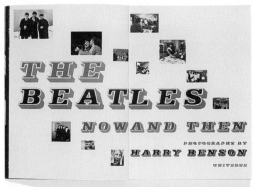

Theodore Roszak:
The Cult of Information,
University of California
Press Berkeley, 1986
D: Laurie Anderson
I: Mirko Ilić

Nathaniel Tripp:
Confluence,
Steerforth Press, 2005
AD: Louise Fili
I: Mirko Ilić

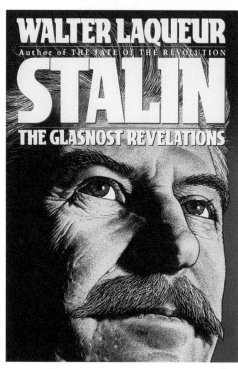

Walter Laqueur: *Stalin,
the Glasnost revelations*,
Scribner/MacMillan, 1990, AD: Wendy Bass,
D & ILLUSTRATION: Mirko Ilić

RIGHT:
Studs Terkel: *The Great Divide*,
Pantheon Books, 1988,
AD: Louise Fili

Philip Augar: *The Greed Merchants*,
Portfolio, 2005, AD: Joseph Perez

John Anderson:
Follow the Money,
Scribner, 2007
AD: John Fulbrook

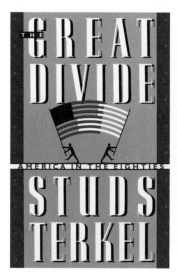

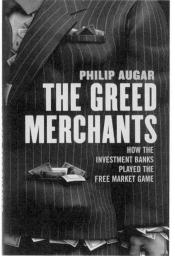

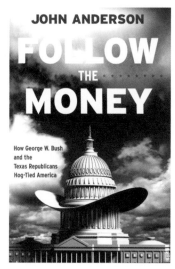

254

Kay-Yut Chen, Lead Economist, HP Labs, and Marina Krakovsky

SECRETS OF THE MONEYLAB

HOW BEHAVIORAL ECONOMICS CAN IMPROVE YOUR BUSINESS

With a foreword by George A. Akerlof, Nobel Prize–winning economist and author of *Animal Spirits* and *Identity Economics*

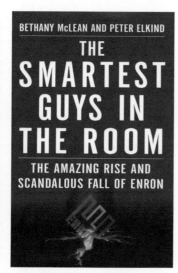

BETHANY McLEAN AND PETER ELKIND

THE SMARTEST GUYS IN THE ROOM

THE AMAZING RISE AND SCANDALOUS FALL OF ENRON

NETFLIXED

The Epic Battle for America's Eyeballs

Gina Keating

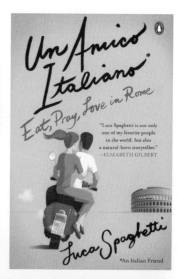

Un Amico Italiano*

Eat, Pray, Love in Rome

"Luca Spaghetti is not only one of my favorite people in the world, but also a natural-born storyteller."
—ELIZABETH GILBERT

Luca Spaghetti

*An Italian Friend

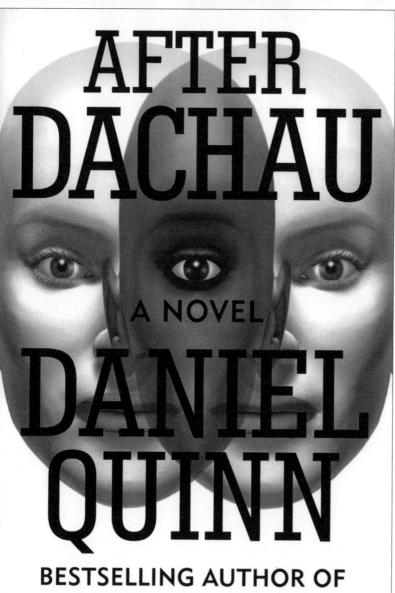

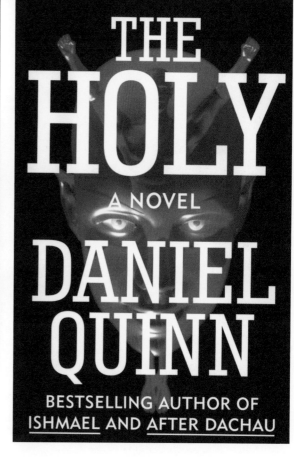

Daniel Quinn: *The Holy*, and
Daniel Quinn: *After Dachau*,
Zoland Books, 2001
AD: Louise Fili
D: Chad Roberts
ILLUSTRATION: Mirko Ilić

Kay-Yut Chen & Marina Krakovsky:
Secrets of the Money Lab, 2003;
Bethany McLean & Peter Elkind:
The Smartest Guys in the Room, 2010;
Gina Keating: *Netflixed*, 2012,
ALL: Portfolio-Penguin, AD: Joseph Perez
TOP RIGHT:
Luca Spaghetti: *Un Amico Italiano*,
Penguin (USA), 2011, COVER LETTERING:
Nicky Lindeman, ILLUSTRATION: Mirko Ilić

Tribes

We Need **You** to Lead Us

Bestselling author of *Purple Cow* and *The Dip*

SETH GODIN

THE END OF THE FREE MARKET

Who Wins the War Between
States and Corporations?

IAN BREMMER

"Brilliant and
indispensable."
—Nouriel Roubini

"A powerful and important book." —Former U.S. senator Bill Bradley

THE POSTCATASTROPHE ECONOMY

REBUILDING AMERICA AND AVOIDING THE NEXT BUBBLE

ERIC JANSZEN

RED AND BLUE AND BROKE ALL OVER
RESTORING AMERICA'S FREE ECONOMY

CHARLES GOYETTE
NEW YORK TIMES BESTSELLING AUTHOR OF
THE DOLLAR MELTDOWN

Seth Godin: *Tribes*,
Penguin, 2008,
AD: Joseph Perez,
ILU: Mirko Ilić

The End of the Free Market, 2010
The Postcatastrophe Economy, 2010
Red and Blue and broke all over,
Sentinel-Penguin, 2012

ALL THE DEVILS ARE HERE
THE HIDDEN HISTORY OF THE FINANCIAL CRISIS

BETHANY McLEAN
BESTSELLING COAUTHOR OF
THE SMARTEST GUYS IN THE ROOM
AND **JOE NOCERA**

GRAPEVINE
The New Art of Word-*of*-Mouth Marketing

Dave Balter & John Butman
founder of BzzAgent

"The rapidly growing field of word-of-mouth marketing has been desperately missing one thing: hands-on experience. This book fills that gap."
—Emanuel Rosen, author of *The Anatomy of Buzz*

FROM THE AUTHOR OF THE *NEW YORK TIMES* BESTSELLER *PERFECTLY LEGAL*

FREE LUNCH

HOW THE WEALTHIEST AMERICANS ENRICH THEMSELVES AT GOVERNMENT EXPENSE (AND STICK YOU WITH THE BILL)

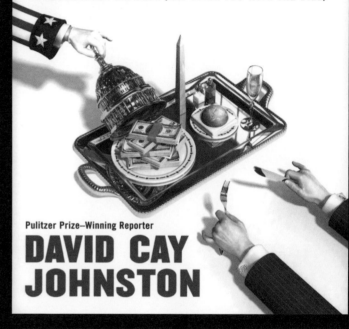

Pulitzer Prize–Winning Reporter

DAVID CAY JOHNSTON

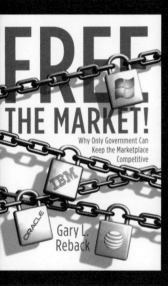

FREE THE MARKET!

THE MARKET!
Why Only Government Can Keep the Marketplace Competitive

IBM
ORACLE
Gary L. Reback

"The most amazing fact about Shirky's incisive manual for building a better world is this: it's just possible that everything he promises may be true." —*THE GUARDIAN*

COGNITIVE SURPLUS
How Technology Makes Consumers into Collaborators

CLAY SHIRKY
Bestselling author of *Here Comes Everybody*

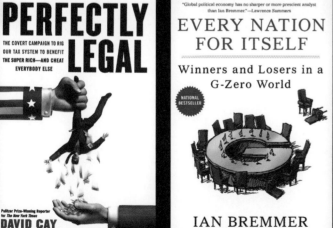

PERFECTLY LEGAL
THE COVERT CAMPAIGN TO RIG OUR TAX SYSTEM TO BENEFIT THE SUPER RICH—AND CHEAT EVERYBODY ELSE

Pulitzer Prize-Winning Reporter for *The New York Times*
DAVID CAY JOHNSTON

"Global political economy has no sharper or more prescient analyst than Ian Bremmer."—Lawrence Summers

EVERY NATION FOR ITSELF
Winners and Losers in a G-Zero World

NATIONAL BESTSELLER

IAN BREMMER
Author of *The End of the Free Market*

DELAY DENY DEFEND

WHY INSURANCE COMPANIES DON'T PAY CLAIMS AND WHAT YOU CAN DO ABOUT IT

JAY M. FEINMAN

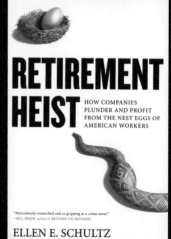

RETIREMENT HEIST
HOW COMPANIES PLUNDER AND PROFIT FROM THE NEST EGGS OF AMERICAN WORKERS

"Meticulously researched and as gripping as a crime novel."
—NELL MINOW, author of *WATCHING THE WATCHERS*

ELLEN E. SCHULTZ
Award-Winning Reporter for *The Wall Street Journal*

All the Devils are Here,
Portfolio-Penguin, 2003

Grapevine, 2009

Cognitive surplus, 2011

Free Lunch, 2007

Delay Deny Defend, 2010

ALL:

Penguin (USA)

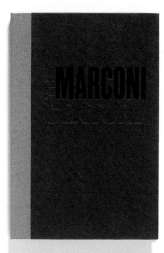

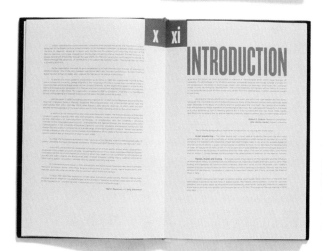
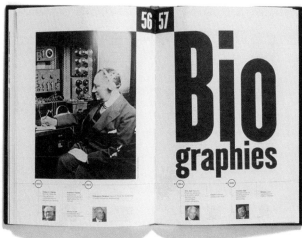

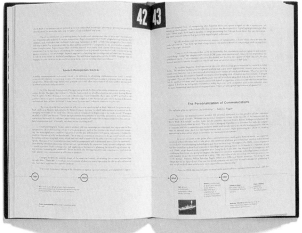

The Marcony Century,
Marconi Foundation at
Columbia University, 2004
Photos of the second edition:
Marconi Society. Inc, 2005
AD & D: Mirko Ilić
D: Helen Wu & Jee-eun Lee

"I do take various fonts from my friends and fool around with them, but when I make a book or anything else, I buy these fonts. When I want to send a design with a certain typeface to the printer, I like to have proof confirming that I have bought that specific font. It's quite simple, I wouldn't like anyone to treat my art differently so why would I do it to someone else?"
—MIRKO ILIĆ

Among friends and colleagues, Ilić is known as a walking encyclopedia of design work. As he has said, he often may not know the author's name, but can give precise details of a graphic solution or a book in which a reproduction was published. He began to use this talent in recent years by collecting materials and editing books on the list of his top goals. In cooperation with the prolific Steven Heller, he created *Genius Moves—Icons of Graphic Design* (North Light Books, 2001) in the British edition titled *Icons of Graphic Design: A Showcase of Innovative Designs*, (Thames & Hudson, 2001), which follows a repetition of ideas through the history of graphic design. The material in the book is sorted chronologically and each selected work is followed by a picture of the design that preceded it or was a direct influence for that work, as well for similar ones that were created later.

A second book with Heller, *Handwritten—Expressive Lettering in the Digital Age* (Thames & Hudson, 2004), followed the evolution of different forms of handmade typography from manuscripts to embroidery.

Design of Dissent, a collaboration with Milton Glaser, pointed to various examples of politically engaged use of graphic design and visual communication at a time when corporations dominated design and advertising.

"I persuaded Milton to jointly make a book on political design, which is interesting to both of us. In doing so, we were not interested in just American political design, but also in experiences from around the world. We obtained, for example, works from Iran, Libya, former Soviet countries, virtually from all over the world. Two designs were sent from China as well, although it is still difficult to get this kind of design from that country."

In the early 2007, Mirko and Heller collaborated on a unique idea for a book called *The Anatomy of Design—Uncovering the Influences and Inspirations in Modern Graphic Design* (Rockport, 2007). The book can be seen as a continuation of their first one. In the current flood of monographic publications that deal with specific well-known designers, periods or themes, *Genius Moves* and *The Anatomy of Design* stands out as an attempt to establish connections between the works, i.e. introduction and development of historical consciousness that is often lacking to young designers.

In *The Anatomy of Design,* the authors conducted a kind of "anatomy class" in forty-nine cases of contemporary graphic design—every page of the book shows, and in specific ways, reveals the origins, sources, role models, and forerunners of the parts out of which some design works were made, their predecessors, conscious or unconscious influences and inspirations.

The book was laid out so that each left page folds out and each segment (marked on the edge with its own color) actually occupies the space of four pages. With the information about the author and the work, and short text that describes specifics of the origin or context of the work, it points to several key elements that seemed important to the authors and whose genealogy they followed with a series of visual examples that can be seen only when the left side is unfolded.

The selection of items includes all kinds of design works: posters, books, CDs, and record covers, packaging. Things for different purposes and different clients, from *Adbusters* to advertising, from pop singers to cultural alternatives. As pointed out by authors in the introductory text, the works that serve as examples are not necessarily some canonical points of the contemporary design, but they were chosen as well-conceived, well crafted examples of various methods and approaches that are frequently used and that enabled authors of the book to extract several "genealogy" lines, for example in the stylistic and thematic approach, visual motifs, typography, color treatment, a variety of printing "special effects" and so on. ▶

"Success is always the same—there is no difference between success in Zagreb and success in New York. My success in Zagreb is dearer to me than that in New York because it happened first. People remember their first love more than some other loves. Success is the same everywhere, the same gimmicks, the same tricks, the same feelings, only the results differ. Back at home, one can be successful at what he does and not have a penny, and in some other parts of the world success produces money."

—MIRKO ILIĆ, "BECAUSE OF MY ILLUSTRATIONS TRANSVESTITES HAVE ORGANIZED DEMONSTRATIONS IN NEW YORK," PLUS 7, *NOVI LIST*, RIJEKA, JUNE 10, 2000

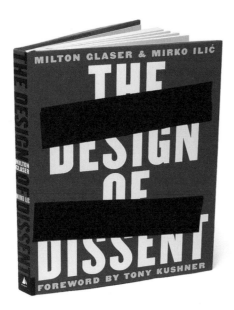

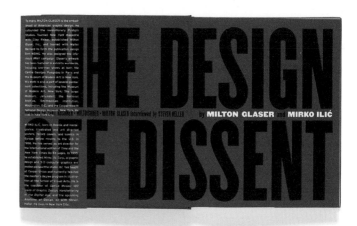

> "Content is very important to me. I am not interested in pure design that much, it's a bit of a bore. I've always felt that my design has to be against someone. This is probably because I grew up where I grew up."
>
> —MIRKO ILIĆ, "GIVE ME A DEADLINE AND MONEY," *ORIS* NO. 2, ZAGREB, 1999

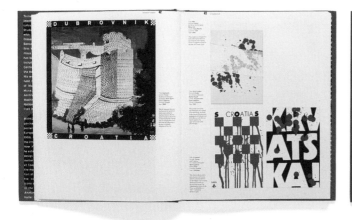

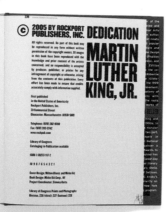

ACKNOWLDGEMENTS

JESSI ARRINGTON • AMY AXLER
SIMONA BARTA • DANA BARTELT
AMIR BERBIĆ • TERRENCE BROWN
ASJA DUPANOVIĆ • EKREM DUPANOVIĆ
STEVEN HELLER • ALEXANDRA KANE
ČEDOMIR KOSTOVIĆ • DEJAN KRŠIĆ
JEE-EUN LEE • MARIJA MILJKOVIĆ
DAOUD SARHANDI • ARABA SIMPSON
STAFF OF TIPOGRAFICA MAGAZINE
SCHOOL OF VISUAL ARTS • GARTH WALKER
LAETITIA WOLFF • HELEN WU

CONTENTS

COMMUNISM 1
PALESTINE AND ISRAEL 12
EX-YUGOSLAVIA 26
IRAQ WAR 52
PEACE 86
EQUALITY 130
FOOD 134
ANIMALS 148
CORPORATE WORLD 160
MEDIA 166
GUN CONTROL 170
RELIGION 176
GOVERNMENT 210
U.S. PRESIDENTIAL ELECTION 220
Foreword: TONY KUSHNER 224
MILTON GLASER Interviewed by STEVEN HELLER 232
Directory of Contributors 236
Acknowledgments 238

Milton Glaser & Mirko Ilić: *Design of Dissent*, Rockport, 2005, COVER DESIGN: Milton Glaser & Mirko Ilić, BOOK DESIGN & LAYOUT: Mirko Ilić Corp.

Steven Heller & Mirko Ilić:
The Anatomy of Design
— Uncovering the Influences
and Inspirations
in Modern Graphic Design,
Rockport, 2007
AD & D: Mirko Ilić
D: Mirko Ilić Corp.
PHOTO: Luka Mjeda

Reproduced spreads show
works of the authors from
the former Yugoslavia:
CD *Burek* designed by
Fabrika from Sarajevo
book *Contributions to
Cultural Strategy of City of
Rijeka* designed by Dejan
Dragosavac.

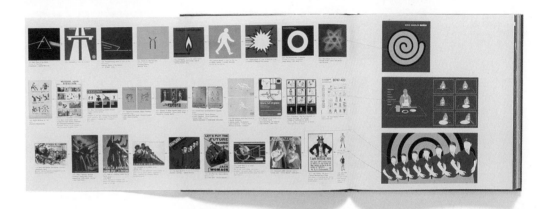

"I met Mirko first as a man, and
only then as a designer. We
were introduced by a mutual
friend, and I soon realized
that Mirko was a generous
person—sharp, fun, realistic,
and (as a result from all of the
above) of left-wing views like
me. And then, little by little, I
began to discover what kind
of an extraordinary designer
and teacher he was. One
day I dropped by his studio
and saw pages of a book he
was working on with Steven
Heller pasted on the walls.
The project was extremely
ambitious: to follow the usual
graphic formats back in history,
until their earliest appearances.
It looked almost like sketches
for a book on Jung's archetypes.
But I'm sure that Jung never left
his ideas so that guests could
see them, like sheets spread on
a rope to dry in the sun."
—MOMUS

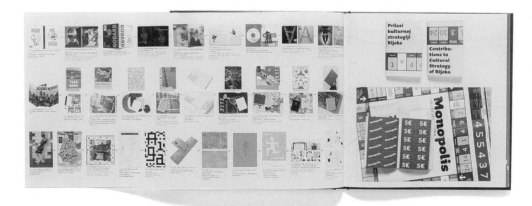

Atheneum Hotel,
logo, 1993
commissioner: Pentagram
AD: Colin Forbes,
Michael Gericke
D: Michael Gericke
ILLUSTRATION: Mirko Ilić

Atlas Print Solutions,
logo, 2010

Palladin,
visual identity, 1999

The Joule,
hotel visual identity, 2006

5K Films Inc.,
logo, 2002

Swiss Army Card,
logo, 2007
CLIENT: Paradoxy Products

Spread,
restaurant/lounge logo,
Spread, Inc., 2002
AD: Mirko Ilić
D: Heath Hinegardner,
Mirko Ilić

Summit,
visual identity
Summit/The Broadmoor,
2006
AD: Mirko Ilić
D: Clint Shaner, Mirko Ilić

The Big Red,
logo, 2009
CLIENT: Charlie Palmer
Group and the Joule
D: Mirko Ilić, Jee-eun Lee

30 for 30,
logo, 2008
CLIENT: ESPN
AD: Walter Bernard
D: Mirko Ilić

UNLESS STATED DIFFERENTLY:
AD & D: Mirko Ilić

Design Is a Good Idea

WHAT BENNY GOODMAN SAID ABOUT SWING can be said for Mirko Ilić's work: "It is as difficult to explain as the Mona Lisa's smile or the nutty hats women wear— but just as stimulating. It remains something you take five-thousand words to explain then leaves you wondering what it is."

Mirko's many design ideas could be—according to the famous advice of Bob Gill—transmitted via telephone and still inspire. As witnessed by Luka Mjeda, they often really did so. While Mirko was in Milan, work on *Panorama*, he still had to create covers for *Danas* in Zagreb. The team would agree over the phone, and Luka would do it in Zagreb. But, as **Gill** also knew well, the idea needed to be properly visualized as well.

Gill, an American, was an important figure in the development of the idea-based design approach. With Alan Fletcher and Colin Forbes, he founded studio Fletcher/Forbes/Gill in London in 1960, out of which, a few years after Gill left, Pentagram was developed.

"Gill and his colleagues aspired to produce designs that were surprising and original graphic solutions to communication problems. This required the designer to let go of any preconceptions about how design is supposed to look and, clearly, if a designer has a strong personal style, then he is starting with the assumption that a design should look like one of his own designs..."[01]

Gill said: "Drawing [illustration] is like design, it's a process. It's a tool, not the goal. Design and illustration are ways of showing views. So if you do not have an opinion, why would you start the process? Ironically most people involved in design are adopting their value system based on their environment; from magazines such as *Graphis*. At the end, it results in everyone doing the same design—which I think is boring. So, if you are not interested in what is now considered to be a 'good design' and if you let the design develop from an idea, you can achieve something original."

Idea-based design was so successful in the market that it represented, in the Anglo-American world of the sixties and seventies, the dominant approach to graphic design, especially in advertising. But in the late seventies many young designers—especially in Britain and on the west coast of the United States—began to question the belief.

During the last decades of the twentieth century, back at the time when Ilić was making his name, a series of famous designers appeared with distinctive personal styles. Among the first to become famous was Neville Brody with his works for the magazine *The Face* and independent record companies. However, in New York in the eighties, Tibor Kalman revived the tradition of idea-based design, with work that was smart, witty, humorous, and rooted in vernacular and popular culture. An autodidact in the field of design, he opposed the conventions and the complacency of the American design scene entrenched in advertising, had very strong opinions, and did not hesitate to express them at the cost of conflict.

Kalman was also an ardent advocate of design with socially valuable content, so after studio M &Co closed, his associates—like Sagmeister, who opened Sagmaister Inc. in 1993—strengthened that current in the New York design. This was the atmosphere in which Mirko began to practice design on the American scene.

"Designers, in my opinion should have no style, except a general way of thinking. I've always tried to have no style. The idea must determine the form and not the opposite."

—MIRKO ILIĆ, "SEVERAL SHARP WORDS AT THE EXPENSE OF SLOVENIAN DESIGNERS," FINANCE, LJUBLJANA, JUNE 7, 2000

Under/Stand Design, t-shirt, *Emzin*, December 2001

01 | Poynor in Sagmeister: *Handarbeit*, pp. 66–67

**MAINGATE
LAKESIDE RESORT**

Bochic, fine jewlery, logo, 2011

Andrew Young & Co. Inc., logo, 2006

Richfield, logo, 2010

Tihany Design, logo, 2006

Charlie Palmer Restaurant Dallas, Texas, logo, 2007

Maingate Lakeside Resort, logo, 2011

"It took me a long time to get design jobs. I first got serious jobs after I started to work at *Time* magazine. I partially accepted that position because I needed a break. I have never met Kalman. It was always interesting to me, I saw several projects, but until *Colours,* I was not engaged. It was *cool,* but still corporate stuff... The biggest thing he did when he closed the studio—was divide his clients between his associates. Stephen Doyle got a part, Sagmeister got his, Studio Seventeen got a part, everyone got something out of it ..."

When it comes to the formal style, Mirko seems to be following Oscar Wilde's maxim that consistency is the last refuge of the unimaginative. He especially emphasizes the issue of communication, in which form itself must be relative to the content.

In the early seventies, Boris Bućan made work that was labeled FACH IDIOT = STYLE [Afterward, Sagmeister formulated similar thought as *Style is fart*]. Ilić took the message to heart. He persistently avoided a distinctive style that could easily be mistaken as a stamp of distinction, but also become a *fach-idiot*. Rather than development of a personal style, his work represents continuous exploration of different strategies, procedures, methods, tactics, schemes, and forms of creative expression. Perhaps because each new task required a new type of response and reaction to a specific problem in a specific context, he was never satisfied, as he often said, with work he had already completed, that he only saw flaws in them.

"I would like to have a style. It would have been much easier. Unfortunately I think that style is a pattern, you solve everything based on it and things work. It is wonderful to be a designer if you know in advance how you will solve any problem that you come across. Exactly because I do not have a style, I often make a lot of bad things. I do illustration under the pressure of impossible deadlines, other clients want something as well, so I would probably screw something up... If I had a style, it would be snap—snap—snap based on the pattern and it would be done correctly. But that's boring to me. Things do repeat in my work, but only because I bump into a subject that requires a response similar to something that I have already made. I do not have four aces, and things are not always the same; I have some mixed cards that do not always win for sure, but combinations are more interesting. There are times when certain things begin to resemble one another, but often I make one thing and then in two years the other..."

Despite the dozens of different styles and approaches he has used over the years, his work is recognizable more for his way of thinking than his drawing style. Moreover, some of his drawing styles seemed so deceptively simple that others often tried to mimic him; of course without a whole lot of success. "It is easier to steal the hand than the brains, and thus it is easier to steal the style than the idea ..." he said in an interview with Igor Masnjak.

In critical reviews of Ilić's work, a frequent comment is that some of his colleagues are better pure drawers than him; that his drawings are "rigid," "stiff," somewhat schematic. However, somewhat paradoxically, it is exactly these characteristic that made him a better illustrator, more suited to the printed mediums. In the illustration as "applied graphics," some traditional pure artistic values—such as stroke, gesture, expression, coloring, and skills of noting details—are often not important, and indeed they may stand in the way of communicating an idea. This was precisely the problem of the domestic painters who worked at *Start*. A "beauty of the stroke" does not mean much to a good illustrator. More important is what he has to say and how he presents it.

Ilić frequently cited American illustrator Brad Holland as a role model and who encouraged him, but this influence was not noticable in the visual results or even in the technique. He shares with his Holland the ability to condensie an idea, to synthesize and abstract each concept or problem, to conceptually and visually strip it to the core. He is able to distill the message to the simplest form, to reduce it to a simple image that clearly carries a complex message. Ilić's clean, coldly precise drawing, devoid of any superfluous expression, stripped of all unnecessary details, conveys the idea so effectively.

In the article "The Steamroller of Branding" (*Eye* no. 53, 2004), designer Nick Bell divided his colleagues into two major groups—"The agents of neutrality" and "The aesthetes of style." First consider that there is no role for self-expression in design, while others are consumed by the formal aspects of design. Both views are apolitical in their own way, ready to serve all types of clients without a lot of thinking. However, as Bell points out, there is a third group whose voice is less heard—"the champions of diversity," those who are ready to defend the content from the reduction to the lowest common denominator implemented by steamrollers of branding and corporate identity. Often, they are designers who work in the area where success is not measured only by the number of copies sold. They design exhibitions, magazines, catalogs and similar publications, i.e., they are more engaged in creating things than how to sell something that already exists to as many people as possible.

From his comics on, Ilić's work was characterized by the belief that the idea was most important, but also the understanding that content and form cannot be separated. In an interview with Glaser, a seemingly contradictory view of his, one certainly complex and often elusive to the people from the world of corporate design, was brought into focus. On the one hand, it is the position of a "journeyman," "mercenary," a man who works for others by order. When you add often repeated assertions that he had "no style," "that style was not important to him," "that he was not interested in style," it seems as if we are dealing with a typical "advocate of neutrality." On the other hand, he is very interested in the "formal aspects of design," shifting boundaries, expanding knowledge, discovering as yet unknown or underutilized and forgotten opportunities. In the collision of these apparent contradictions, his actual position is that of the "advocate of diversity."

As Heller pointed out, Ilić's conceptual precision, sharpness (often expressed through sarcasm), rough and sometimes sophisticated culturally-informed humor fits within the spirit of New York very well. Ilić is also original in his constant striving to overcome set limits or self-imposed limitations, but without refraining from intelligent reliance on the past, the history of design, and the traditions of visual communication. While doing so, he is not only borrowing and quoting, but he is, above all, taking over the creative process, upgrading and reinterpreting along the way. His work is not distinguished by constant stylistic traits such as a favorite typeface or typical color palette, but primarily, by linking content and form; a way of thinking that leans to the more complex, requiring a second or even third glance.

He mastered a skill of looking at all things in two ways: one is the awareness of a wider picture, context, and the other looking only at what is directly in front of the eyes. Design students at the Department of Visual Communications at Split Art Academy could see this when he caught them by surprise, commenting on their work without talking about big concepts as they might have expected. He was unerringly focused on the details, about which students used to achieve quick results with a computer, did they not think for a second: some alignement, unncessary line, some spacing or kerning?

And when he held a workshop in the Art Directors Club, for younger teens from New York City public schools, he talked a little about craft, but tried to encourage them to think about the content and role of visual communication, but also that they could build a career in design as well, and that it was not an area exclusively reserved for white boys from rich families. ▶

The Orphan Society of America, logo, 2004
Auschwitz Jewish Center, logo, 2001
Jewish Film Festival, Zagreb, logo, 2012
Raphael Lemkin Center, logo, 2008
AIRP, logo, 2008
AIC Foundation, logo, 2008

D: Mirko Ilić, Leen Sadder

THE TIME

The Time Hotel, New York,
Adam D. Tihany International Ltd.
1999
logo
card
door signs
key card
laundry bag

THE TIME
224 W 49th Street
New York, NY 10019
Tel 212.246.5252

Insert and
Remove
Keycard
Magnetic
Stripe Down

Introduzca y quite la tarjeta

Introduire et retirer la cart-clé

カードを挿入し 引き出す
插入及拉出匙卡，磁條向下

Turn Handle
While Green
Light is
Flashing

Gire la perilla cuando
destelle la luz verde

Tourner la poignée au
clignotant vert

緑のライトがついている時に
ハンドルを回す

當綠燈亮時扭動房門把手

MAID SERVICE REQUESTED

DO NOT DISTURB

...ANING LAUNDRY/DRY CLEANING SERVICE LAUNDRY/DRY CLEANING SERVICE LAUNDRY/DR...

THE TIME

VIKRAM CHATWAL

224 West 49th Street New York, NY 10019   Tel 212.632.9053   Fax 212.974.3922   E-Mail vchat@aol.com

ULRICH R. WALL
General Manager

Tel 212.320.2940
Fax 212.320.2941
E-mail uwalltime@sprynet.com

224 West 49th Street New York, NY 10019

THE
TIME

224 West 49th Street New York, NY 10019

The Time Hotel, New York
Adam D. Tihany International Ltd.
1999.
stationery
guest gift package
matchbox
fax paper

FROM

COMPANY

TO   FAX #

DATE + TIME

I WILL BE HERE UNTIL

PRIVATE IN-ROOM FAX #

PAGES INCLUDING COVER

224 West 49th Street   New York, NY 10019
Tel 212.320.2925   Fax 212.320.2926
Reservations 1.877.TIME NYC

Sparkling colorful jewels
and playful monkeys
stealing from one another
are the key themes of the
visual identity for newest
version of the New York
restaurant *La Cirque*. Ilić
kept the old logo, which he
said looked like someone
doodled it on the napkin,
but that very roughness
gave it warmth and charm.

La Cirque, New York,
restaurant visual identity,
2006, AD: Mirko Ilić
D: Mirko Ilić Corp.

Giselle Ceniza
Senior Designer

TIHANY DESIGN
135 West 27th Street
New York, NY 10001
tel: 212 366 5544
fax: 212 366 4302
gceniza@tihanydesign.com

TD – Tihany Design,
visual identity
and promotional booklet,
Tihany Design, 2006
AD & D: Mirko Ilić,
Various photographers.

"I met Mirko several years back and was immediately charmed by his 'retro socialist' sense of humor. Getting to know him, I realized that he is actually a 'rebel retro socialist,' one with a sharp mind, tongue, and enormous design talents. It will suffice to take a look at his incredible illustrations to glimpse into the complex soul of a genius artist, social critic, and keen observer of our times.

In time, we became friends and collaborators. Mirko does all the graphic design work for my firm, my friends and clients. Once you 'hook up' with him, it is hard to let go. He has a quick wit and keen instinct of who you are and what you need and has no problems telling you when you are wrong. His total honesty is sometimes off-putting but always welcome. Mirko is, in every regard, an authentic voice and talent whom I respect beyond measure."

—ADAM TIHANY

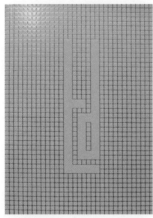

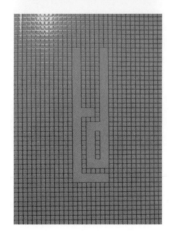

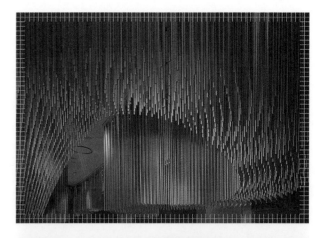

Each year promotional booklets with new photographs are printed with a similar design but a different color for the cover.

Summit restaurant,
visual identity
Summit/The Broadmoor,
2006
AD: Mirko Ilić
D: Clint Shaner, Mirko Ilić

Charlie Palmer at the Joule restaurant,
visual identity, 2008
AD: Mirko Ilić
D: Mirko ilić, Jee-eun Lee

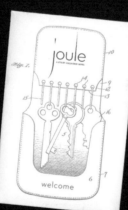

The Joule Hotel,

visual identity, 2008

AD: Mirko Ilić

D: Mirko Ilić, Jee-eun Lee

next vintage

Next Vintage Wine Shop is the perfect solution for the home diner or host who wants the full wine experience but doesn't know exactly where to start when it comes to adventurous pairings. The temperature-controlled, 13-foot high glass and polished steel showcase housed in the hotel's lobby, is staffed by the restaurant's sommeliers, and features a rotating selection of wines which extend far beyond typical wine store selections.

Until now, those exceptional lists were only offered to restaurant diners. Now, Palmer brings them directly to you at competitive retail pricing. Featuring weekly wine tastings and instruction and an array of winemaker dinners throughout the year, Next Vintage has become the authority on fine wines from regions spanning the globe.

nextvintage.com

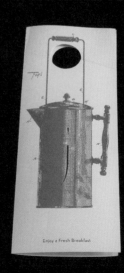

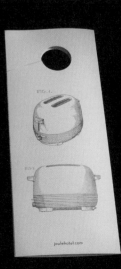

LA FONDA DEL SOL

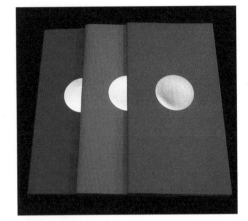

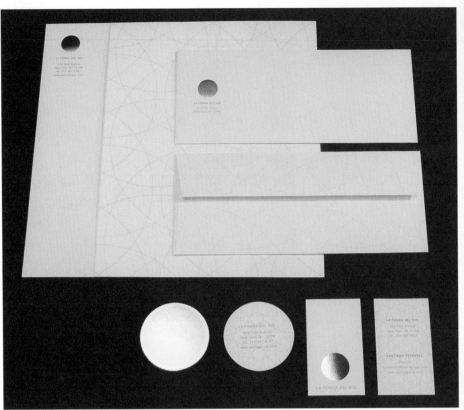

La Fonda Del Sol restaurant, visual identity, 2008, AD: Mirko Ilić, D: Mirko ilić, Jee-eun Lee

"I would describe Mirko as a walking encyclopedia of the visual, as someone who sometimes has a painful 'no bullshit' approach, as a leftist and activist, as a person not ashamed to ask when he does not know, as a huge source of knowledge free to take from as much as you need, as my mentor and friend.

Our working relationship has ranged from occasionally in Belgrade to almost daily in New York and I often relay to my friends two stories about Mirko which on the surface were not related to design.

One was in Belgrade: I witnessed a discussion on what career to choose, what to do in life, what decisions to make... At one point, Mirko just stopped the conversation: 'Ok, come now and turn yourself inside out like a sock, and take a look at what is inside. Maybe you won't like what you see, but that's it and you need to do it. And no lying.'

The other was in New York: An enormous number of people pass through his studio on 32nd Street and a significant number of them are seeking some kind of help. I am among the latter, and once I just wanted to thank him for everything that he has done for me. 'You are welcome' he said, 'but I would not have been able to help you if you did not help yourself first.'

Design is not just the visual. Design is solving problems.

—ALEXANDER MAĆAŠEV

5K Films Inc.,
film production
visual identity, 2002
AD & D: Mirko Ilić

www.levycreative.com • **LEVY CREATIVE MANAGEMENT** • info@levycreative.com
300 East 46th Street • Suite 8E • NYC, NY 10017 • telephone: (212) 687 6463 • fax: (212) 661 4839

Levy Creative Management, 2000

memo, notice of the office move

AD: Mirko Ilić,

D: Heath Hinegardner, Mirko Ilić

The notice was printed in four fluorescent
colors and part with information was die
cut in the shape of the letter L.
Colorful pieces were then inserted in
transparent envelopes.

Foundation for the Advancement of
Veterinary Research for Companion Animals

Jennifer Chaitman, VMD
President
1520 Spruce Street, apartment #109, Philadelphia, PA. 19102
(215) 735-2378   jchaitman@aol.com   www.faver.org

Foundation for the Advancement
of Veterinary Research for
Companion Animals
www.faver.org

FAVeR   Foundation for the Advancement of Veterinary Research for Companion Animals   www.faver.org

FAVeR

The Use of Plasma Cardiac Troponin I (cTnI),
Cardiac Troponin T (cTnT) and Atrial Natriuretic
Peptide (ANP) as Biochemical Markers
of Cardiac Injury Associated with
Doxorubicin Chemotherapy
by Drs. Craig Clifford, Karin Sorenmo, Marc Kraus, et al.

Doxorubicin is a very effective and widely used chemotherapy drug. After several doses it can damage the heart, eventually leading to congestive heart failure and death. Once heart damage is detected by physical exam findings, electrocardiogram or echocardiogram changes, even if no more doses of doxorubicin are given, the heart cannot heal itself. The purpose of this study is to detect early markers of heart damage from doxorubicin before it's too late. ANP, cTnI and cTnT are substances released into the bloodstream when heart cells are damaged or with heart disease. We are measuring these substances in dogs with cancer who are undergoing chemotherapy with doxorubicin. This is the first study measuring these substances in dogs receiving doxorubicin chemotherapy. We are also monitoring patients' hearts with echocardiograms. We hope results of this study will allow us to take a blood sample in dogs receiving doxorubicin and know whether or not their heart is withstanding treatment. If we can pick up signs of early damage before we see irreversible damage on echocardiograms, we can prevent further damage by stopping the drug. The chemotherapy protocol would then be modified to a drug that is heart-sparing.

Evaluation of Plasma Vascular Endothelial
Growth Factor (VEGF), Angiogenin (ANG)
and Basic Fibroblast Growth Factor (bFGF)
levels in Normal Dogs and Dogs with
Hemangiosarcoma, Osteosarcoma,
Mast Cell Tumor and Lymphosarcoma
by Drs. Craig Clifford, Tonatiiuh Melgarejo, Karin Sorenmo et al.

Angiogenesis is the formation of new blood vessels from existing microvessels. Metastasis is the spread of tumor (or cancer) cells, a process where cells leave the original tumor site and travel in the blood to distant sites. Angiogenesis is an essential component of metastasis, providing the principal route by which tumor cells leave the primary tumor site and enter the circulation. Tumors can both induce and inhibit angiogenesis. Angiogenic factors include vascular endothelial growth factor (VEGF), angiogenin (ANG) and basic fibroblast growth factor (bFGF). Angiogenic factors were first described in the mouse just a few years ago and led to studies in humans. People with certain types of tumors have increased blood levels of VEGF. Increased VEGF levels indicate a poor prognosis for numerous tumor types and magnitude of VEGF levels reflect tumor burden, response to therapy, and disease progression. Dr. Clifford has recently discovered elevated VEGF concentra-

FAVeR – Foundation for the Advancement of
Veterinary Research for Companion Animals

visual identity, 2001
AD: Mirko Ilić

D: Heath Hinegardner, Kristina Duewell, Mirko Ilić
SIGN: Keith Haring

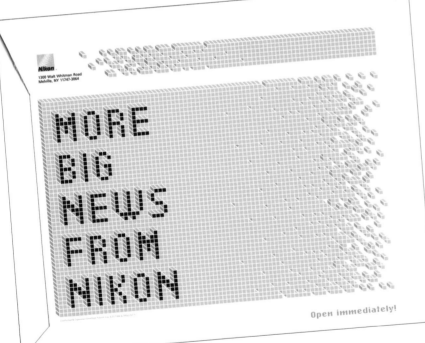

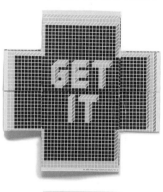

Nikon: Get Digital,
promotional material,
Nikon Inc., 2005
D: Mirko Ilić Corp.

Make It Happen,
promotional material,
Nikon Inc., 2005
D: Mirko Ilić Corp.

Nikon: BIG,
promotional material, Nikon Inc. 2004
CREATIVE DIRECTOR: Michael Mellett
AD & D: Mirko Ilić

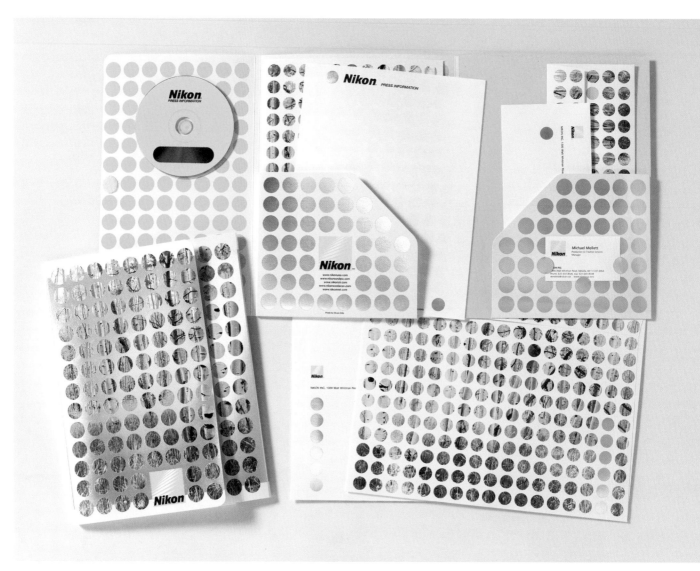

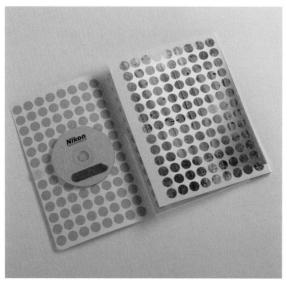

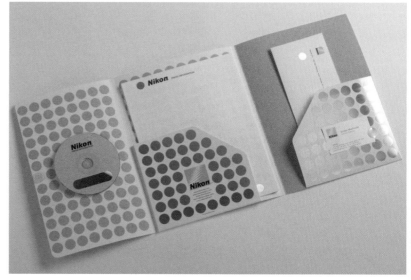

Nikon Digital, Press kit, 2004

AD: Michael Mallett and M.I.

D: Mirko Ilić

First Born Films, title animation, 2012, WITH: Aleksandar Maćašev

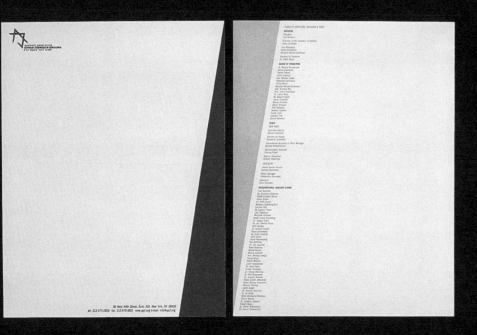

"Design is a different ball game than editorial illustration. Recently, when I was working for the Auschwitz Jewish Center I exercised a lot of restraint. Showing off and getting an award from the Type Directors Club was not on my mind. The type had a very specific purpose, it was chosen for a certain group of people, including older people, who need to be able to read the type. It needed to be of a certain size, not like today's trend, where the type is barely legible. This project for example, has a clear universal function, and it differs from the editorial illustrations I do, which are my personal statements. I'm giving that freedom to myself."

—MIRKO ILIĆ, "MIRKO ILIĆ & MILTON GLASER: THE KING AND THE JESTER," *GRAPHIS* ISSUE #350, MARCH/APRIL 2004, INTERVIEW EDITED BY LAETITIA WOLFF

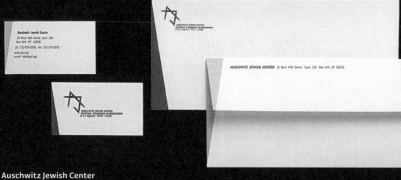

Auschwitz Jewish Center

visual identity, 2001

AD: Mirko Ilić

D: Heath Hinegardner,

Mirko Ilić

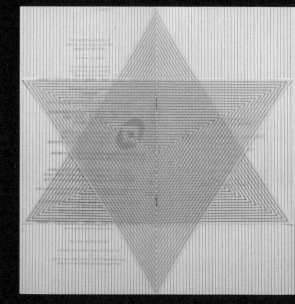

The American Friends of the Tel Aviv Museum of Art

invitation card and menu, 1999

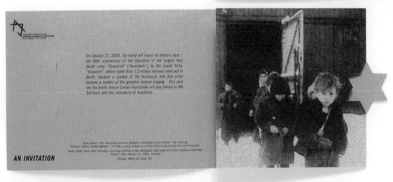

> "It is very easy to stand for gay rights if you are gay; it is very easy to fight for the rights of blacks if you're black; it is very easy to be against discrimination if you are Jewish. It is very difficult if you are on the other side to take that position. Your 'people' will hate you much more than the group you side with because you are a traitor."
>
> —MIRKO ILIĆ, *POLIGRAF*, B 92, BELGRADE, MARCH 16, 2006

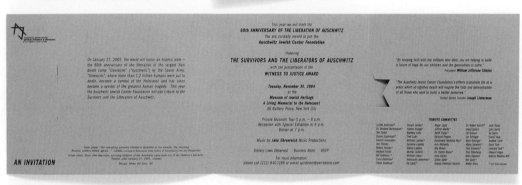

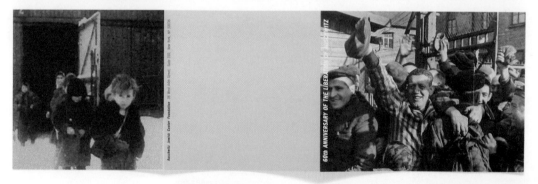

60th Anniversary of the Liberation of Auschwitz, invitation card, Auschwitz Jewish Center Foundation, 2004

The Auschwitz Jewish Center, leaflet, 2004

AD: Mirko Ilić

D: Heath Hinegardner, Mirko Ilić

Jewish Film Festival, Zagreb
logos, 2008–2012
AD & D: Mirko Ilić

6th Zagreb Jewish Film Festival – Tolerance,
t-shirt, badges and festival
programme leaflet, 2012
AD & D: Mirko Ilić

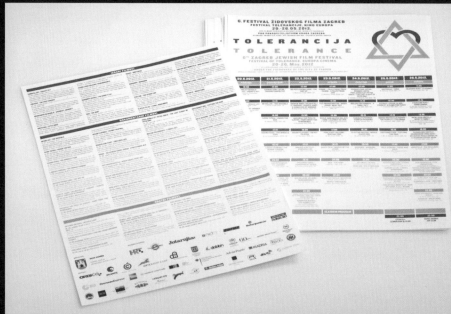

6th Zagreb Jewish Film Festival –

Tolerance,

programme booklet, 2012

AD & D: Mirko Ilić

Scout's Honor, a film by Neil Leifer, 1999, Title sequence,
AD: Walter Bernard & Mirko Ilić, 3D ANIMATION: Lauren DeNapoli,
STUDIO: WBMG, Inc. / Mirko Ilić Corp.

"I am interested in animated film, of course. I'm interested in other things as well, but I am already old and tired. Animation is a time-consuming job. I would have to spend five years of my life before I could see the final result. And in these years, I would have to be something I do not like, the manager."

—MIRKO ILIĆ, "ENVY PECULIARLY MEASURES YOUR SUCCESS", DELO, SATURDAY SUPPLEMENT, LJUBLJANA, JUNE 3, 2000

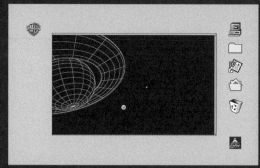

YOU'VE GOT MAIL

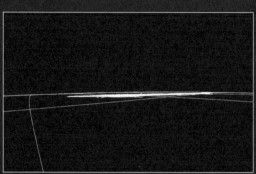

"Milton previously worked on two films for Nora Ephron, so she came in for advice about a new one, and since it was about computers, he said 'why don't we do it with Mirko?'"

—MIRKO ILIĆ

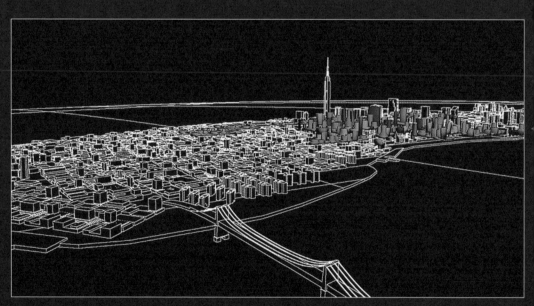

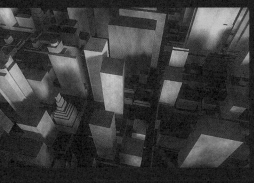

"*I.D.* magazine has described the film animation for the film *You've Got Mail*, which Ilić did in collaboration with Milton Glaser and Walter Bernard, as one of the most creative achievements in the evolution of film opening sequences in recent history."

ANICA TUCAKOV, MIRKO ILIĆ — INTERVIEW, STRIP VESTI # 52

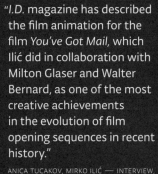

You've Got Mail,
a film by Nora Ephron
Warner Bros, 1998
title sequence
AD: Milton Glaser,
Walter Bernard & Mirko Ilić
3D ANIMATION: Lauren DeNapoli

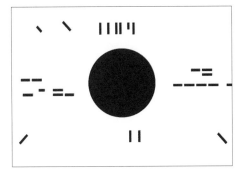

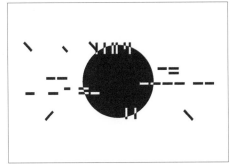

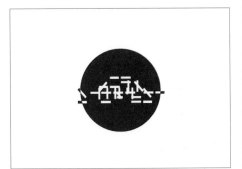

Mirko and I have known each other for almost thirty years, ever since the ancient days of *Polet*. A few years older than me, Mirko was my mentor, role model, and friend through all these years. His early work wrote a new chapter in newspaper illustration in the late seventies and early eighties. Clever ideas with an impressive style are the hallmarks of his work, and from illustrations to design to movie credits, all have brought him international fame. Of course, I was thrilled when he agreed to design the opening sequence for the *Zen Stories* with his New York studio, and I gave him absolute creative freedom. He looked at the rough version of the film and on the spot, with an imagination trained by extreme deadlines, he came up with basic outlines of the concept which contained the very idea of the film. Mirko thought, and I gladly agreed, that Zen, as a philosophy of deep concentration and contemplating the universe through the peace of an emptied mind, is best symbolized by an empty white screen. A dot appears, growing into a round hole incorporating the first frames of the film, symbolizing the creation of the universe. As in all Mirko's work, a richness on numerous levels appears here as well. Graphic signs enter the screen, reminiscent of the Japanese letter forms, and once they meet in the middle of the composition they begin to create Latin letters and print the name of the movie and the names of its authors and assistants. For this opening sequence, Mirko and his studio created special letters that mimic the angular structure of Japanese characters. Together with the formation of letters, the circle in the middle widens so that finally the film material covers the entire surface of the film format. The opening sequence was very successful and it makes me very proud that my film was the inspiration for this outstanding work in the field of film design. I am grateful for the effort, time, and talent that Mirko and his studio invested in the creation of the title sequence for the *Zen Stories*.

—MILAN TRENC

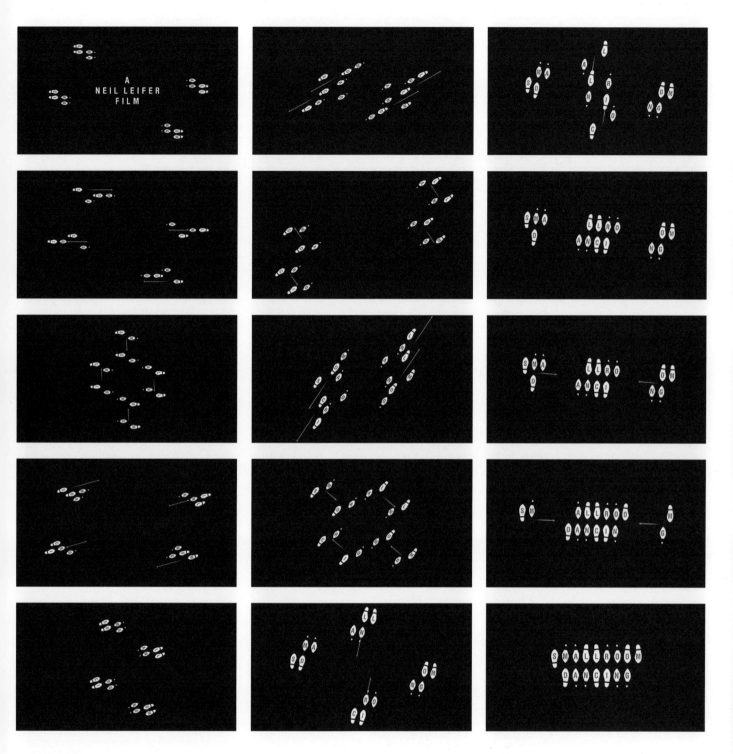

Smallroom Dancing, a film by Neil Leifer, 2002, AD: Walter Bernard, Mirko Ilić, ANIMATION: Heath Hinegardner, Mirko Ilić, STUDIO: WBMG Inc. / Mirko Ilić Corp.

OPPOSITE PAGE:

Zen Stories, a film by Milan Trenc

IMG Media, 2000

CD: Mirko Ilić

ANIMATION: Heath Hinegardner, Mirko Ilić

TYPOGRAPHY: Mirko Ilić

STUDIO: Mirko Ilić Corp.

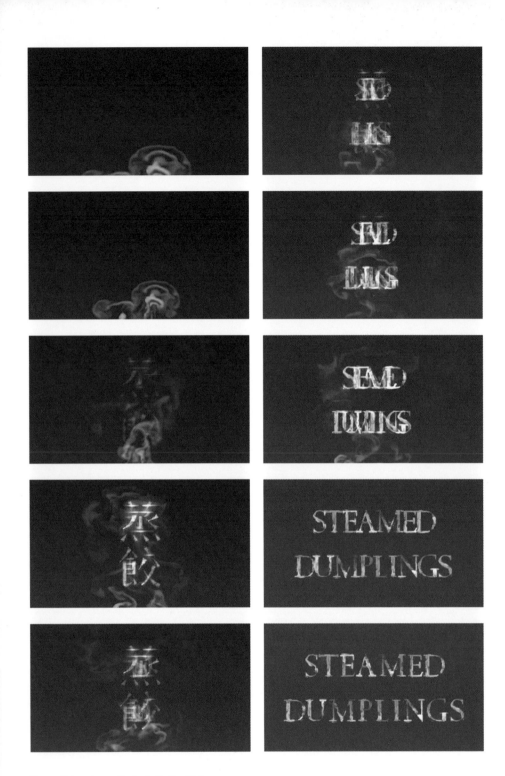

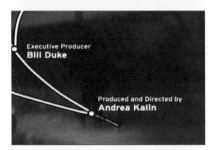

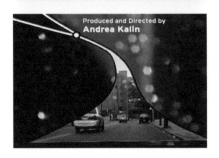

Steamed Dumplings, a film by Neil Leifer, 2003

AD: Walter Bernard, Mirko Ilić, ANIMATION: Lauren DeNapoli

STUDIO: WBMG, Inc. / Mirko Ilić Corp.

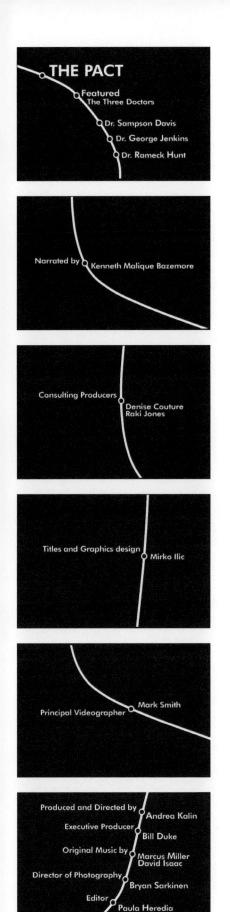

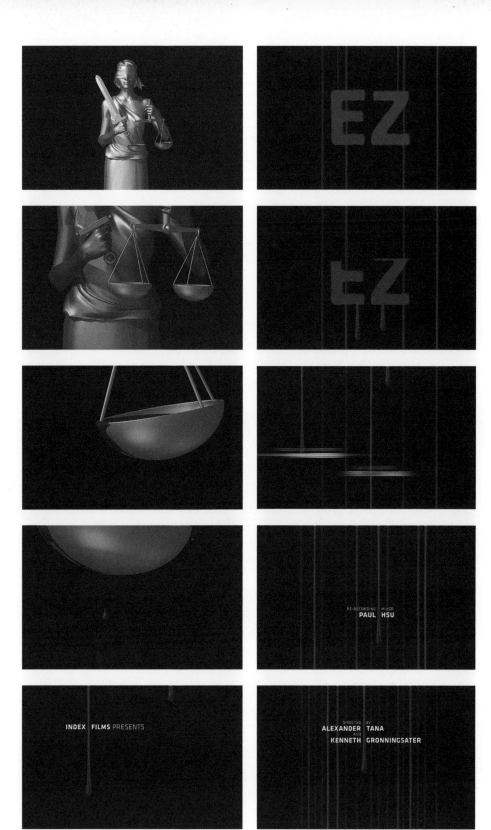

The Pact, directed & produced by Andrea Kalin,
Spark Media, 2006
AD: Mirko Ilić, ANIMATION: Clint Shaner, Mirko Ilić
STUDIO: Mirko Ilić Corp.
Documentary film about the life stories and friendship
between three black boys from the hood, who have agreed
to finish medical university and help other people.

ez, directed by Alexander Tana &
Kenneth Gronningsater
Index Films, 2007
AD: Mirko Ilić
3D: Lauren DeNapoli
2D ANIMATION: Goran Krstić
STUDIO: Mirko Ilić Corp.

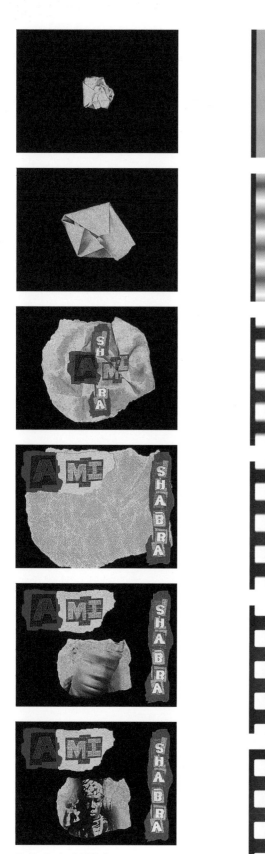

Shabba Ranks: A Mi Shaba,

promo floppy disk, Epic/Sony, 1994

AD & D: Nicky Lindeman, EDITING: Timothy
Manteau, PHOTO: Warren Mantooth,
CONSULTING: Oko & Mano Inc.

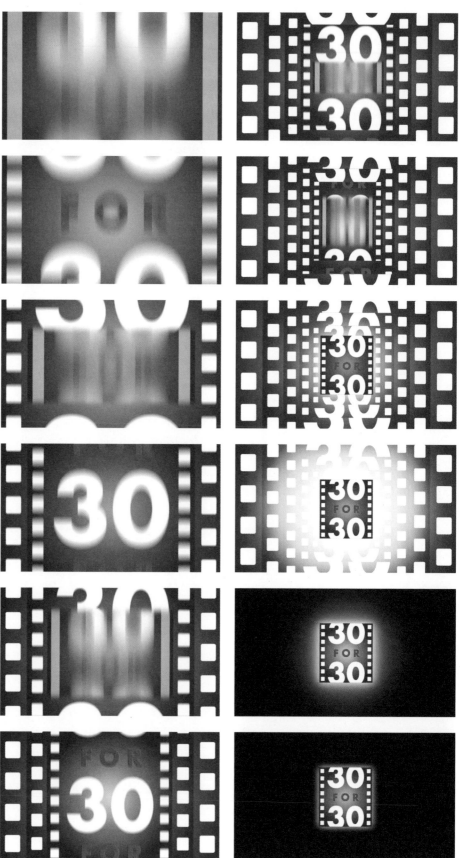

30 for 30, 2010,

CLIENT: ESPN, AD: Mirko Ilić and Walter Bernard

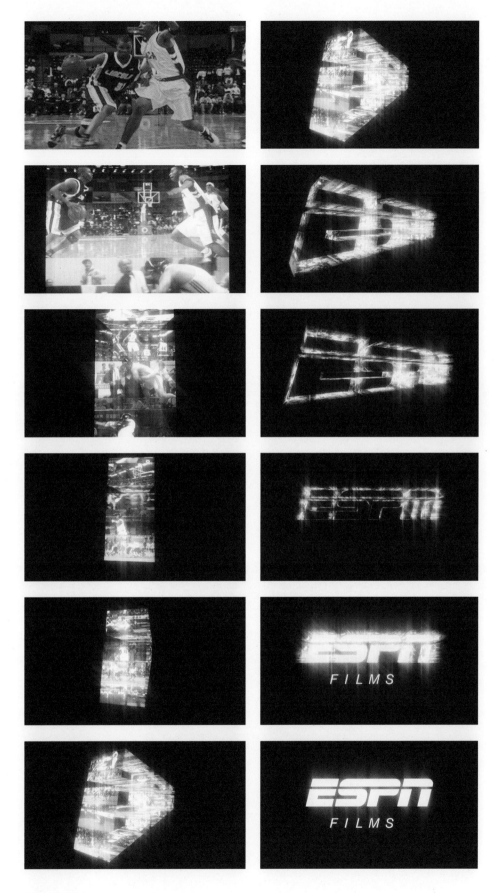

ESPN Films, 2011,

client: ESPN, AD: Mirko Ilić and Walter Bernard

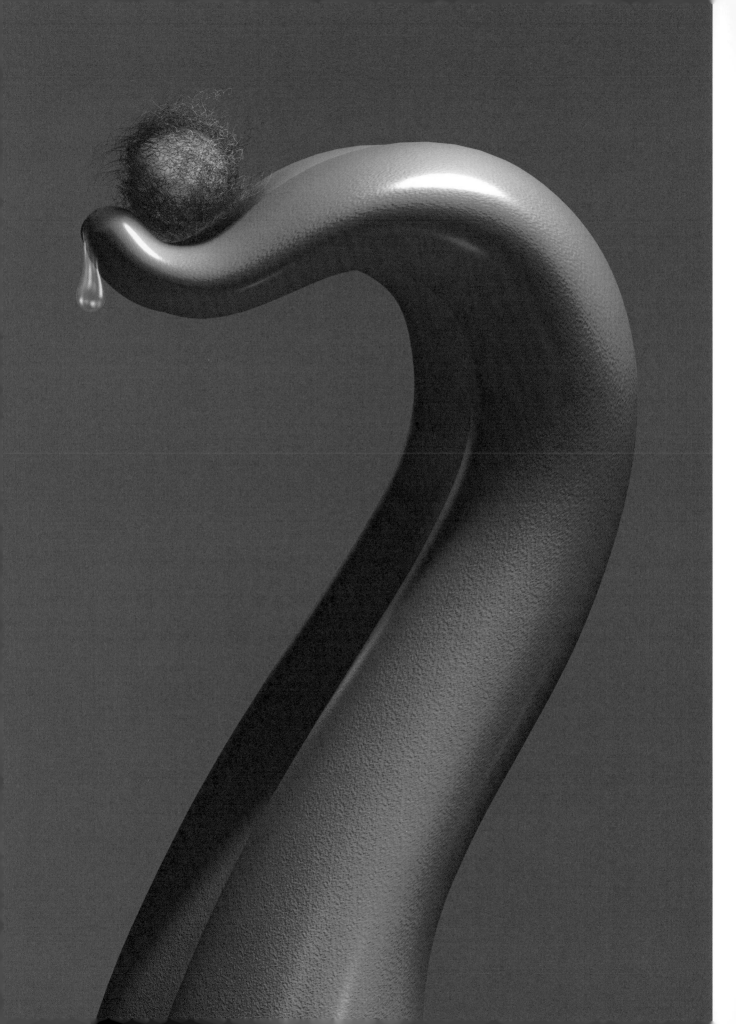

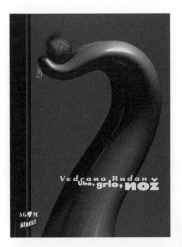

CROATIA IS AN ENTIRELY DIFFERENT PLACE TODAY than when Ilić worked there early in his career. But speaking about his position now one cannot ignore all of the "national questions" surrounding him which were so problematic during Tudman's Croatia—the fact that he was born to the "wrong" ethnicity, in another Republic no less. And the fact that he was part of a family of a military professional. Then there's his indifference toward the representative role of the national culture, and the fact that his first wife, writer Slavenka Drakulić—was part of an infamous media scandal and denounced as one of the "witches from Rio"[01] by her former colleagues and collaborators from publications such as *Pitanja, Polet, Start,* and *Danas.* Ilić was even directly attacked "as one of her husbands who escaped to America." To which he responded: "They forgot to write that I escaped to America in 1986."

The "witches were not the ones who changed themselves for political reasons, they remained essentially the same, they did bend with the wind. They did not follow the system and because of that they ran into a head-on collision with the system. I have said this repeatedly: Slavenka does not need Croatia, she proved herself. Her books are sold all over the world."

The same can be said about Mirko. He does not need Croatia, he has proven himself all over the world as well. After the exhibition of his work, held at the Art Pavilion in 1992, as part of the Zagreb Animated Film Festival where he was a member of the jury, Ilić did not return to former Yugoslavia again for a long time. Occasionally, a random interview with him would appear, but the fact that allready arranged deal about his monograph was suddely ditched by the publisher was a clear sign that Ilić had fallen out of favor with the powers that be.

His American illustrations were being carried by *Novi Danas* and *Forum;* one was even put on the covers of the strange publication *Croatian Political Jokes!* It was not the only example of older work by Ilić being used for new books. Acclaimed writer Theodore Roszak even came to his publishers with a page cut out of a magazine with one of Ilić's illustrations that he had been holding on to for many years and requested that it be used on the cover of his new book.

The former editor at the Jugoton record company, Veljko Despot, asked him to design a visual identity for his new private company, Koncept VD Ltd. (For which, he created a logo where all the letters were made out of two identical elements which could be read both in English and Serbo-Croatian, as Koncept and Concept), and a CD cover for the album *Noč* by Buldožer.

In 1999 designer Ivan Doroghy, marketing manager Robert Jakovljević, and design critic Feđa Vukić launched IDC (International Design Center), a short-term initiative to promote the importance of design. For the promotion of the center, the three authors were commisioned, each poster featuring single concept from the title. Ilić made a poster titled *International.*

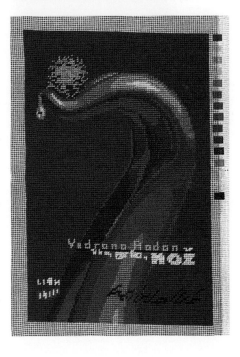

Cover and promo gobelin needlepoint for the book *Ear, Throat, Knife* by **Vedrana Rudan**, AGM, 2002, ᴅ: Melina Mikulić

LEFT:

Hug, 2002,

from the *Sex and Lies* series

By the end of the same year, as a part of the comic book festival "Crtani romani šou," an exhibition was organized to mark the twentieth anniversary of Novi kvadrat. "I came to the opening in a quasi military jacket, a look inspired by the Beatles's song "Sgt. Pepper's Lonely Hearts Club Band" which begins with the lyrics *It was twenty years ago today...* I am very nostalgic when it comes to Kvadrat. The situation with comics is very bad in Zagreb. If you have no money for anything, you definitely don't have it for comics. Everyone who's worth

01 | For specifics of the case see: http://www.women-war-memory.org/en/vjestice_iz_ria/

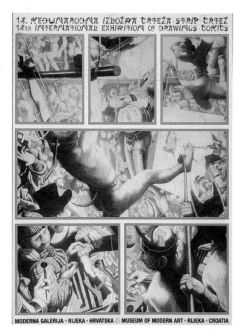

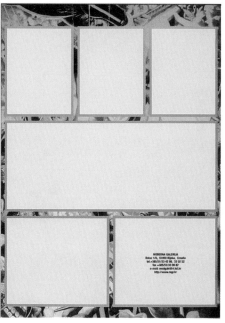

14ᵗʰ International Exhibition of Drawings,

Moderna Galerija, Rijeka, 1999

AD & D: Mirko Ilić

ILLUSTRATION: Davor Vrankić

D: Vesna Rožman

anything is working abroad. So because of this I wanted to support the new generation who invited me as a joke because they thought I wouldn't come. But when I said yes, then Kordej said yes, and everyone else appeared. As I predicted, it was reported all over television and in every newspaper."

Then, on November 27, an innocent victim of the organized crime conflict, a man named Zoran Domini, was passing by the windows of the cultural information center and was killed by a grenade from a rocket launcher.

"We opened the exhibition on Friday night. The exhibition was set up on both sides of the building. Kvadrat was on one side, and on the other were some new kids. The other side was the one that was hit. The local mafia tried to kill, with a rocket launcher, a person they claimed was the leader of a rival clan. And, because they had not trained in the army, they did not know that a rocket launcher should be fired from a distance, so it ricocheted and flew into the window on Saturday at six in the morning killing an innocent passerby. A reporter said to me: *You must be accustomed to these things because you are coming from America?* I have never heard of anyone in America firing a bazooka in a crowded downtown area. Anything can happen, but bazooka shooting? That's something you only see in bad movies. This question contained a desperate need for rationalization: If I said that these things were happening in America every day, she could have said—we are becoming America. Several more bazookas and that's it, dollars are coming too! If politics had any dignity at all, that place would be named after Zoran Domini, the man who was killed there. He was an innocent victim of government's stupidity, because someone did not do his job properly before the explosion."

At the instigation of Karl Rosandić in 1999, Ilić was asked to redesign the newspaper *Večernji list* (Evening Gazette), which had been bought by the Austrian Styria Corporation. In the summer of 2001, the contract was signed and work on the redesign began. Management and the editorial board accepted the proposal for the new design of the newspaper and the accompanying marketing campaign, but after the initial enthusiasm, the design solution soon became a stumbling block. In July 2002, the implementation of the redesign was postponed indefinitely until the arrival of a new office computer system. When *Večernji list* finally appeared with the new design, it was completely different than what Ilić had proposed.

But his frequent visits to Zagreb prompted several smaller projects. He designed the cover for Rujana Jeger's book, *Darkroom*, he also had an exhibition with his work *Sex and lies,* at the Josip Račić Gallery in Zagreb, which led to one of the pictures from the series in the exhibition being used for the cover of the very popular book *Ear, Throat, Knife*, by Vedrana Rudan.

While *Večernji list* went through the redesign process, with secure financial support from a new owner, *Slobodna Dalmacija* had behind it ten years of financial collapse and uncertainty about what privatization would be like and when the government would decide on it. To decide to do a redesign in such a situation might seem brave, but in the long term it proved to be a wise decision by the editor, Dražen Gudić, and the paper's management.

More than just a mere change in appearance, a redesign represents an opportunity for a newspaper to rethink its position. That's why someone from the outside is usually hired for the job as they are unburdened with restrictions or office politics such as "we cannot do that" or "we do things differently." Ilić's concept for the new design of the *Slobodna Dalmacija* represented exactly that out-of-the-box thinking Americans are so fond of.

Of course, as with all change, some people did not like the new look and felt the new *Slobodna Dalmacija* did not look like a national newspaper. In the environment of domestic "entertainment journalism," *Slobodna Dalmacija* had some comparative advantages, of which it was often not aware. They kept room for long articles, and were the only paper that on the last page brought the latest news, instead of a patchwork of sensational news collected from agency services. Exactly because of the limitations of regional character, and its remoteness from the political center, it had the opportunity to become a critical medium, a different voice.

Unlike at *Večernji list*, where the whole editorial system had changed (color printing was implemented and the structure of the paper was redefined), the changes at *Slobodna* were done within the existing—albeit very limited—technological parameters, without any significant editorial interference in the structure of the paper.

The use of dark blue ink was a simple move and it made the paper to stand out at the newsstands. Aside from a patriotic red, white, and blue regional association, the decision was also grounded in the tradition of the paper, harkening back to when it was printed in indigo blue in the early fifties and the satirical section *Pomet*, by Miljenko Smoje, was printed in a light blue. It is interesting to note that in the mid-seventies, back when Ilić did his early works for the *Omladinski tjednik*, art director Mladen Galić used to regularly experiment with colors. The paper was often printed, for example, with no black, instead he used combinations of blue and red, green and red, dark gray and green, brown and orange, purple and yellow. Nikola Kostandinović did a similar thing with *Vidici*.

Although the paper's masthead looked the same at first glance, it had been updated typographically. As a little spite to *Večernji list*, the logo was moved from the top left into the margin. Except the fact that this was not a typical newspaper design, it allowed for the maximum use of space and the

Davor Vrankić: Let Me Make You Real

catalogue, Galerija likovnih umjetnosti,

Osijek, 2010,

AD & D: Mirko Ilić

D: Mirko Ilić and Jee-eun Lee

**Luka Mjeda: C/B Zagreb
(Black and White Zagreb)**,
S.L.M. d.o.o, Zagreb, 2002

Along with the hardcover edition a mini version of the book was published. Dust jacket of the hardcover edition could be used as a poster.

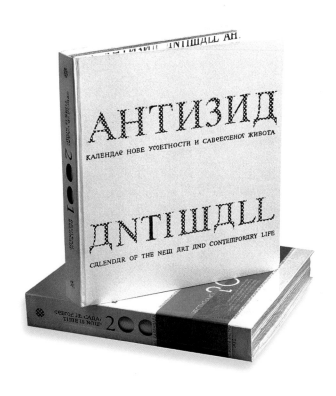

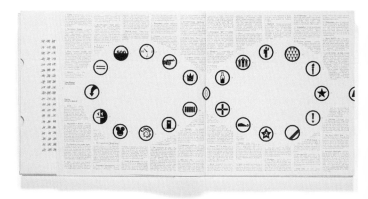

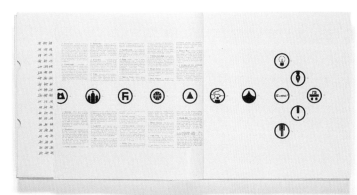

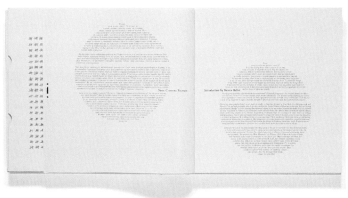

абвгдђежзијклљмнњопрстћуфхцчџω 1234567890
АБВГДЂЕЖЗИЈКЛЉМНЊОПРСТЋУФХЦЧЏω

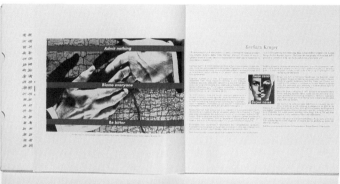

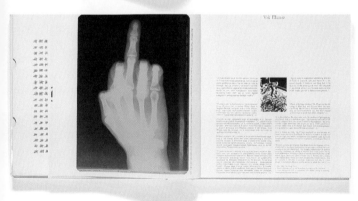

Antiwall, FIA, Publikum, Belgrade, 2000

13 pg. calendar, 48 pg. book

DIMENSIONS: 31× 31 cm book, 60× 60 cm calendar

PHOTOS: Wim Wenders, Natasha Merritt, Björk, Vik Muniz, Oliviero Toscani, Barbara Kruger, David Byrne, Marina Abramović, Tadanori Yoko, Christo & Jeanne Claude, AES Group, Dragan Živadinov

HANDWRITTEN LETTERING: Ringo Takahashi, Ryta Nakazawa, Asa Hasimoto, Jelena Čomba Đorđević

ICONS: Slavimir Stojanović

"Each letter was written by hand, not a single letter was typed. I joked that since we were starting from the beginning we should write by hand like at the beginning of Serbian culture. The other thing we did is transform Cyrillic letters in numbers wherever possible, to give the Serbs that feeling for money, mathematics, and time. And for the English letters we transformed as much Cyrillic letters as possible to give Westerners a little taste of Eastern Europe."

—MIRKO ILIĆ,"AN ANTIWALL ORIGINATING FROM GALLERY WALLS," *VIKEND*, BELGRADE, JANUARY 27, 2001

дбččédđefghijklmnnjoprsštuvzž 1234567890

ДБČČĆDĐEFGHIJKLMNOPRSŠTUVZŽ

front page was opened up. The heading moved to the last page, and became an alternative cover. Red and blue stripes on the spine of the paper created a clearly recognizable visual code, and on special occasions a photograph would be placed over the spine.

The basic idea was to refine the graphics, typography, and overall structure of the page. To emphasize the hierarchy of topics. The simplification of the page layout also accelerated its production and—at least in theory—left more time for fine tuning and finessing the design. The extremely poor print quality was offset by the bold graphic "boxing poster" layout—big headlines, thick rules. The HTF Champion font used for titles was reminiscent of the aesthetics of old wooden letters, although it was completely modern. The body type, HTF Mercury News, tailored for poor quality newspaper printing, was used for the first time because Jonathan Hoefler and Tobias Frere-Jones of the New York type foundry Hoefler & Frere-Jones, gave it to Mirko for review before it was officially released for distribution.

As Ilić pointed out, in both redesigns his biggest problem and the conflict—which was described by the critics within the news desk as the designer's interference with editorial strengths—was exactly the passivity of the newspaper editors, as if redesign meant just a transfer of the same old content into a slightly different form and printed in some new fonts.

Despite everything, the redesign was mostly maintained until the arrival of the new owner and editor, when in only a few days almost all the rules were broken. Soon after that, the paper was again entirely redesigned.

Some more conflicts and controversies on the Croatian design scene continued after the exhibition *Europa 2020*, while more active contacts with younger representatives of the scene resulted in the organization of lectures by Nigel Holmes, Rick Poynor, and Lazar Džamić, participation of Laetitia Wolff in the jury of ZGRAF 9 and bringing the Art Directors Club and the Type Directors Club exhibitions, which would have beeen far more difficult without his intervention. Ilić gave a number of interviews and his work was featured in journals, but equaly important for his continued presence was his role as a promoter and supportter of young designers.

An obvious symptom of Ilić's tenuous position in Croatian culture was that he was often denied the status of a designer, where, in a typically reductionist understanding of the profession, the job of an illustrator was treated with characteristic disdain forgetting that it was his work in political illustration that significantly influenced the role of illustrations in newspapers and magazines, representing its brightest period prior to the onslaught of photos and digital technology.

The attitude toward Ilić in post-Yugoslav countries, especially in Croatia and Serbia, is also symptomatic of the difference between Croatian and Serbian nationalism. While the Croatian approach is an exclusivist one, concerned about the purity of the nation, and in pursuit of reaching an imaginary purity of Croatian culture, with purging, cleansing, and exclusion of words, language, people or historical events, the Serbian approach is imperialistic and therefore necessarily partly inclusive. Thus, in Zagreb, Mirko was not accepted at the exhibition of Croatian design and he cannot get a certificate of citizenship and passport through a normal procedure, while in Belgrade he was offered membership to the Art Directors Club and received honors and awards. Ilić was eventually offered a Serbian passport and citizenship but he refused it. Referring to this, he often gives different variations of the following statement: "I am an American, and for the last twenty years I had only one passport, American." Interestingly, the same statement subtly changes its meaning when spoken in Zagreb or Belgrade. In Zagreb, it has an ironic tone—you do not give me

Test prints for testing masthead for the paper and weekly supplements with different possibilities of positioning the ads and treatments of the headline.

AD & D: Mirko Ilić

D: Dejan Dragosavac Ruta, Dejan Kršić

INFO-GRAPHICS: Nigel Holmes

  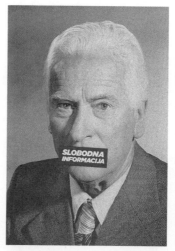 

Redesign of
Slobodna Dalmacija,
July 2003
AD & D: Mirko Ilić
D: Dejan Dragosavac Ruta,
Dejan Kršić, Mirko Ilić
graphic redaction of SD,
graphic editor
Slobodan Brkljača

**Posters for the
promotional campaign**,
AGENCY:
McCann-Erickson Croatia
AD & D: Mirko Ilić
CW: Dražen Gudić, Mirko Ilić
D: Dejan Dragosavac Ruta,
Dejan Kršić
PHOTO: Dag Oršić

Gavrilović, billboard, 2005
AGENCY: McCann Erickson
Croatia
In this pop-art
interpretation of the
Gavrilović trademark, raster
points are replaced with
actual size scans of the
famous Gavrilović salami.

Autumn in Zagreb *International Multicultural Encounters*

20.09–08.11.2008

FAR LEFT:

Karl Jaspers:
The Question
of German Guilt,
AGM, 2006

LEFT:

YES.ZGB - Autumn in
Zagreb,
visual identity, logo,
programme booklet cover,
2008,
AD & D: Mirko Ilić

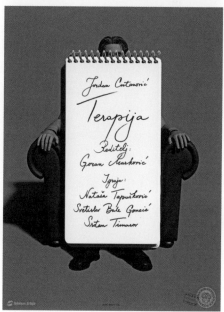

"The design scene in Croatia became very serious. But, serious is not always the best approach to design, it can mean being too far on the safe side. When you're a pro, and you aim for a certain level you do not want to go below, it often means that there is no going beyond that either. No serendipity, no fooling around. To be a pro means to lose that something that made you get into design in the first place—the game. So you become another cog in the production process. The high level of professionalism in design often means the loss of individuality. You have five or six top designers, but you are not sure what is whose work because you cannot identify an individual way of thinking. Ljubičić is recognized by little red squares that he promotes as a recognizable Croatian identity, but one needs some time to figure out who is who in the new generation. And that's the problem, alternatives are missing."

—MIRKO ILIĆ, "CROATIAN DESIGN IS BETTER THAN AMERICAN," NEDELJNA DALMACIJA, SPLIT, APRIL 12, 2002

A.N. Ostrovsky: Wolfs and sheeps

Kerempuh Theatre, poster, 2008

AD & D: Mirko Ilić

ILLUSTRATION: Mirko Ilić

In Therapy

Atelje 212, poster, 2009

AD & D: Mirko Ilić

TYPOGRAPHY: Sandra Hadžismajlović

ILLUSTRATION: Mirko Ilić Corp.

SAV TAJ CRTEŽ

26. II – 19. IV 2009., Dolac 1/2

Utorak-nedjelja od 10-13 / 17-20 sati

Design: Mirko Ilić Corp.

(SU) ŽIVOT

Plakat međunarodnih izložbi crteža

4.-22. III 2009., Mali salon, Korzo 24

Svakim danom od 10-13 / 17 -20 sati

60 godina MMSU-a u Rijeci

40 godina Međunarodne izložbe crteža

Realizaciju izložbi omogućili su Grad Rijeka, Primorsko-goranska županija i Ministarstvo kulture Republike Hrvatske.

LEFT:

**All that Drawing -
international drawings
exhibition**,
poster,
MMSU, Rijeka, 2008,
AD: Mirko Ilić,
ILU: Mirko Ilić

RIGHT:

**Nadežda Petrović
Memorial, Čačak**,
poster, 2007
AD: Mirko Ilić,
D: Mirko Ilić,
Aleksandar Maćašev

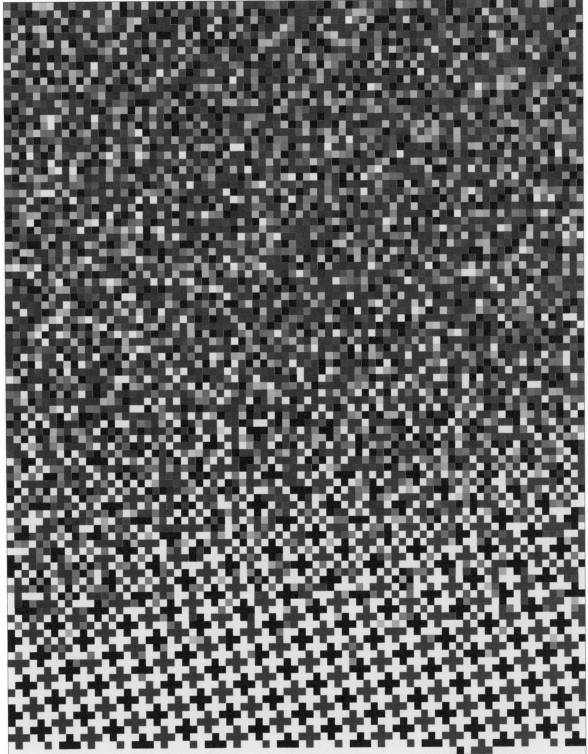

MEMORIJAL
NADEŽDE
PETROVIĆ

Transformisanje sećanja. Politike slike 22. Septembar - 4. Novembar 2007.
Transforming Memory. The Politics of Images September 22 - November 4 2007
24. MEMORIJAL NADEŽDE PETROVIĆ, ČAČAK
24. NADEŽDA PETROVIĆ MEMORIAL, ČAČAK

Fikret Atay, Yael Bartana, Michael Blum, Mariana Castillo Deball, Mounir Fatmi, Ghazel, Irena Kelečević,
Irena Lagator, Moataz Nasr, Sean Snyder, Grupa Spomenik / Monument Group, Milica Topalović,
Florin Tudor & Mona Vatamanu, Urtica, Luca Vitone

Kvart, logo, 2008

Kvart no. 13, magazine
cover, September 2009
ILLUSTRATION: Mirko Ilić

Here and there,
film logo, 2007, AD: Mirko Ilić
D: Mirko Ilić, Trevor Gilley

Reflektor, logo, 2011
AD: Mirko Ilić, D: Jee-eun Lee

a passport, you do not want to accept me again as part of your culture, but I do not need it anyway, I have an American passport that you would want to have. In Belgrade, it means "you earnestly wish to appropriate me on the basis of that same element that prevents my admission to Croatian citizenship, a random fact of my parents' ethnic origin, but I am not yours. I am an American now."

In Belgrade in 2005, at the initiative of Anica Tucakov, a retrospective exhibition was held at the Museum of Yugoslavia, followed by a few smaller projects, including an exhibition of sketches, drawings, and computer generated illustrations called *Štapom po pesku* (With a stick in the sand), and an exhibition of album covers called *Greatest Hits* in 2008. These projects were well-promoted and caused a lot of media attention and Ilić renewed some old—and made new—contacts which would bring him to Belgrade frequently in the coming years, among which were Mia David, Maja Lalić ,and Borut Vild. The design of graphic materials for the retrospective exhibition was made by the young designer Aleksandar Maćašev, who met Mirko for the first time on that occasion. This was the beginning of their collaboration, which ultimately resulted in the Aleksandar moving to New York, where he works on his own design and art projects and occasionally partners with Ilić.

As a direct result of these visits to Belgrade, he was officially commissioned for several projects, such as the logo for the Ministry of Culture, the logo for the Museum of History of Yugoslavia, and a visual identity of the Memorial of Nadežda Petrović. In 2012, he designed the visual identity for the 52nd October Salon, and the new visual identity for LDP, the Liberal Democratic Party headed by Čedomir Jovanović.

But so far, the most media noise was caused by the fact that he was engaged as a creative consultant for the redesign of *Politika*, the oldest daily newspaper in Serbia. The work on the redesign was launched in September 2006, and the first redesigned issue of *Politika* appeared on *Politika's* 103rd birthday, on January 25, 2007. Art Director Borut Vild, and designers Olivera Batajić and Vedran Eraković tried to uphold the tradition of a serious daily newspaper (broadsheet, instead of the current global trend to be tabloid size), but at the same time to give it modern look and typographic treatment. The famous type designer Jovica Veljović was commissioned to create two new fonts, Politika sans and Politika serif. Like all redesign projects, this one has caused much controversy and various reactions. A part of the audience complained as expected, while the other welcomed the new revised and brighter look. Apart from several comments in newspapers and on the website *Tipometar*, fellow designers, did not publicly respond, but insulting comments directed toward Ilić were often posted in various blogs, as if he was the principal author and the only one to blame for all changes.

Talking about this, he said: "I did not redesign *Politika*, I was a consultant. Borut Vild redesigned it, a Slovenian who lives in Belgrade and is currently the creative director of all *Politika's* editions. Why did they call me? For all kinds of reasons; respect, experience, I can often achieve a little more than a local designer. In American football, there is a player who runs in front of the person carrying the ball, a blocker who clears the way so the ball carrier gets to score a touchdown. I'm very good at blocking. In any conflict with editors, I am always on equal ground, while local designers aren't. Local designers must often fight with editors, and so they can call on me. I can clean up the area very well. The design of *Politika* is changed, cleaned up, so the newspaper is easier to read. Today, *Politika* looks very modern and clean. They made a positive change. Part of the media attacked me because they were afraid, and at one point they even argued whether a foreigner could and should redesign the oldest Serbian newspaper. They opposed the redesign because they did not want any change. Fear of change is very important. No one likes to have somebody walk into their apartment in the middle of the night and move the furniture around, they are afraid that when they go to the bathroom at night they will trip and fall over the table. However, once they fall over that table then they know the table is there and everything becomes OK again. The problem is the first two or three nights. On the other hand, the announcement of design changes also suggests changes in content. These may be slow, but still they happen, and that brought some opposition, too."

In an interview for the *Novosti—Independent Serbian Weekly Magazine,* published in Zagreb, he said: "If you look at first ten questions in this interview, all of them really are political. And people ask me why I am involved in politics. When one is coming from such an environment where politics are obviously more important than the economy, because you wouldn't normally be asked who you are but how much money can I make with you, then that remains etched somewhere in you. If someone in Croatia or Serbia wants to offend me, they call me a faggot. If needed, I am a Croatian or Serbian faggot. All that tells you is that, unfortunately, you have to be politically involved."

In addition to interviews, he was also busy working. He created, pro bono, the visual identity for the Jewish Film Festival in Zagreb and for the Zoran Đinđić Foundation. With TV station B92, he was one of the initiators and major media figures who supported and promoted the initiative to save and create a landmark out of the area known as Staro Sajmište (Old fairgrounds), which during World War II was used as a concentration camp. In cooperation with Milton Glaser, he designed the logo for the project.

Ilić has also aided the work of local designers and artists in various ways, and in doing so has overseen the development of the scene. He designed the logo for the band Darkwood dub; the poster illustration for the movie *SOS* by Slobodan Šijan, logos for the movie *Here and There,* the poster for the play *In Therapy,* the logo for the magazine *Kvart,* and the cover for the 13th issue of *Kvart,* the magazine for architecture, design, art, and lifestyle (which, sadly, was discontinued after the 18th issue). However, one of the offshoots of *Kvart* is the conference *Designer, Author, or Universal Soldier,* which was started in 2010. With his enthusiasm, connections, and penchant for connecting people, Ilić has not only has brought Steven Heller, designers Paul Buckley and Ingsu Liu, exhibitions of illustrations by Milton Glaser, *75 years of Penguin,* and *The Design of Dissent* to this small, non-profit initiative.

On initiation of the project, Borut Vild says: "As always, Mirko called me late at night, 'Hey, I have an excellent exhibition of Milton Glaser in Ljubljana. A great documentary about him goes with it, and I could say something as well. What do you think, could we find a space for it in Belgrade?' Of course, I immediately accepted. With Mia David, editor in chief of *Kvart,* Maja Lalić from *Mixer,* and designer Isidora Nikolić, we began to think about a neat spot. Short on time, of course. Maja proposed, and then provided the emptied space of a socialist mega-store *Beograd* in the downtown pedestrian zone. Mia proposed that we expand the list of lecturers. Isidora said 'Aaaaa, we must have workshops for students.' And we added workshops. We realized that we had something good, and that it would be nice to share this with colleagues and design students from the region. So in two months, *Vojnik* (Soldier) was created. And it remained. Now, Mia and Isidora won't let me change its name."

Through this conference, Ilić has achieved one of his permanent goals: to help young and talented authors. As he says, "A lot of different people helped me, so why not give back. I cannot give them back directly, but I can give it back through someone else." And he always adds, "If someone is not good at what he does, whatever I do I cannot help that person." ▶

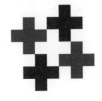

MEMORIJALNI CENTAR SAJMIŠTE

LOGOS: **Ministry of Culture of the Republic of Serbia**, 2005 • **Museum of History of Yugoslavia**, 2006 • **Zoran Đinđić Fund, Belgrade**, 2006 • **Nadežda Petrović Memorial**, 2007 • **Memorial Center Sajmište, Belgrade**, 2008, AD & D: Mirko Ilić, Milton Glaser

52.OKTOBARSKI SALON
VREME JE DA SE UPOZNAMO
MUZEJ 25. MAJ, Botićeva 6 · 20.10.-4.12. 2011. Beograd · 10.11.-4.01.2012. Ljubljana

52.OKTOBARSKI SALON
VREME JE DA SE UPOZNAMO
MUZEJ 25. MAJ, Botićeva 6 · 20.10.-4.12. 2011. Beograd · 10.11.-4.01.2012. Ljubljana

52 October Salon Annual Exhibition,

visual identity, billboards, catalogue,

Kulturni centar Beograd, 2011

AD: Mirko Ilić

PHOTO: Mirko Ilić

D: Mirko Ilić and Sandra Milanović

PHOTO OF BILLBOARDS: Senja Vild

ules of *Western Impressions*: the game is base
ents, which make it a microcosm which functic
e are six players, each representing an India
icans (soldiers, cowboys, etc.). Each player is
ules and partly a free agent, making their o
imstances (e.g. in some cases a player will
ies or allies, in other cases that will be dete

As a reference to the main subject of the

exhibition, obedience to authority, conformism,

social responsibility, as well as disobedience and

non-conformism, thruout whole catalogue all

interpunction signs are set in red.

VREME JE DA
SE UPOZNAMO

Izložbeni prostor: Muzej „25° Maj" – Muzej istorije Jugoslavije

IT'S TIME WE
GOT TO KNOW
EACH OTHER

Exhibition venue: Museum „25° May" – Museum of Yugoslav History

Kustosi/Curators: Galit Eilat & Alenka Gregorič

Amir Yatziv

Detroit, video, photography, drawing on paper, 2009

'Detroit' is a 1:1 simulation of a Palestinian city, the Gaza or other identical Arab situation. Amir Yatziv's *Detroit* installation consists of a map – which the artist found in this military training area – a video piece and photograph. The title of the installation was borrowed from the Israeli Defence Force's (IDF) training area near Ze'elim in the country's southern region. Is it accidental that an IDF training area was named after the American city of Detroit, once a bustling metropolis, and now a ghost town of sorts?

In the video work Yatziv presents the architectural plans for 'Detroit' to various urban planners, without mentioning what this plan represents – asking them instead to analyse the city for him. All the planners express varying measures of discontent with the city plan, but none realise that it is a city constructed for the sole purpose of simulation. The mosque architect is baffled by the fact that such a call mosque was erected for a city of such a small scale, whereas another urban planner wonders why, in this new city, no road was paved to facilitate vehicular traffic between the commercial centre and the residential neighbourhoods.

The training city 'Detroit' is intended to prepare soldiers for combat in a built environment. The setting resembles a Muslim quarter, thus meeting the user's needs in a simulation which would furnish them with the fantasy of an Arab city. The essence of this city is replaced by its fictive image. 'Detroit' even contains live targets. A private company supplies extras with an 'Eastern' (Arab) look who play the Palestinians in the simulation. Is 'Detroit' a simulation that went out of control during the operation in Gaza 'The Gazan 'Detroit' is devoid of flowering gardens, the city's residents are mere actors, and the houses contain no signs of life. The simulation prepares the fighter for 'better' confrontation in real time, striving to neutralise the element of surprise in battle by exercising – dulling the shock of encounter with the real. The simulation enables distant confrontation, based on previous experience, and not on the initial encounter in the battlefield. At the same time, it might establish automatic patterns of action and cause numbness to real effects.

Amir Yatziv's recent works document military re-enactments in Europe and other historical events that suggest that, in dealing with even the most personal events like death and bereavement...

Amir Yatziv (born and raise in Kermat, Israel, 1972) currently lives and works in Berlin. He studied at the Bezalel Academy of Arts & Design Jerusalem (2004 >> 2008) and Computer science IDC Herzelia, Israel (1988 >> 2001). His recent solo exhibitions include: Historein

LDP! LIBERALNO DEMOKRATSKA PARTIJA

Liberal Democratic Party, visual identity, 2011
AD: Mirko Ilić
D: Mirko Ilić and Aleksandar Maćašev

ABOVE: "For" and "Against" voting plates.
ON THE RIGHT: Delegates voting on LDP congress.

"I would not accept a job to rebrand Serbia, to change the image of Serbia in the world, because it must be done by people in Serbia. I could be an advisor to see what they do and how they do it. However, as I repeat over and over again, to redesign means to tailor a new dress, but if the lady does not take a shower, the dress will start stinking in three days. The redesign of Serbia should be a change of political structure. Free political structures will bring so much change to Serbia, which cannot be achieved with any design. Not voting for idiots is more important for the image of Serbia than any color or form… The citizens of Serbia have to make their own smart choices in terms of selecting their government. To decide who and what they are, to project that image to the outside world and the design and promotion will happen. The best designed country in the world, at one point, was most probably Nazi Germany. Total design. Real branding. But it did not help much in the projection towards the world. On the contrary! It is not a matter of the design, but of what (and whom) that design represents."

—MIRKO ILIĆ

LEFT:
LDP billboards on Belgrade streets, PHOTO: Senja Vild

PP. 316–317: **International**, poster for *International Design Center*, Zagreb, 1999

Acknowledgments

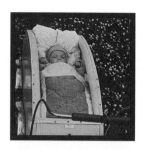

The first Croatian edition of this book was published as:
Mirko Ilić: Strip / Ilustracija / Dizajn / Multimedija 1975–2008
Agm & Profil International, Zagreb 2008. That version would not have been possible without the publisher **Janislav Šaban**, support from editor **Kruno Lokotar**, and the cover design, layout, scanning and prepress work of **Mario Aničić** and **Jele Dominis**.

This edition was made possible thanks to the enthusiasm of the **Mikser** team, **Maja Lalić**, **Mia David**, translator **Jasmina Ilić**, and designer **Andrej Dolinka**. For additional translations we are grateful to **Jele Dominis** and **Graham McMaster**, and for use of the typefaces (Brioni, Typonine Sans), thank you to **Nikola Djurek** of **Typonine** foundry.

The author and publisher are also very thankful for the contributions from: **Olivera Batajić Sretenović, Inoslav Bešker, Mario Bošnjak, Art Chantry, Nicholas Currie Momus, Veljko Despot, Slavenka Drakulić, Lazar Džamić, Milton Glaser, Darko Glavan,** *Graphis* magazine, **Nigel Holmes, Rujana Jeger, Zrinka Jurčić Tatomir, Pero Kvesić, Julie Lasky, Tomaž Lavrič, Borislav Ljubičić, Aleksandar Maćašev, Robert Massin, Branko Matan, Rick Poynor, Karlo Rosandić, Ines Sabalić, Stefan Sagmeister, Željko Serdarević, Slavimir Stojanović, Nedjeljko Špoljar, Adam Tihany, Milan Trenc, Borut Vild,** and **Laetitia Wolff**

The fact that the U.S. edition of this book makes any sense at all to an international audience is the result of the hard work and understanding of its editors **Aaron Kenedi** and **Buzz Poole**, and the keen eye of copyeditor **Georgia Cool**.

Special thanks to **Steven Heller** for his selfless help. And above all, thanks to **Mirko Ilić** for his inspiration and support, and to everybody at **Mirko Ilić Corp.** who worked on the many projects presented in this book and provided material for it: **Lauren Denapoli, Heath Hinegardner, Jee-Eun Lee, Marija Miljković, Clint Shaner, Ringo Takahashi, So Takahashi,** and many others.

Special thanks also to the photographers: **Dražen Kalenić, Vladimir Miladinović, Luka Mjeda, Goran Pavelić Pipo, Milisav Vesović, Velizar Vesović, Srđan Vuković, Andrija Zelmanović**; as well as the numerous journalists, editors, newspapers and magazines who published interviews and articles about Ilić.

For archive material we would like to thank:
Janja Bjelopavlović | **Teatar &TD**
Charlotte Frank | **Grafička zbirka NSK**, as well as the staff of the technical department of the **National and University Library, Zagreb**:
Tanja Šimić | **Croatian Radio-Television**
Marija Šimun and **Siniša Škarica** | **Croatia Records**
Koraljka Vlajo | **Arts and Crafts Museum, Zagreb**

These days, Mirko Ilić's design and art work can be found in numerous museums and collections around the world, the largest collection of which lives in the **Museum Of Modern and Contemporary Art** in Rijeka, Croatia.

PAGE 319

PHOTO: Luka Paić

PAGE 320

The Flight of the Spermatozoon, *Playboy*, 2007

AD: Rob Wilson

ILLUSTRATION: Mirko Ilić

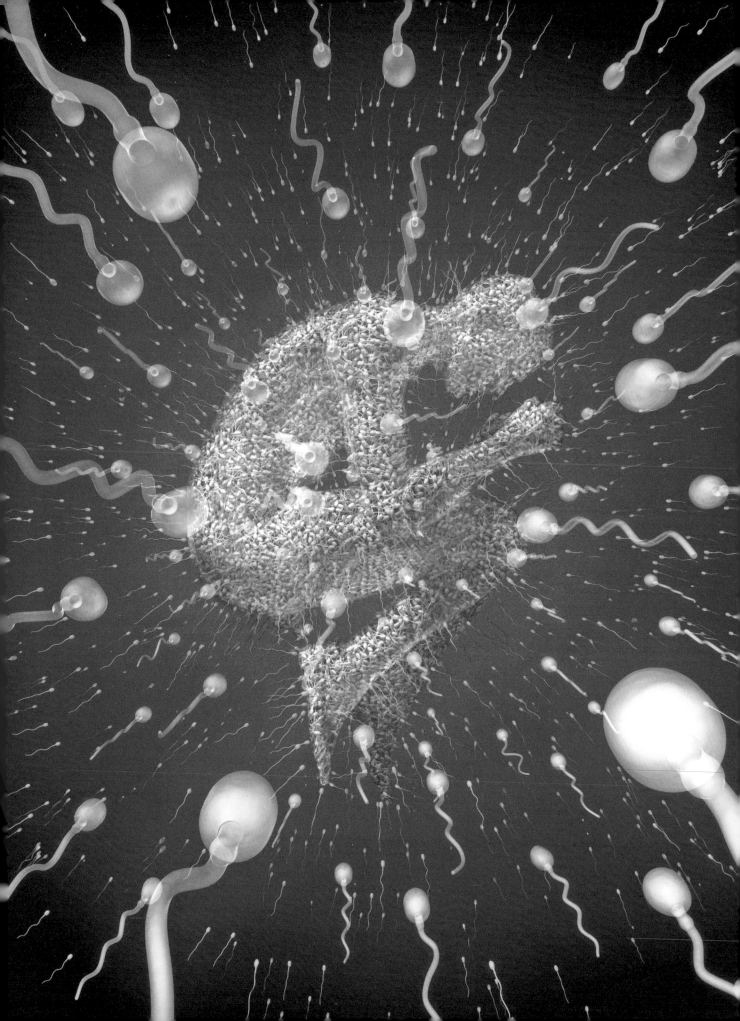